Things You've Always Wanted to Know About Food & Drink

Other Books
by Helen McCully

Nobody Ever Tells You These Things
  About Food and Drink

Cooking with Helen McCully
  Beside You

The Other Half of the Egg
  (*with Jacques Pépin*)

The Christmas Pony
  (*with Dorothy Crayder*)

Things You've Always Wanted to Know About Food & Drink

by Helen McCully

Holt, Rinehart & Winston
New York Chicago San Francisco

Portions of this book have appeared in
House Beautiful *magazine*.

Published simultaneously in Canada
by Holt, Rinehart and Winston of
Canada, Ltd.

Library of Congress Catalog
Card Number: 77–155524

Designer: Ernst Reichl

ISBN: 0–03–091354–3

First Edition

Printed in the United States of America

Preface

Some six years ago, about the time I joined *House Beautiful* magazine as Food Editor, an old friend, John Ellestad (then, too, an editor on the magazine), and I were discussing food. We both agreed that all too often it was difficult, if not impossible, to find the answers to questions that come to a cook's mind when shopping or cooking. Together, and almost in one voice, we said, "Nobody ever tells you these things."

Subsequently, I suggested to Sarah Tomerlin Lee, then *House Beautiful's* Editor-in-Chief, that answering these puzzling questions might make an interesting and useful column in the magazine. She agreed and "Nobody" as a regular monthly feature was born. In 1967, "Nobody Ever Tells You These Things About Food & Drink" became a book. Today, it is available both in hard covers and paperback.

Now, five years and hundreds of questions later, here is a companion to the original "*Nobody*," illustrated, as is true of the earlier volume, with a collection of recipes. This is a completely new book, with the answers to hundreds of questions—a continuation, if you will, of the first "*Nobody*." Have you wondered why the bones of perfectly cooked chickens are sometimes pink? What you can do about the mildew on olives? If there's a substitute for lard in cooking? How much gelatin to use?—And how to use it? How to determine when a custard is properly baked? If butter can be frozen?

Tracking down the answers to questions such as these is endlessly fascinating and has led me down many a winding and intriguing path. Not only that, it has led to many exceptional and extraordinarily helpful people—far too numerous to thank here—but without whom this book could not have existed.

If you seriously care about food and cooking, I can't help but believe you will find this book as well as the first volume a storehouse of useful, stimulating information.

HELEN McCULLY
New York, 1972

Contents

Things You've Always Wanted to Know About Food & Drink

Weights and Measurements

About Recipe Measurements

To an English woman in the kitchen a cup is a teacup but to an American, a cup is a standard 8-ounce measuring cup for both liquid and dry measurements holding 16 standard tablespoons. In France, on the other hand, the cook measures by liter for liquid ingredients and by grams for dry measure.

For certain dishes precise measurements are a downright necessity (cakes, certain types of breads, puddings, etc.), but there are many instances where precise measurements are sheer nonsense—if not illogical. When Elizabeth David asks in, *Spices, Salt and Aromatics in the English Kitchen* (Penguin), "What is the difference between a suspicion and a pinch? How much more is a good pinch?" I agree with her this is a ridiculous nomenclature. When I see a recipe calling for 1 teaspoon of minced parsley, I'd like to shake the writer. Who, in his right mind, would even consider chopping a few parsley sprigs, then measuring out exactly 1 teaspoon? Why not say a few sprigs minced? Why not, indeed? In most cooking a little more or less of this or that isn't going to make one iota of difference in the finished dish. Cooks should learn to use their heads. At the same time, their tongues. You cannot season with salt and pepper, for example, without tasting the food before it is presented—then, if necessary, adding more of the seasonings. "Taste as you go" should be every cook's slogan, etched on the wall of every kitchen.

I do not mean to suggest that the cook go off half cocked and dump in 1 cup of cognac when all the recipe calls for is ¼ cup. A lot is not necessarily better than less. But I do mean to suggest that if a recipe calls for 2 tablespoons of lemon juice, you simply squeeze half a lemon and let it go at that. Or if the recipe says "a few twists of the pepper-mill," you don't grind in the whole lot.

I string along with the British in that I think in many instances ingredients should be listed by weight, rather than by measure. This is particularly true of fruits and vegetables. After all, you don't buy 3 cups of apple slices, but, rather, so many pounds, and the recipe should indicate that so many pounds add up to so many cups, sliced. Common sense plays an enormous role in the kitchen and it should play an equivalent role in the written recipe.

Within a relatively short time the metric system will be established throughout the world and with it will go the old familiar way of measuring. I believe it is not a moment too soon for cooks to begin to familiarize themselves with this system. A metric chart follows which will help you with cookbooks not published in this country and will assist you when we, too, adopt this simpler measuring system based on tens and their multiples.

I am also including a list of equivalent British measurements which will illustrate my point about the comparative ease of listing recipe ingredients by weight, rather than by measure. The list, of course, will also be invaluable when using cookbooks published in Great Britain.

British Measurements Compared

SOLID MEASUREMENTS

BRITISH	AMERICAN (approx. equivalents)
1 pound butter or fat	2 (standard 8-ounce) cups solidly packed
½ pound butter or fat	1 cup solidly packed
¼ pound butter or fat	½ cup solidly packed
2 ounces butter or fat	¼ cup (4 tablespoons)
1 ounce butter or fat	2 tablespoons
1 pound caster sugar	2⅓ cups superfine granulated sugar
½ pound caster sugar	1 cup plus 3 tablespoons
¼ pound caster sugar	8 tablespoons
2 ounces caster sugar	4 tablespoons
1 pound plain flour sifted	4½ cups sifted flour
¼ pound plain flour sifted	1 cup plus 4 tablespoons
2 ounces plain flour sifted	8 tablespoons
1 ounce plain flour sifted	4 tablespoons
¼ ounce plain flour sifted	1 tablespoon
¼ pound dry grated cheese	1 cup
½ pound rice, raw	1 cup

LIQUID MEASUREMENTS

BRITISH	AMERICAN
1 gallon = 4 quarts = 8 pints	1½ gallons = 5 quarts = 10 pints
1 quart = 2 pints = 40 ounces	1 quart, 8 ounces = 2½ pints = 5 cups
1 pint = 20 ounces	1 pint, 4 ounces = 2½ cups
½ pint = 10 ounces	10 ounces = 1¼ cups
¼ pint = 5 ounces = 1 gill	5 ounces = ⅝ cup
2 ounces = 4 tablespoons	4 tablespoons = ¼ cup
1 tablespoon = ½ ounce	1 tablespoon = ½ ounce
1 tablespoon = 4 teaspoons	1 tablespoon = 3 teaspoons

Weights and Measurements

A pinch = ½ to ⅛ teaspoon, or as much as can be picked up between thumb and forefinger

3 teaspoons = 1 tablespoon

4 tablespoons = ¼ cup or 2 ounces

5 tablespoons plus 1 teaspoon = ⅓ cup

8 tablespoons = ½ cup or 4 ounces

16 tablespoons = 1 cup or 8 ounces

Breadcrumbs

1 slice firm, day-old bread, grated in electric blender = ¼ cup crumbs

Butter, Lard, Margarine, or Shortening

1 ounce = 2 tablespoons or ¼ stick

2 ounces = 4 tablespoons, ¼ cup, or ½ stick

4 ounces = 8 tablespoons, ½ cup, or 1 stick

½ pound = 16 tablespoons, 1 cup, or 2 sticks

1 pound = 2 cups or 4 sticks

Cheese

¼ pound Cheddar or Swiss = 1 cup grated

½ pound cottage = 1 cup

3-ounce package cream = 6 tablespoons

Cream

1 cup or ½ pint heavy cream = 2 cups whipped

Eggs

4 to 6 whole shelled eggs = about 1 cup

8 to 10 egg whites = about 1 cup
12 to 14 egg yolks = about 1 cup

Flour

1 pound white all-purpose = 4 cups sifted
1 pound cake flour = 4¾ to 5 cups sifted

Fruit

1 pound, 3 medium apples = 3 cups sliced
1 pound, 3 medium bananas = 2½ cups sliced
1 medium lemon = 3 to 4 tablespoons juice *
1 medium lemon = 1 tablespoon grated rind
1 medium orange = ⅓ cup juice *
1 medium orange = 10 to 11 sections
1 medium orange = 1 tablespoon plus 1 teaspoon grated rind
1 medium grapefruit = ⅔ cup juice *
1 medium grapefruit = 10 to 12 sections
1 pint box berries, except gooseberries = 2 cups

    * All citrus fruits boiled for about a minute yield a larger amount of juice. However, the rind *cannot* be grated after boiling.

Pasta

1 8-ounce package macaroni or 2 cups uncooked = 4 to 5 cups cooked
1 8-ounce package noodles or spaghetti, or 2½ cups uncooked = 3 to 4 cups, cooked

Rice

1 cup uncooked long grain rice = 3 cups cooked
1 cup parboiled or converted = 4 cups cooked rice
1 cup precooked rice = 2 cups cooked
1 cup brown rice = 4 cups cooked

Sugar

1 pound brown, firmly packed = 2⅓ to 2½ cups
1 pound confectioners' unsifted = 4½ cups
1 pound granulated or superfine = 2¼ to 2½ cups

Unflavored Gelatin
1 envelope = 1 tablespoon. This amount will "gel" 2 cups of liquid.
(If sugar is used, it should be counted as part of the total liquid.)

Chocolate
1 ounce semisweet chocolate pieces is the equivalent of 1 ounce of
any sweet cooking chocolate or 1 square, 1-ounce size, semisweet
chocolate.

Nuts
1 cup or about 5 ounces, by weight, grated with a hand-operated
grater yields 2 cups grated.
1 cup or about 5 ounces, by weight, grated in the electric blender,
yields about 1½ cups grated.

Parsley
1 cup parsley sprigs = ½ cup minced parsley

Vegetables and Fruits
1 pound dry white beans, or 2 cups uncooked yields 6 cups cooked
1 pound dry kidney beans, or 2⅔ cups uncooked yields 6¼ cups cooked
1 pound dry lima beans, or 3 cups uncooked yields 7 cups cooked
3 medium tomatoes = 1 pound
3 medium sweet potatoes, or 1 pound = 3 cups sliced
3 medium white potatoes, or 1 pound = 2⅛ cups sliced
3 medium peaches make 1 pound, or 2 cups of sliced peaches, or one
cup of mashed
3 to 4 medium oranges make 1 cup of juice
2 medium oranges make 1 cup of bite-sized pieces
1 medium orange makes 10 to 11 sections
1 medium orange yields 4 teaspoons grated rind
1 medium orange unpeeled make ⅔ to ¾ cup purée

What are cup equivalents to can sizes?
¾ cup = 6 ounces
1 cup = 8 ounces
1¼ cups = 10½ ounces
1½ cups = 13 ounces
1¾ cups = 15½ ounces
2 cups = 1 pound

2½ cups = 1 pound, 4 ounces
3½ cups = 1 pound, 13 ounces
5¾ cups = 2 pounds, 14 ounces
12 cups = 6 pounds

What is the metric system of measurement? The average housewife
uses measurement units every day—units of length, weight, volume,
and temperature. She measures the length of her curtains in inches,
buys a 5-pound roast for dinner, uses standardized cups and spoons
to measure the ingredients for her cake, bakes it in a moderate 350° F.
oven, then takes the temperature of her sick child to be sure it is
no higher than the normal 98.6° F. She has been doing these things
all her life and she does them without thinking about them.

She may never have heard of the metric system of measurements,
although 90% of the earth's population is either using it now, or is
committed to using it in the future. Since the United States is consid-
ering the possibility of joining the rest of the world by adopting it also,
the housewife should know something about it. It's simply a system of
measurement based on units of 10, and it has been almost universally
accepted because it is consistent, logical, and much easier to work
with than our customary system.

Think of the confusing multiplicity of numbers the housewife has
to remember if she wants to convert any of those measurements she
uses every day: 12 inches in a foot, 3 feet in a yard, 5,280 feet in a
mile; 8 ounces in a cup, 16 ounces in a pound or a pint, 2 pints in a
quart, 4 quarts in a gallon; and who remembers how many pounds in
a long ton? Or how many feet in a rod?

On the other hand, if a housewife were using the metric system,
she would only have to remember one number: 10 (and its multiples). In the metric system the multiples of 10's are always designated
by the same prefix, regardless of the base unit being used. The most
commonly used prefixes are:

kilo = 1000.0
deci =   0.1
centi =   0.01
milli =   0.001

Thus, a kilogram is 1000 grams, and a centimeter is one one-hundredth of a meter. Obviously, to make a conversion from a meter to a
centimeter, it is only necessary to move the decimal point.

The housewife would use the following metric units: The meter (and its multiples) for length; the gram and kilogram for weight; the liter and milliliter for volume; and temperature Celsius.

Let's consider each of these units. First, the meter for length (which is equivalent to 3.3 feet or 1.1 yard in our system). One thousand meters are one kilometer, used for measuring large distances, as between cities. A speed limit would be set at so many kilometers per hour. For smaller measurements, the meter is divided into 10 decimeters, 100 centimeters, and 1000 millimeters. Cloth and paper goods would be measured in centimeters; the length of an object smaller than a centimeter, for instance a cigarette, would be designated in millimeters. That's all: the base unit times 1000; or, one-tenth, one-hundredth, or one-thousandth of the base unit.

Next, the gram and kilogram (1000 grams; equivalent to 2.2 pounds, in our system) for weight. Meat and butter would be weighed in kilograms; smaller units would be weighed in grams. Again, that's all. Then, the liter (1.056 quart, or roughly equivalent) for volume. The liter contains 1000 milliliters (ml). Most liquids would be measured in liters (1000 ml), ½ liters (500 ml), or ¼ liters (250 ml). Finally, let's look at temperature, comparing Fahrenheit with metric (Celsius):

	Fahrenheit °	Celsius °
Water freezes	32	0
Water boils	212	100
Normal body temperature	98.6	37

The use of metric greatly simplifies ordinary calculations. A housewife could easily compare quantities and prices if commodities were unit priced in metric: if length were measured in centimeters, weight in kilograms or grams, and volume in liters or milliliters.

But when a society changes from customary measurement to metric, the transition period is confusing, for one is thinking in customary terms and making complicated conversions to metric. During this period, it is helpful to rely on accurate conversion charts and tables. Then, as rapidly as possible, it is best to discard them, and forget about feet, quarts, gallons, and miles. Think metric, and all you have to remember for conversion is the number 10, and its multiples.

Written by Mrs. Florence M. Essers of the Metric Study Team, U.S. Department of Commerce, National Bureau of Standards

U. S. Customary Units, and Possible New Measures for Metrication in Home Preparation of Food

U.S. Customary Units	Possible New Standard Measures (in Milliliters*)	
	I †	II ‡
1 quart	1000.0	1000.0
1 pint	500	500
1 cup	250	250
¾ cup	187.5	
⅔ cup	166.7	
½ cup	125	
⅓ cup	83.3	
¼ cup	62.5	
1 tablespoon	15.6	
1 teaspoon	5.2	
½ teaspoon	2.6	
¼ teaspoon	1.3	

* The milliliter (ml) is a unit of measurement equal to 0.03381 liquid ounces.
† The measurements of column I are based on a 250-ml cup, marked off into ¾, ⅔, ½, ⅓, and ¼ units.
‡ The incomplete measurements in column II are based upon the metric system, but because it may be awkward for the homemaker to deal with odd-sized metric units, accurate and acceptable measurements in round numbers will eventually be worked out.

Do package labels give the number of servings?   The manufacturer is not required by law to list the number of servings in a package, but if he does, then he must give the size of the servings, stated in some common measure such as ounces or cups or tablespoons. Homemakers unaccustomed to thinking in terms of weight measurements should immediately learn that 8 ounces is 1 cup or 16 tablespoons, thus making it relatively easy to compare prices of a product packed in different-size containers.

What is a "jumbo" pound?   A pound is a pound is a pound, to paraphrase Gertrude Stein. But you've brought up a good question, particularly significant since the new Fair Packaging and Labeling Act went into effect July 1, 1968.

The Economic Research Service of the U.S. Department of Agriculture sums it up concisely: "The net contents of the package, unless specifically exempted, must be listed on the principal display panel, which is the part the shopper usually sees when the product is on the supermarket shelf. They must be shown in terms of total ounces, followed by a separate statement showing pounds and ounces; in bold-face type in a color that is in distinct contrast to the rest of the label; in a type size that is easy to read." What this means: You don't have to hunt all over a package to find out exactly how much and what it contains. It is against the law to use misleading terms, such as "jumbo pound" or "giant quart." A "jumbo pound" contains exactly 16 ounces, like every other pound, and a "giant" quart, the standard 32 ounces, just like every other quart.

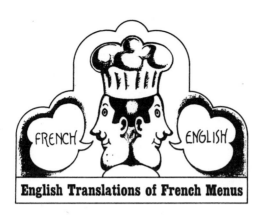

English Translations of French Menus

Can you give me the English meanings of words frequently found on French menus? It would be impossible to give you a complete list but here is an edited list of foods that appear frequently on French menus in the United States.

Agneau, Lamb
Ananas, Pineapple
Artichaut, Artichokes
Asperges, Asparagus
Bar rayé, Striped Bass
Bisque, Thick cream soup
Bouquetière, Vegetable garnish
Caneton, Duckling
Champignons, Mushrooms
Crème Chantilly, Sweetened whipped cream
Consommé en tasse, Consommé in a cup
Crevettes, Shrimp
Épinard, Spinach
Escargots, Snails
Foie de veau, Calf's liver
Forestière, Mushroom garnish
Fromage, Cheese
Fruits de mer, Mixed seafood, hot or cold
Glace, Ice cream

Grenouille, Frogs' legs
Huîtres, Oysters
Jambon de Bayonne, Smoked ham
Langouste, Rock lobster
Moules, Mussels
Mille-feuille, puff pastry
Petits pois, Young peas
Pigeonneau, Squab
Plat du jour, Specialty of the day
Poisson, Fish
Pommes de terre, Potatoes
Potages chauds, Hot soups
Potage du jour, Soup of the day
Poularde, Chicken
Praires, Clams
Ris de veau, Sweetbreads
Rognons de veau, Veal kidneys
Rouget, Red snapper
Saucisson, Sausage
Saumon fumé, Smoked salmon
Soupe à l'oignon, Onion soup
Suprême de volaille, Breast of chicken
Terrine, Pâté in a terrine
Truffes, Truffles

Housekeeping

How long can you store foods in the freezer? The recommended *maximum* storage times for frozen foods, *held at 0° or below,* are these:

MEATS

Beef *	6 to 8 months
Fresh pork *	3 to 4 months
Lamb *	6 to 7 months
Variety meats (liver, heart, tongue, etc.)	3 to 4 months
Veal	3 to 4 months
Smoked Hams, picnics, and slab bacon (whole, halves, or quarters)	Not to exceed 60 days
Other cured and smoked meats	Not to exceed 60 days
Sliced bacon	Not recommended for freezing
Bologna, frankfurters, or wieners	Not recommended for freezing
Fresh pork sausage	Not recommended for freezing
Poultry	
Giblets	4 months
Chicken	6 to 12 months
Turkey	6 to 12 months

* Except when ground.

BAKED GOODS

Cakes, cupcakes	2 to 3 months
Pastry (baked or unbaked)	2 months
Cookies (baked or unbaked)	9 months
Breads (all kinds)	3 months

15

FROZEN FRUITS, VEGETABLES

Citrus fruits, juices	4 to 6 months
Other fruits	8 to 12 months
Vegetables	8 to 12 months

OTHER FOODS

Prepared main dishes	3 to 4 months
Soups	4 months
Stews	4 months
Leftover creamed dishes	1 month
Sandwiches	2 weeks
Butter	2 months
Ice cream	1 month

Does freezing kill bacteria in foods?   No. According to the U.S. Department of Agriculture, it simply stops bacteria from multiplying, which is why it is so important to maintain strict sanitation in preparing food for the home freezer and to freeze only high-quality food.

What is meant by freezer burn?   It's a term used to designate foods, particularly meats, that have dried out in the freezer because they have not been wrapped and sealed properly. Although the food is still edible, it will lack flavor (may even be off-flavor), and the texture will be stringy. A grayish-looking surface is the sign to watch for. Frost-free freezers are more apt to cause this because they are kept free of accumulated frost by fans which, as must be obvious, are drying. Hence the very special need to use proper materials or containers, well sealed. To forestall freezer burn, moistureproof, transparent quilted bags, tied securely with rubber bands or metal closures, and freezer foil or several layers of Saran Wrap, securely taped, are recommended for meats with the bone in; freezer tubs or jars securely sealed can be used for meats cut off the bones, if large enough to accommodate the meat.

How much food can you safely freeze at one time?   The U.S. Department of Agriculture suggests that you limit the amount of food to two pounds per cubic foot of total freezer space.

Is there any advantage in buying frozen fruits, vegetables, shellfish loose in plastic bags?   Yes. There are two major advantages. First, with individually quick-frozen foods (the trade refers to them as I.Q.F.), you can use as much as you want from a package and return the remainder to the freezer; second, you can tell instantly if the food has thawed en route, then refrozen, because it will refreeze into a block. Obviously, you will not want to buy food that has thawed and refrozen, because, as everybody knows, refreezing can affect quality.

How do you freeze individual foods? Meat patties, small steaks, pastry shells, cookies, etc. should be placed on a baking sheet so each one is separate, then put in the freezer until frozen. Once frozen, place pieces of Saran Wrap or aluminum foil between the individual foods (this makes separation easier when you come to use them), then stack them. You can use the drugstore wrap or the butcher's wrap (see below).

How do you wrap foods for freezing? Three accepted methods are: the drugstore wrap, the butcher's wrap, and the freezer bag. The drugstore wrap is done like this: Take a piece of foil or Saran Wrap large enough to encompass the food. Bring the front and back edges together, pulling tightly. Turn under, making an inch fold. Continue folding until the wrap adheres snugly to the food. Then smooth with your hands to press out the air. Next, fold ends into triangles, again pressing out any air. Bring each of the triangles to the center. Seal with freezer tape and label with name, date, and weight. The butcher's wrap is done like this: Place the stack diagonally on its side on a piece of Saran Wrap or foil generous enough to encompass the food completely. Bring back corner forward, pressing snugly to the food. Fold in from each side in turn, drawing tightly around the food. Pull up remaining side, seal with freezer tape, label with name, date, and, if necessary, weight. With a freezer bag which should, obviously, be large enough to enclose the food, squeeze out all air by pressing the bag to the food, then fold the end over and seal with freezer tape. Label with name, date and weight.

What foods do not freeze successfully? Salad greens, cucumbers, radishes, cabbage, tomatoes, bananas, pears, hard-cooked eggs, onions, celery, cottage cheese, mayonnaise, egg yolks, salad dressing, and fried foods (except potatoes and onion rings), root vegetables.

Do you consider an oven thermometer essential? Ovens—at least, *my* oven—seem to fluctuate greatly and a thermometer is a foolproof means of determining whether your oven temperature is correct or not. Personally, I never attempt to cook anything anymore without checking my oven with an oven thermometer. The thermometer I use, and recommend, is Taylor's mercury thermometer, which registers from 100° to 700°.

Is there any way to protect the stove and other equipment from the spatter when you fry or sauté? A fine cook of our acquaintance uses shirt boards, which he stands up in what he hopes will be "the line of fire." Although the boards may not catch all the grease, he reports they minimize the problem. Bachelor girls should cultivate boyfriends. Lacking boyfriends, buy a "spatter preventer," available in stores specializing in fine cooking equipment.

How do you clean carbon steel knives? With Scotch-Brite scouring pads, the dandiest scrubbers your knives ever met. Reusable, washable, rustproof, and splinterproof. Just wet the pad, dip in water, and your knives will clean up like new. Loads of other uses, too, such as cleaning barbecue grills, ovens, pans, broilers. Recommended highly by such knowledgeable people as Ann Roe Robbins, New York's well-known cooking school expert. Cleaning your knives every time you use them is a good habit to establish and so easy with these efficient scouring pads. Available in all supermarkets.

How do you sharpen your carbon steel knives? With Carborundum knife sharpeners. Use the short kitchen sharpeners for small knives, such as paring; the carving knife sharpener (this resembles the old-fashioned sharpening rod, or steel, as it is often called) for carving knives, French chef's knives, boning knives, etc. These sharpeners with sturdy handles that fit your hand are very easy to use and the combination of silicon and carbon makes a perfect abrasive to give a fine edge to any knife. To keep your knives on the *qui vive*, as it were, do as all good chefs do: sharpen them each time they are used. Clean and wash them immediately after using.

What is a porte-couteau? A knife rest, commonly used in France, on which to rest one's knife between courses or on which to rest a carving knife.

Should you cool hot foods before refrigerating them? No. The sooner you get the foods (meats, vegetables, etc.) into the refrigerator, the better they will be when you come to eat them up. Cover securely, of course. In the old days of iceboxes with poor insulation, cooks did not refrigerate immediately because it tended to melt the ice, but that problem doesn't exist today.

How can you clean rubber sink and stove mats easily? Soak in bleach water (about ¾ cup of the bleach to a gallon of water), then wash thoroughly. If stains are stubborn, a little judicious rubbing with a scouring pad should clear them up.

Do you use baking soda other than for cooking? Yes. It's the great cleaner and sweetener of all time and in these days when all of us are concerned or should be, about pollution, baking soda is the answer to many kitchen needs. Allow about 3 teaspoons to 1 quart of water to wash the refrigerator, plastic dishes, stainless steel surfaces, bread boxes and cookie jars, coffeemakers, teapots, glass surfaces, etc. And if your feet are tired after a long day, soak them in a mixture of soda and water in the same proportions.

How can you remove wax stains from table linens? The fabric experts at the U.S. Department of Agriculture say to do this: "Scrape the spot with a dull knife. Then place the stained cloth between two clean *white* blotters or several layers of facial tissue and press with a warm iron. To remove the slight stain that remains, sponge with a grease solvent. The same procedure works for other fabrics."

Is it true that ice trays should be filled with hot water rather than cold? We queried the General Electric Company on this and they answered us with a positive "No!" This is especially important with modern ice trays, which have a thin coating of wax to prevent the ice cubes from adhering to the tray or grid and make shucking easier. Hot water would remove the wax. They also tell us that trays should never be filled beyond the top edge of the grid, to preclude the water's freezing into a solid sheet of ice on top. This not only makes it harder to shuck the ice; it will tend to distort the bottom of the tray.

What utensils should you use for pickling and preserving? Only en-

ameled ware, glass, aluminum, stainless steel, or stoneware utensils.
Brass, copper, iron, or galvanized utensils are apt to cause unattractive color changes or they will react with the acid or salt to produce
unwholesome substances.

Cooking Terms and Techniques

What is a calorie? Food is the source of energy for the body, and the energy value of food is measured in the form of the heat it will provide when it is burned up or oxidized by the body. A calorie is the unit used to measure this energy (heat), as an inch is a unit of length, and a minute is a unit of time. It is defined as the amount of heat required to raise the temperature of a kilogram of water (about one quart) one degree centigrade. You gain weight when your food provides more energy—or calories—than the body uses. The extra energy is stored mainly as fat. About 3,500 extra calories produce a pound of fat.

What is the difference between "enriched" and "fortified" foods? According to Cornell University's Consumer Education Program (New York City): "Enriched foods (chiefly those made from cereal grains) are nutritionally improved by the addition of extra amounts of thiamine, riboflavin, niacin (all B vitamins), and iron, all four of which must be included for a product to be labeled 'enriched.' These particular vitamins, so important to your well-being, change into energy in the body, keep your nervous system on the *qui vive*, and help to keep appetite and digestion normal. 'Fortified' is applied to foods where one or more ingredients have been added to provide certain nutrients that may or may not be present naturally in the food." Two examples are vitamin D, the vitamin we get from sunshine, which is added to milk; and iodine, which is added to table salt. The latter is especially valuable to people living in what is known as the "iodine belt" where there is little, if any, natural iodine in the water and foods.

How can you tell when foods have "turned"?   There are many signs. Your nose is a big help and you can always taste such things as milk, cream, or soup. If meat or poultry in a broth has soured, it will ferment—which you can actually see working. As for meat or poultry, the color changes, looks "different" and there is some odor.

What are food additives?   The National Academy of Sciences defines a food additive as a "substance or mixture of substances, other than a basic foodstuff, which is present in a food as a result of production processing, storage, or packaging." The oldest known additive is salt, which can perform two functions: enhance the taste of the food and/ or preserve it.

How did the word restaurant originate?   It derives from the French, *restaurer,* meaning "to restore." In 1765, according to *Larousse Gastronomique,* a man named Boulanger (incidentally, his name means "baker"), a soup vendor, called his soups *restaurants,* i.e. restoratives. He wrote on his sign, "Boulanger sells magical restoratives" which he embellished with a culinary joke in Latin: *Venite ad me; vos qui stomacho laboratis, et ego restaurabo* which loosely translates into: "Come to me, you with tired stomachs, and I will restore you."

Where does the word grocer come from?   Believe it or not, it's right from the 14th-century pepper and spice trading in England. After peppercorns had made that long trip from the East to London, they were bought and sold by the Guild of Pepperers, who sold the pepper by the gross (in modern terms, this would mean wholesale). Peddlers would buy pepper from the "grossers" to sell to housewives. Thus, grocers. In France they had spice sellers; the French word for grocer is still *épicier.* As a matter of interest, today Americans consume 44 million pounds of black pepper and about 3.5 million of white. Black is lustier than white, but white is preferred in white dishes, and today all good cooks use peppermills to season their cooking. And just remember when you are cooking that pepper and chicken were made for each other.

What does brasserie mean?   It's the French for brewery, brewhouse, or beershop. In modern terms a brasserie is a café or restaurant where sturdy foods, with all kinds of drinks—not only beer—are served. France is cluttered with them, the most famous being the Brasserie Lipp in Paris, familiar to many Americans. The first brasserie in the United States, which turned up in New York a few years ago, is open twenty-four hours a day, 365 days a year.

What does maison mean on a restaurant menu? Originally it meant a dish that originated with the chef of the restaurant. Today it is a convenient label for any dish without a special name, concocted out of ingredients available in the restaurant at the moment.

What is boui-boui? In the middle of the 1880s in France, the life style then known as *la belle époque* was colored by luxury and ornamentation. Surfeited with extravagances, connoisseurs searched out tiny cafés—restaurants they named *boui-boui* (pronounced bwee bwee)—where simplicity replaced luxury. Marble tables and wooden benches amused and delighted the customers who were bored with the ornate. Today, we have a Boui-Boui at 69 West 55th Street, New York City, where you can have omelettes, sweet and savory, escargots, Welsh rabbit (French style), and elegant fare such as *poulet champenoise* (chicken cooked in champagne) and steak bordelaise.

What does provençale mean in cookery? The term is applied to dishes of southern France (Provence is a former province of southern France), containing garlic, sometimes tomatoes, and olive oil.

What exactly is a casserole? Both the *Oxford English Dictionary* and the *Dictionnaire de l'Académie des Gastronomes* say it is the diminutive of *casse*, old French for an open-mouthed pan, bowl, or basin, with or without a cover. Hence the many French recipes that call for a casserole. The cast-iron Dutch oven, familiar to many American cooks (once popular but used less today because iron discolors foods cooked with wine or eggs), is a casserole in the French sense. In the United States today, however, casserole usually means a one-dish meal made with two or more ingredients cooked in a casserole or bake-and-serve dish.

What does réchauffé mean? Obviously, it's French; and it means food that has been warmed over. It is in contrast to *les restes,* meaning "the remnants," the French expression for foods left over from one meal which the thrifty French cook turns into a delicious aftermath. The *Dictionnaire de l'Académie des Gastronomes* designates the using up of leftovers as a fine art and "one of the most precious talents of the economical housewife." There is, as a matter of record, a French book called *Manières d'Accommoder les Restes* (Ways to Do Up the Remainders).

What's the difference between mix and blend in cooking? None. But with the advent of that remarkable piece of equipment, the electric blender, "blend" has become, to many cooks, synonymous with blender. For that reason, it would seem to make sense if all recipes specified "mix" to indicate combining two or more ingredients thoroughly.

What does dot mean? Literally, to dot food with bits of fat or cheese.

What does papillote mean in cookery? It means several things; among them an envelope of parchment paper, usually encasing a veal chop or sometimes a fillet of fish. Thus, food cooked in paper is called *en papillote.* It is presented at the table in the paper and the guest removes the paper himself. It also means a paper frill used to adorn a lamb chop or the bone of a ham—its *raison d'être* being strictly aesthetic. It can also mean a Christmas bonbon rolled in a piece of paper, then decorated with a drawing and inscribed with a motto, the whole wrapped in colorful paper with frills at both ends.

What does à point mean in cooking? It simply means the dish has been cooked to the right stage.

What is toss? It simply means to mix gently with a fork and a spoon or two forks. Salad, for example, is tossed lightly to coat the ingredients with the dressing.

How do you deep-fat fry? Pour the oil in, or add the shortening to, a regular deep-fat fryer, deep electric skillet, or deep heavy pot. For most deep-fat frying 365° is about the right temperature. If you go beyond that, the fat will burn. If you do a lot of frying it is almost essential to have a thermometer designed for deep frying. Most thermometers on the market used for this purpose are also designated as candy thermometers which means they can be used in making frostings, etc. Lacking a thermometer, you can test the temperature by dropping a one-inch square of bread in the fat. If it browns in one minute, the fat is heated to 365°.

What does mignonnette mean, culinarily?   The word derives from the French *mignon,* meaning "tiny." In the kitchen it means ground pepper, *une petite mignonnette.*

What does chow mein mean?   Grace Zia Chu, author of *The Pleasures of Chinese Cooking,* and Johnny Kan, famed San Francisco Chinese restaurateur, tell us that chow mein refers to stir-fry, the original Chinese cooking technique that came as a result of the invention of the *wok,* centuries ago. The *wok* is the all-purpose cooking pan of the Chinese kitchen.

How can you keep olives once the bottle is opened?   Throw the lid away and refrigerate the olives. They will keep indefinitely but if the brine evaporates and the olives are exposed they will mildew. So, if necessary, add a little water to the brine, with some salt.

Are cold consommé and consommé en gelée the same?   No, indeed. Consommé, meaning a clear soup, can be made with a beef, fish, chicken, or game base, plus vegetables, strained, but not clarified. These are simple consommés. Then there are double consommés (see below).

Are double consommé and condensed beef broth (bouillon) comparable?   In many respects. Consommé or bouillon (they are synonymous) is a soup made with beef, poultry, game or fish bones, vegetables, and seasonings, and simmered for a very long time to concentrate the flavors, then strained. The French call this *consommé simple.* It can be drunk as is or it can be used as a base to make other soups, to cook other foods, to make sauces, etc. Double consommé is *consommé simple* that has been clarified to remove all extraneous matter, which further concentrates the flavors. The result is an absolutely clear, usually golden, liquid that may or may not "gel" depending on the amount of natural gelatin derived from the ingredients used. It can be served hot or cold, with or without garnishes, and it is, of course, the base for savory aspics. Innumerable clear soups call for double consommé, a familiar one being madrilène, meaning Madrid style, made with chicken consommé flavored with fresh tomatoes, sweet tomatoes, and sweet red peppers; traditionally served cold. Condensed beef broth, also called bouillon, and condensed chicken broth, both commercial canned products, strained but not clarified, are so highly concentrated they can be diluted with water, half and half. However, this writer prefers to use them full strength. They, too, can be clarified and used as you would double consommé. Lacking homemade broth, these are well-qualified substitutes. As a matter of record, there is no commercial fish bouillon on the market, but clam juice is a reasonable equivalent.

Does the clarification of stock (broth or bouillon) reduce the volume? Yes. Clarifying, as you know, removes the solids from the stock and, as a consequence, at least a third, and sometimes a half or even more can be lost. So figure in those terms if you intend to use the cleared stock in specific quantities, such as in aspics. It is well, too, to remember that clarifying also reduces the strength, so seasonings should be added more generously prior to clarifying and adjusted to taste once you have achieved the clear, amber liquid.

What are croquettes? A mixture of finely chopped, cooked meat, fish, shellfish, poultry, game, or potatoes, bound together with a very thick sauce, then cooled. The mixture is then shaped, dipped into egg, and breadcrumbs, then deep-fried. Entrée croquettes are always served with a compatible sauce.

ANITA ODEURS' POTATO CROQUETTES

5 Idaho potatoes	1 large clove garlic, peeled and
3 eggs, separated	minced (optional)
¼ cup (½ stick) butter, softened	Commercial, unseasoned bread-
Salt	crumbs
Freshly ground pepper	Vegetable shortening
Freshly ground nutmeg	

Peel the potatoes, quarter, and drop into boiling salted water. Bring to a boil again. Reduce heat to moderate, cover, and cook until the potatoes are tender when pierced with the point of a small knife. Drain immediately and dry quickly by shaking the pan over a high heat or out the window. Put through a potato ricer, then mix in the yolks and butter well *with a fork* because you do not want too creamy a mixture. Add salt, pepper, and nutmeg to taste. Stir in the garlic, then shape the mixture into tubes about

1″ in diameter and 3″ long. Dip in the egg whites, then roll in the bread-crumbs. Place on a baking sheet, cover wth Saran Wrap, and allow to dry overnight or for several hours.

To fry, heat the shortening to 400° on the thermometer. Fry the croquettes, a few at a time, until golden. Drain on paper towels. Makes 24.

N O T E : Croquettes can be fried ahead, refrigerated, then heated in a 400° oven; or frozen and reheated in a hot oven.

What is bagna cauda? Essentially a dip, it is one of the famous specialties of the province of Piedmont (Italy). Made with olive oil, butter, anchovies, and garlic. The sauce is served hot with raw celery, cabbage, peppers (both cooked and raw) with a strong coarse red wine. Not usually served at meals but rather when someone feels hungry and thirsty. For garlic eaters, it's a blissful feast.

What is saltimbocca? From the Italian, it means, literally, "jump into the mouth." It is made with thin slices of veal and raw or cooked ham, sage leaves, salt, pepper, butter, and Marsala. Served with croutons of fried bread.

What is duxelles? Created by La Varenne, a famous gastronome and 17th-century author (*La Cuisine Française*) who dedicated his creation to the Marquis d'Uxelles, his master, it is a mixture of raw minced mushrooms, shallots, onions, and parsley, seasoned with nutmeg, salt, and pepper. Used to stuff large mushroom caps and such vegetables as onions or tomatoes; with or without breadcrumbs to stuff chicken or game; combined with a béchamel sauce to make meat or potato croquettes; as a foundation for various sauces, or turned into a sauce by the simple addition of cream or wine and served with meat.

DUXELLES

1 pound fresh mushrooms, finely minced (whole, or stems only)
4 tablespoons (½ stick) butter
2 tablespoons vegetable oil
3 tablespoons minced onion
3 tablespoons (about 8 cloves) minced shallots

Salt
Freshly ground pepper
Freshly ground nutmeg
8 to 10 parsley sprigs, minced

Twist the mushrooms, a few at a time, in a clean linen towel to extract as much juice as possible—a lot will emerge.

Heat the butter and oil in a heavy enameled skillet. Add the onions and shallots and cook over a high flame for about a minute. Add the mushrooms, reduce heat to moderate, and sauté, stirring frequently, for 6 to 8 minutes or until the mushroom pieces begin to separate from each other and brown lightly. Season to taste with salt, pepper, and nutmeg. Stir in the parsley. Cool. Refrigerate in covered jar, or freeze. Makes 2 cups.

What does Florentine mean in cookery? A garnish of spinach in one form or another.

What does à la Hongroise mean? In the Hungarian style. According to *Larousse Gastronomique*, "Dishes prepared *à la hongroise* are always cooked in a cream sauce, seasoned or garnished with paprika." Eggs, fish, meat (other than pork), poultry, and vegetables such as cauliflower can all be prepared *à la hongroise.*

What does chasseur mean gastronomically? *Chasseur* is French for hunter; in the French kitchen it means hunter's style. *Sauce chasseur* consists of minced shallots and mushrooms, sautéed, reduced with white wine, enriched with meat extract and parsley.

Are stuffing and dressing the same thing? Yes. They both mean the filling used to stuff poultry, meats, fish, game, eggs, etc. The term stuffing is always used in the United States and, apparently, today in England, although at one time dressing was preferred. However, the *Oxford English Dictionary* still seems to prefer dressing over stuffing. Forcemeat, one of the oldest terms in cookery, was once used by the British (*Mrs. Beeton's Cook Book* is our reference) and in *Larousse Gastronomique* the listing reads, "Forcemeats or Stuffings." The French, of course, is *farce*. Dressing also means a sauce. You "dress" a salad, vegetables, etc.

What does "chantilly" mean in French cooking? It has three meanings: *crème chantilly*, meaning whipped cream sweetened with sugar; *mayonnaise chantilly*, mayonnaise made with lemon juice rather than vinegar and mixed with whipped cream; *hollandaise chantilly*, hollandaise sauce mixed with whipped cream.

What is bean curd? Known as *dofu* in Chinese dialect and *tofu* in Japanese, it is made from soybean milk and can be compared to cottage cheese. Available dried in packages; fermented or fresh in cans; also by the piece, in stores specializing in Chinese and Japanese foods.

What does noisette mean in cookery? *Noisette,* the diminutive of *noix,* meaning nut, is the French for hazelnut, which we in the United States call filbert; it also means hazel-colored or brown. *Beurre de noisettes* is a mixture of butter and browned filberts that have been pulverized. Used in soups and sauces, *sauce noisette* is hollandaise sauce made with *beurre noisette* (brown butter) or *beurre de noisettes. Pommes de terre noisette* are potatoes shaped to look like nuts, then browned lightly in butter. *Pommes de terre noisette* are used as a garnish in the professional kitchen. Also, *noisette* can mean small pieces of lamb, mutton, veal, beef, or, sometimes, fish.

What is falernum? A syrup made of spices, sugar, and citrus acid, with 5% alcohol, which originated in Barbados, West Indies. Used primarily to make rum drinks: daiquiris, rum sours, and Collinses. Cooks, however, also use it to baste chickens, to glaze hams, and to garnish fresh fruits.

Is petite marmite a soup or a pot? *Marmite* is French for a big pot used for making soups or stocks. *Petite marmite,* like *pot-au-feu* (literally, pot on the fire), is a kind of homemade family soup made with beef, chicken giblets, vegetables, and a simple consommé. *Pot-au-feu* provides two dishes: a delicious soup that can be garnished in many ways, and meat and vegetables; it is classically made with beef and chicken. *Poule-au-pot* (chicken in a pot) is essentially the same, except that the chicken is stuffed.

What does "try out" mean? This is a term used when cubes of pork, suet, bacon, etc., are browned over a low heat to extract as much fat as possible to use for cooking. The browned cubes are called "cracklings" and are frequently used to season peas, lentils, and other legumes or in soups. "Render" means the same thing.

What exactly is mincemeat? You have to go back a long way. "Mynce pyes" were served at the crowning of Henry V in the 15th century. The original combination was something to give one pause: duck, rabbit, pigeon, goose, partridge, curlew (apparently the equivalent of the modern quail), neat's tongue (actually, ox tongue), woodcock, and blackbird. The whole bound together with flour and butter. By Samuel Pepys' time, mince pies were essentially meat dishes flavored with spices and fruits. His wife, he reported in his diary for Christmas 1666, had overslept because she had sat up until four o'clock that morning to see the mince pie properly finished for dinner.

Mince pies have had rough sledding. They were banned in Cromwell's day; and in this country in the middle of the 19th century, there were no mince pies in New England because of a religious argument over the shape and meaning of the pies. The variations on the recipe are almost endless but, essentially, it is a mixture of dried fruits (raisins, citron, currants), beef and suet, apples, almonds, sugar, spices, and brandy, etc., baked in pastry. The modern ready-to-use commercial mincemeats are so good it seems almost ridiculous for a woman to make her own.

What does corned mean?   Cured by soaking in a salt solution or brine. Corned beef, for example.

How should cocoa be stored?   As with chocolate cocoa does not "weather" well if exposed to high temperatures or humidity. Suggested temperatures are 60° to 70°. The flavor is not affected by temperature or humidity but the cocoa tends to lump or lose color. It is best to store it in glass, plastic, or metal containers tightly sealed.

What does rougail mean?   It's straight out of Creole cookery and means a sort of condiment, highly spiced, actually an appetite stimulant, that is served with rice à la creole. Rougail is made with green apples, eggplant, salt cod, tomatoes, and shrimp.

What is tahini?   Also spelled *taheeni*, it is a paste made of sesame seed oil mixed with lemon juice, garlic, salt, and chopped parsley. Used extensively in Near Eastern cookery as a dressing for fish or meat, with vegetables such as cauliflower or eggplant, and on salads.

How do you tie a collar around a soufflé dish?   Cut a wide piece of strong baking parchment or waxed paper long enough to go completely around the mold and overlap well. Then fold the paper two or three times, depending on the width of the mold and how high you want your soufflé to rise above the mold. Apply the strip of paper to the outside of the mold, pulling the paper together securely and tightly so that the soufflé mixture cannot run down between the paper and the mold. Secure the paper collar with a piece of string, tying it very tight.

What is a soufflé mold? A straight-sided earthenware dish is the classic French mold, originally white only (in our slightly prejudiced opinion, still preferable) but now available in colors and with designs of all kinds (good and bad). They range in size from 1½ cups (for individual soufflés) to 2 quarts. Sizes beyond that are much too large for cooking a *hot* soufflé. The larger sizes can, of course, be used for cold soufflés or for casserole dishes. Glass soufflé dishes, 1- and 1½-quart sizes, are new and very chic. You'll find they cook much more quickly than the standard porcelain soufflé molds.

When is a soufflé done? If you're nervous and many people are when they make soufflés, you can open the oven door after 20 minutes, *not before*, to see how it's coming along. In 25 to 30 minutes, if properly prepared, it will have puffed at least 2 inches above the rim of the mold and the top should be nicely browned. If you cook it another 4 to 5 minutes it will not sink as rapidly when taken from the oven but you will have a firmer soufflé. We belong to the school that likes a creamy center.

CHEESE SOUFFLÉ

¾ cup Swiss cheese, freshly grated, or half Swiss and half Parmesan (about 6 ounces)	½ teaspoon salt Dash white pepper, freshly ground Pinch cayenne pepper
3 tablespoons butter	Pinch nutmeg, freshly grated
3 tablespoons flour	4 whole eggs, separated
1 cup milk	3 extra egg whites

Butter the inside, curves and all, of a 1½-quart soufflé mold. Add 2 or 3 tablespoons of the cheese. Tip the mold back and forth to coat the bottom and sides well. Best done over waxed paper. Give the mold a good bang to dump out any excess and combine with the remaining cheese. Refrigerate the mold.

Melt the butter in a medium-size saucepan. Stir in the flour and cook, stirring constantly with a wooden spatula, for about 2 to 3 minutes, to cook the flour. Do not allow it to brown. Add the milk and beat with a wire whip over moderate heat until the sauce is smooth. Continue cooking, beating constantly, until the sauce (béchamel) is very thick. Take off the heat. Stir in salt, peppers and nutmeg. Add the egg yolks, one at a time, beating hard with the whip after each addition. Stir in all the cheese except about 1 tablespoon. (*The soufflé can be prepared to this point and set aside, the surface sealed with Saran Wrap to prevent a skin from forming.*)

Beat the egg whites with a rotary or electric beater or in the electric mixer until they hold firm, shiny peaks when the beater is held straight up. Add about a third of the beaten whites to the sauce and beat into it vigorously with a whip. Finally, fold in the remaining whites with a rubber spatula.

Pour the batter into the prepared mold. Sprinkle remaining cheese over the top. Place the soufflé on the middle rack of a preheated 400° oven. Immediately turn the heat down to 375° and bake for 25 to 30 minutes; this will give you a creamy center. If you like it firm, bake an additional 5 minutes. Serve immediately. Serves 3, or you may be able to stretch it to 4.

Why are soufflé molds chilled? It is the contention of chefs (and all chefs chill molds for hot soufflés) that a cold mold helps to puff the soufflé and, further, helps to make it rise straight up.

Do you tie a paper around the mold for hot soufflés? We don't because it is not necessary if the soufflé has been prepared correctly in the first place. However, a paper *is* necessary for a cold soufflé (sometimes called iced or frozen soufflé), which is not a true soufflé. It's a fake and the paper is used to give it height, as if it had been baked. Actually, a cold soufflé belongs to the mousse family.

SOUFFLÉ GLACÉ GRAND MARNIER

1¾ cups sifted confectioners' sugar   ½ cup Grand Marnier
8 egg yolks   3 cups heavy cream

Make a collar (see pages 30–33) for a 1½-quart soufflé dish. Set aside. Combine the sugar and egg yolks in a large bowl and beat with an electric beater or, if you have one, in an electric mixer for 25 to 30 minutes. The mixer is a big advantage here because of the long beating time. At this point, the mixture should have a pastelike appearance and be very thick and creamy. Begin to add the Grand Marnier very slowly in a steady stream, beating constantly. When all the liqueur has been incorporated, beat 5 minutes longer.

In another bowl, whip the cream with a rotary or electric beater until it begins to take a shape. Add to the egg mixture and beat together for 3 to 4 minutes.

Spoon the mixture into the mold right up to the edge of the mold. Place it and the surplus in the freezer for 15 minutes. By this time the mixture in the mold will have become firmer and will not run. Now take the remaining mixture and fill the "collar", right to the brim. Return to the freezer and freeze until firm. About 5 minutes before serving time, remove the soufflé from the freezer and place in the refrigerator. At serving time, remove the collar, taking great care. Serve directly from the mold. Serves 8.

Are there many types of timbales?   Timbale means, literally, a round receptacle, and comes from the Arab-Persian word *atabal,* tambour, which means, among many things, a drum. In French culinary parlance, it is a preparation of any kind cooked or served in a deep crust. Small or large, cooked before or after filling, timbales can "carry" such different mixtures as fish, shellfish, chicken, game, noodles, macaroni, truffles, vegetables, or sweet mixtures made with chestnuts, rice, fruits, ice cream, etc. There are, of course, porcelain timbales but the accepted form is an edible timbale crust. There is also Swedish timbale, a paper-thin shell made of egg batter, cooked on a timbale iron (the shapes vary) in deep fat, in or on which creamed foods are served. The smaller, more decorative of these fried timbales are often sprinkled with confectioners' sugar while still warm and served as a confection with tea or coffee. There is still another type of timbale, made with rice, macaroni, spaghetti, halibut, or lobster, which is molded in darioles, small cup-shaped molds, and baked in a pan of hot water. These are served as garnishes to meat dishes or as luncheon dishes accompanied by a suitable sauce.

How do you unmold a jellied dish?   Whether it's an aspic or a mousse, you use the same technique. First, rinse the serving plate in cold water. This makes it easier to slide the mold into the center of the plate in case you missed it. Once the mold is in place, wipe the serving plate dry. Now, to unmold, dip the mold briefly into warm, *not hot,* water almost to the level of the top of the mold. Then loosen around the edge with the tip of a small spatula. Wipe the mold off and place the serving dish on top of the mold. Invert. Give it a good shake, holding the mold tightly in place. If this doesn't work, repeat the operation.

Another way: Wring a cloth out in very hot water and wrap around the bottom of the inverted mold, taking care not to apply the heat too long or the shape of the mold will be ruined.

N O T E : Metal molds unmold more easily than earthenware because metal conducts heat more readily.

Does the size of a jelly kettle make any difference? Yes. A large, heavy 6- to 8-quart kettle with a broad, flat bottom is absolutely essential in jelly-making. This size allows the juices and sugar to bubble and cook quickly. See utensils used in pickling and preserving, pages 19–20.

How do you know when jelly has reached the jellylike point? Dip a large metal spoon into the boiling syrup. Tilt the spoon until syrup runs from the side. When jellying point has been reached, the liquid will not flow in a stream but will divide into two distinct drops that run together and "sheet" from the spoon. Thermometers are helpful when cooking jelly, but the "sheet" test should be made, too, because the jellying point is not always the same. The jellying point is usually eight degrees above the boiling point of water, whatever the locality.

Why does my jelly sometimes cloud? For one or more of the following reasons: pouring the jelly mixture into the glasses too slowly; allowing the jelly mixture to stand before pouring into glasses; improperly straining juice, leaving pulp in it. Jelly makers may be interested to know that jelly that sets too fast is usually the result of using fruit that is too green. By the way, cotton swabs are the handiest thing for cleaning rims of jars before sealing.

Why is my jelly sometimes too soft? It might be for several reasons, according to the U.S. Department of Agriculture: (1) there was too much juice; (2) there was too little sugar; (3) the mixture was not acid enough; (4) you made too big a batch at one time. If it's too stiff, just the opposite is true, or you used too much pectin, or you overcooked it.

How do you sterilize jars and lids? Wash the jars thoroughly in soap and warm water. Rinse well. Place a folded cloth or rack in the bottom of a deep kettle. Add jars, open end up, and cover with water. Bring to a boil and boil 15 minutes. Jars should remain in the hot water until ready to use. Lift from water with tongs and turn upside down on a cloth only long enough to drain. Fill at once. Drop the lids into boiling water but do not boil or the rubber will soften.

N O T E   W E L L : *Dishwashers are not hot enough to sterilize.* Jars must be actually boiled.

How do you use paraffin in jelly-making? Since paraffin is highly flammable it should *never* be melted over direct heat. The most practical way we have discovered is to take a small "tired" saucepan. Place the paraffin in it, then place the pan in a saucepan of hot water to melt. Any paraffin left over after the jelly has been sealed can be kept in the pan until it is needed again.

How do you seal jelly paraffin? Although some recipes specify two layers of paraffin, experts tell us that this is too heavy and will not hold the seal. Therefore, to seal properly, rotate the glass after the hot paraffin has been added so it can "climb the glass" and make an airtight seal.

How do you test the seal of jars? About 12 hours after sealing the jars, remove the band. If the center of the lid is down and stays down when pressed, the jar is vacuum sealed. It then, if you like, can be stored without bands.

How do you seal jars when preserving and pickling? The important thing you must remember is that everything should be boiling hot as you pack and cap and that you should seal one jar at a time. Recipes should all indicate how much head space to leave. Wipe top and threads of jar with a clean damp cloth before capping or use a cotton swab dipped in hot water. Once filled, add the lid, then the screw band. To cool, stand filled jars upright on cloths or wood, a few inches apart, out of drafts.

Is there an easy way to extricate jam or jelly from a jar? Yes. Place the jar, uncovered, in a small pan of hot water over low heat. As soon as the bottom of the jam or jelly begins to melt, turn it out.

How much gelatin do you use to "gel" 2 cups of liquid? One envelope of unflavored gelatin will "gel" 2 cups of liquid. If sugar is an ingredient, it should be counted as part of the total liquid because, when dissolved, it liquefies. This will give you a fairly firm jelly. If you want a less-firm jelly (soup, for example), allow 1 envelope for each 3 cups of liquid; for a firmer jelly (to coat a mold, for example), allow 1 envelope for 1½ cups of liquid.

Are vegetable and hydrogenated vegetable shortening the same thing? Yes. Hydrogenated simply means that hydrogen has been added to the oil to change it from a liquid to a solid, in other words, to harden it.

Should vegetable oils (also called cooking and salad oils) be refrigerated once opened? Yes, says the U.S. Department of Agriculture. Also lard, butter, margarine, and drippings. Well covered, of course.

N O T E : Do not freeze the oils. All others can be frozen.

Where does most of the olive oil come from? France produces very little olive oil and exports only a small percentage of the world's production; California, the only American state that grows olives, produces even less. The big producers are Spain and Italy. Italy produces a good one-third more than Spain (1967 figures), although Spain exports more oil to the United States than Italy. The U.S. Department of Agriculture tells us that both Italian and Spanish oils are of good quality and comparable if you take into consideration the many grades available.

ELEANOR HEMPSTEAD'S
OLIVE OIL PICKLES

4 quarts tiny cucumbers (no more than 3 inches long), sliced very thin
8 onions, peeled, and sliced very thin
1 teaspoon powdered alum *
Salt
2 tablespoons celery seed

2½ tablespoons mustard seed
1½ teaspoons turmeric
1½ teaspoons curry powder
2 tablespoons sugar
Dash Tabasco
1 teaspoon black pepper, freshly ground
2½ cups olive oil

Pickling Sauce:

1 pint vinegar
½ cup dry mustard

Place the prepared cucumbers and onions in a large kettle. Sprinkle with the alum. Cover with cold water. For each gallon of water, add 2 cups of salt. Cover and allow to stand 24 hours. Drain.

Mix together all the remaining ingredients and stir until dissolved. Pack six sterilized pint jars with the drained vegetables. Cover with the pickling sauce, making sure the vegetables are completely covered, leaving ½-inch headroom. Seal at once. When cold, label and store. Allow to season a few weeks before using.

* Available in drugstores.

What is virgin olive oil? The first pressing and, therefore, the best quality. However, the Agricultural Research Service of the U. S. Department of Agriculture tells us: "There are many grades of virgin oil, depending on its acidity and other factors. Quality is affected by many things—weather, the season, the year, the area, the variety of olive, and the crop condition." Not unlike wine. And, again like wine, one year the yield may be good, another year it may not be good at all.

Is there any substitute for lard in cooking? No. Lard has a distinct flavor all its own and it is used in cooking for precisely that reason.

What is sweet oil? It's an old-fashioned term for oils such as olive or vegetable that you may run into when you read an old recipe. In all likelihood it was originally a pharmacist's term.

Are shortenings and oils reusable?   If they've been used for deep-fat frying they can be reused provided proper care is taken. Once you've finished cooking, allow the fat to cool, then strain through several thicknesses of cheesecloth into a dry container. (The original can makes a perfect container.) Store the used fat in the refrigerator or a cool, dry place. With proper care, the fat can be reused a number of times but it's a good idea to add some fresh shortening with each reuse.

N O T E :   If the reused fat starts to foam or darken when it is heated, it is no longer usable and should be discarded.

What is safflower oil?   The oil pressed from the seeds of the safflower, a thistlelike plant which bears colorful blossoms which, as the flowers mature, form clusters of large, white seeds. Safflower oil contains an exceptionally high percentage of linoleic acid—the poly-unsaturated fatty acid. One of the popular margarines is made with safflower oil. Also a salad dressing.

Why does chicken, meat, or fish broth sometimes turn sour almost the minute your back is turned?   Because it's allowed to cool too slowly in too warm a temperature. The faster you can cool off broth (stock or bouillon), soups, sauces, gravies, etc., the less danger there is of bacteria multiplying. The cooling process starts from the outside and works toward the center. If there is a large quantity, such as broth or soup in a large kettle, the center remains hot a long while and it takes a very long time for the cold to penetrate to the center. Ideally, the Poultry and Egg National Board tells us, chilling should be done immediately and, if possible, in smaller quantities, giving the liquid an occasional stir to speed things up. Setting the pan of liquid in a large pan filled with ice and water (the way you chill champagne) does the trick quickly and effectively. The treacherous holding zone—and it *is* treacherous—is from 45° to 120°, the temperature range in which bacteria thrive. A warm kitchen would probably register anywhere from 70° up—obviously, within the danger zone. Broth that has been refrigerated, or even frozen, should always be brought to a hard rolling boil and allowed to boil several minutes before using, to inhibit any lurking bacteria.

What are tapas?   You might say they are the equivalent of our appetizers or hors d'oeuvre. In short, small bits and pieces of delicacies served with drinks in Spain at all taverns (*tascas*). The *Sandeman Newsletter* says, "They range from the most exotic food from the sea, air or land; from small garden snails prepared in olive oil to delicious tiny steaks or Spanish cheese and ham with *picos* (bread sticks) and those wonderful Seville olives, pickled or stuffed with red peppers or anchovies, to tiny baby eels which have made their way across the Atlantic from the Sargasso Sea, prepared with garlic and oil and served sizzling hot."

What is wheat germ?   It is the germinating part of the wheat seed which, because it contains wheat germ oil, is discarded in milling white flour. A rich source of the B vitamins, vitamin E, iron, phosphorous, potassium, and other essential nutrients, it is used as a breakfast cereal and in cooking.

If it's corn flour, is it cornstarch?   Not necessarily. In England corn flour is what we in the United States call cornstarch, a refined starch obtained from the endosperm of corn. Its main use is as a thickening agent in gravies, sauces, stews, puddings, and pie and cake fillings. Unlike wheat flour, it gives a translucent finish to sauces and gravies. Corn flour in the United States, on the other hand, is milled from whole corn, either white or yellow, to a fine consistency and smooth texture. Like brown and white rice flour, potato flour and soya, corn flour is a substitute for wheat flour in baking and a godsend to those individuals on a gluten-free diet.

What is semolina?   Made from the same hard wheat (durum) used to make pasta, the grain is ground roughly, not reduced to a fine powder, and the granules are of various sizes which are separated by sieves. Thus we have fine, medium, and coarse flour. In France, semolina is called *semoule de blé dur* (hard wheat); *semolette* is the Italian name for the same product. A light amber or yellow, semolina is excellent in milk puddings, for thickening soups, and for savory dishes with grated cheese.

What is farina?   According to Law's *Grocers Manual,* "A Portuguese word for 'meal.' The term literally means flour of any species of vegetable tuber or starch root, such as sago, tapioca, arrowroot, and sometimes includes rice, wheat flour, bran, semolina, or wheat pastes." In the United States farina means either white corn meal used for puddings and desserts or a wheat product used as a breakfast cereal (cream of wheat).

What is matzo meal?   It is actually cracker meal—not just any old crackers, but crackers made from flour and water with nothing else added. The meal is ground into various grades. For example, there is a fine matzo cake meal. Matzo meal is used to make meat balls and meat loaves, and is frequently used as a coating in place of flour or breadcrumbs.

Beverages, Wines, and Spirits

What is the nutritive value of orange juice?   Orange juice, like grape-fruit juice, is the best natural source of vitamin C, the vitamin that "cements" between the cells of tissues, bones, teeth, and blood; helps to keep gums healthy and the body resistant to infection, and to heal wounds. Both orange and grapefruit juice give important amounts of vitamin A and many of the B-complex vitamins, as well as appreciable amounts of minerals.

What are "orange drinks"?   Available powdered or frozen, some are known as orange-flavored breakfast drinks. Orange in color and flavor, they have little or no natural orange juice. Vitamin C is added to many; thiamine, vitamin A, and dried pulp to some. Nu-tritionally they are less desirable than orange juice, regardless of the amount of vitamin C, because they lack many other vitamins and minerals. Another group: canned or bottled orange-flavored fruit drinks, which generally contain some full-strength juice. All the normal substances of the natural fruit are present but in smaller amounts. Sugar is generally added, and if they are enriched with vitamin C, the label usually indicates the amount in each serving. Finally, there are presweetened soft-drink mixes to which water is added to make them drinkable. At this time you cannot tell from the label of any of these orange drinks how much orange juice is in the product.

41

How much citrus fruit should one drink every day?   For good health, *and this applies to all ages,* drink a 4-ounce glass of orange or grapefruit juice or eat a large orange, ½ grapefruit, or 3 tangerines. Because you do not store vitamin C in your body, it must be replaced each day. Other good sources of vitamin C include cabbage, potatoes, tomatoes, melons, strawberries and, of course, lemons and other members of the citrus family.

In what forms are citrus juices available?   In terms of juices only, citrus is the name that encompasses oranges, grapefruit, tangerines, lemons. The frozen concentrated juices include orange, grapefruit, grapefruit and orange, and tangerine. The concentrates, available in 6- to 32-ounce cans, are usually reconstituted but they can be used in the concentrated form where called for. All must be stored in the freezer. Chilled, pasteurized orange juice or citrus juices are either all fresh or a blend of fresh and reconstituted. They come in 8-ounce and quart containers and must be stored in the refrigerator. Canned orange, grapefruit, and tangerine juices as well as blended grapefruit and orange juice, sweetened or unsweetened, are available in cans from 8 to 46 ounces. Chill before serving. In all these forms the vitamin C content (ascorbic acid) is comparable to fresh. Lemon juice is available in lemon-shaped plastic containers (4½ ounces), canned (5½ ounces), bottled (one and 1½ pints), and as frozen concentrate (5¾ ounces).

Is chocolate milk the same thing as chocolate drink?   No, although both are made from whole milk with chocolate and sugar added. *Today's Food Market,* published by Kansas State University, says: "With chocolate drink, sometimes called chocolate dairy drink, the amount of butterfat is less than 3¼% required in whole milk. The drink may also be made of skim milk, which has no butterfat at all."

What is the difference between apple juice, apple cider, and sweet cider?   Apple juice, from the first pressing of apples, pasteurized, commercially made, is packed in vacuum-sealed cans and bottles. Some processors leave some of the pulp in the juice, which makes it somewhat cloudy; others clarify it. Apple cider, unclarified and unpasteurized, most often made at a farm mill, is packed in unsealed glass or plastic containers. It must be kept refrigerated in order to prevent fermentation. Sweet cider, more generally known as pasteurized apple cider, packed in sealed cans or bottles, is similar to apple juice. Fermented or partially fermented cider put up and sold at roadside stands is often referred to as "country cider."

What is hard cider?   Apple cider that has attained some degree of alcohol fermentation. Other countries do not define cider as we do. In England, for example, cider is the juice from apples which has fermented. It cannot be, as here, simply fresh juice from apples. The hard cider generally available in this country is medium-dry hard cider (less than 7% alcohol by volume) imported from England. Sold in wine and liquor stores. However, you may be able to track down some hard stuff locally if you have a friend at a cider mill.

What's the difference between fruit juice, fruit punch, and fruit drink? *Fruit juice* is composed of pure fruit juice and some pulp. If sugar is added, the label will say so. *Fruit punch* is a mixture of different juices, the juice listed first being in the greatest proportion. Read the label to determine which juices are used. Fruit drink can be artificially flavored with *none* of the natural fruits as an ingredient or it may contain *some* fruit juice. However, water is the chief ingredient in most fruit drinks. The difference in content makes the difference in price.

How do you make a good cup of tea?   Freshly boiled water and an immaculate cup or teapot are prerequisites. Bring fresh, cold tap water to a rolling boil. Preheat the cup by rinsing it out with hot water. Add one level teaspoon of loose tea or one tea bag to a teacup. To make tea in a pot, rinse out the pot with boiling water, add 6 level teaspoons (or 6 tea bags) to a 6-cup pot. Fill with boiling water. Always allow the tea to steep three to five minutes, and stir before pouring.

What makes black, oolong, and green tea different?   They all come from the same tea bush but they are treated differently after picking. *Black tea* is oxidized, turning the leaves black and producing a rich, hearty flavor. *Oolong tea* (usually found in stores specializing in fine foods), semi-oxidized, has partly brown and partly green leaves. The brew is much lighter in color. *Green tea,* not oxidized, has green leaves and it, too, brews light.

How much ice should you order for a cocktail party? It depends, somewhat, on the staying power of the guests but, in general, you can figure on 25 pounds for 20 people or slightly better than a pound per person.

What are prairie oysters? An old American non-alcoholic concoction heavy drinkers often lean on following an ill-advised night. *The Wise Encyclopedia of Cookery* writes, perhaps with tongue in cheek: "It is based on sound-reasoning and usually affords some measure of relief." If the emergency should confront you, drop an egg into a wine glass, taking care not to break the yolk. Then add a teaspoon of vinegar, allowing it to slide down the side of the glass. Then add salt and pepper to taste. To drink it, swallow the egg first, before the vinegar. It's possible the hangover is preferable.

Is eggnog an American drink? Let's put it this way, it has become a traditional American Christmas drink, although it is generally conceded by most authorities to derive from the simple English posset of the 17th century, a combination of hot milk, eggs, sugar, nutmeg, and sack or ale. However, the Americans put their imprint on it about 1825 when they substituted headier spirits, such as rum or Bourbon, for the gentle sack. The word eggnog is derived, according to some sources, from egg and nog (a strong ale) but, according to others, nog is an abbreviation of noggin, a mug or cup; it also means a small quantity of liquor (usually a quarter of a pint). Recipes for eggnog in early American cookbooks were usually found in the chapters devoted to the sick.

Who invented the cocktail? There seems to be little question that the cocktail is an American invention. The name applies, of course, to mixed alcoholic drinks as well as to mixed fruits in syrup, with or without a liqueur flavoring, and to shellfish (oysters, clams, shrimp, crabmeat, etc.) served with a cocktail sauce. Generally, it is something planned to pique one's appetite. There are innumerable stories as to the invention of the alcoholic cocktail. One legend credits it to Betsy Flanagan who (in 1779) had a name for making a good mixed drink. In her tavern near Yorktown, N.Y., she kept a glass filled with cock's feathers on the bar thus the cognomen. Both Maryland and Kentucky also claim the honor. As for the origin of the name, Joseph D. Vehling, in *America's Table*, says "this ugly Americanism belongs in the stable," adding, "the name has nothing whatsoever to do with a cock's feathers but refers to the strong stuff roughshod horse dealers give to old nags before parading them in front of a prospective buyer to make the horse prance and 'cock its tail.' "

What is the origin of the Gibson Cocktail? Nobody seems to know who dropped the first olive into a martini, but there are two opinions as to who is responsible for the onion. It is said that Charles Dana Gibson, the famous illustrator of beautiful women, had the olive replaced by an onion at the Players Club in New York. Another story goes that Ambassador Hugh Gibson, when a young foreign-service officer stationed in Vienna in the late twenties discovered, as have many before and since, that martinis prior to lunch are lethal, if you plan to do any work afterward. Rather than eliminate his preluncheon martini he beguiled the bartender into making his weaker than those of his confrères and to separate his from the others by the addition of an onion. Whichever Gibson was responsible, the name has stuck.

Do we have vintage wines in the United States? Alexis Lichine writes in his excellent *Encyclopedia of Wines and Spirits:* "Vintage is the *vendage* or gathering of the grapes. Hence the wines from grapes of a specific harvest, the date of which will be shown on the label." By California law, 100% of the grapes must be of the year; in other countries laws are different. For example, in France, there is often a blending of the years. In Europe, where the weather is notoriously unpredictable, the variations in the weather may so affect the harvest that the yield from one year to another may vary greatly. Hence, the good and the so-called bad years, although it is worth noting that almost every French wine carries its vintage on its label. In California, however, the weather follows a predictably reliable pattern that is reflected in the even quality of the wines, year in and year out. Nevertheless, California vintners often date their wines for the orientation of customers interested in old wines or in cellaring wines for further aging. In that sense, we do have vintage wines.

Is it true wine is now available in cans? Yes. The French tried the experiment but without success.

How do you choose a good corkscrew? Mr. Frank Schoonmaker, the wine authority, says: "You should choose a corkscrew that is at least

2¼″ long but, better, 2½″ so that the worm will transpierce the entire length of the cork (corks vary from 1¾″ to 2½″ long). The worm, or screw, should be a perfectly regular wire helix (spiral) with a uniform hollow core about ⅛″ across, extending from the shank all the way down to the point. You should, in other words, be able to insert an ordinary paper match into this core without difficulty, and the point of the worm, it is most important to note, should *not* be centered but follow exactly the same spiral path as the rest of the worm. Two other dimensions, both of which can easily be checked with a pocket ruler, are also major contributing factors to a corkscrew's effectiveness. Too narrow or slender a worm has an insufficient grip and a tendency to pull through, or rip out the center of the cork without pulling it; too wide or too broad a worm is likely to break an old cork, rather than bringing it out intact, as a good corkscrew should. The simplest of all is the waiters' pocket corkscrew, but it is difficult for the novice to use. The one most liked by most women is probably the type that lifts its 'wings' as it penetrates the bottle. The cork is extracted by closing the wings." Of the new cork extractors, greatly improved over the original models, Mr. Schoonmaker says, "Nothing nearly as satisfactory exists for tired old corks in distinguished old bottles."

What do you do when a cork breaks in a wine bottle?　Stick a skewer or sturdy needle (a knitting needle would work fine) through the cork to release the immediate pressure behind it. Then you can use an ordinary corkscrew (not a cork extractor) to get the cork out in the usual way.

When should a Beaujolais be uncorked?　Chef Jacques Pépin, who grew up in that section of France, tells us that Beaujolais wines are drunk young and—unlike Bordeaux or Burgundy wines, which should be uncorked a couple of hours before serving to allow the wine to breathe—the fruity character of a young Beaujolais, its special attraction, is at its best if the wine is uncorked five or ten minutes before it is poured. He also says Beaujolais should be cool—not cold—when served.

How do you open a champagne bottle?　One thing you don't do and that is make it pop. Very bourgeois. First, remove the wire cap. Then, holding the cork in your left hand, the bottom of the bottle in your right at a 45 degree angle, turn the bottle slowly while you gradually ease out the cork. Turning the cork, rather than the bottle, may break off the top of the cork.

How can you tell if champagne is "corky"? Corkiness imparts a slightly vinegary taste, extremely unpalatable. So you smell the wine to determine if it's "corky." Always wipe the lip of the bottle before serving this or any wine.

What is the difference between brut and extra dry champagne? These are both unsweetened dry white wines, with brut a shade drier. Incidentally, these are the two most popular champagnes imported into the United States. *Sec* and *demi-sec* are sweeter and *doux* is the sweetest of all. The sweetening, it is perhaps well to point out, is referred to as *liqueur d'expédition*, the addition of which makes the difference between dry and sweet.

What are rince-verres? Bowls of varying types, usually crystal, often colored, partly filled with water and used to rinse glasses at the dinner table. They have two "lips" on which to rest the stem of the glass. So, no matter how many different wines are served at a meal, there are only two wine glasses at each plate, one for white wines, one for reds. *Rince-verres* are used widely in Europe. *Monteith* (also spelled *Monteigh*) is another name for a large rinsing bowl and it is usually made of silver, but sometimes of porcelain.

What is the best sherry to use in cooking? Sherry is called for in the preparation of certain dishes because of its nutty flavor. The sherry with the most characteristic nuttiness is amontillado, a fairly dry sherry, which would be used in either an entrée or a sweet dish. After the dish has been fully cooked, a little more sherry should be added because the wine loses some of its flavor and aroma during cooking, which is true of all wines.

How much wine do you use in cooking? If the recipe doesn't specify, as a rule of thumb use ¼ cup of Burgundy per pound of meat in pot roast or stews; the same amount of a dry white wine per pound with boiled, sautéed, or fricasseed chicken; in sauces, 1 tablespoon per cup; in soups, 1 teaspoon per serving; with fruits, 1 tablespoon per serving.

What wines are used in marinating?   Dry red wines with dark-colored meats such as beef or venison; white for lighter ones, such as lamb, veal, or fish.

How do you read a French wine label?   The label is important because it can give you a good idea of the quality of the wine. On a fine French wine, the label will tell you the name of the vineyard (often designated by its estate name, its *château*); the label may also—but doesn't always—include the town and district in which the vineyard is situated. Labels on superior wines may say *Grand Vin, Grand Cru,* or *Premier Cru* (*cru* means "crop"), terms authorized in certain districts. When a label says *Appellation Contrôlée* (controlled name) it is telling you that the wine actually comes from the place the label says it does—therefore the wine is not a blend of wines from various districts, products obviously inferior to good unblended wines. The initials V.D.Q.S., meaning *Vin Délimités de Qualité Supérieur* (superior wines from a delimited area), used instead of *Appellation Contrôlée,* denote lesser wines on the whole—although they often are good ones. Usually the label on a bottle gives the year—that is, the wine's vintage —but that does not necessarily mean a good wine, because wines have good and bad years. If the name of the vintner is on the label, it indicates that he stands behind the wine. If *Mise en Bouteilles au Château* is printed on the label, it guarantees that the wine was bottled on the estate producing it but does not guarantee that the wine is good, although the estate's reputation is behind it.

How do you chill gallon jugs of white wine?   In the refrigerator, but since they are rather awkward to handle, we suggest decanting the wine into bottles with screw caps, such as soda bottles. By doing this they can be laid on their sides in the bottom of the refrigerator and are always chilled when needed. Incidentally, this is a good inexpensive way to buy wine and most of the American vintners now bottle their wines, both red and white, in gallon and half-gallon jugs.

Is a Pouilly Fumé wine the same as a Pouilly Fuissé?   No. They are both excellent dry white wines produced from different grapes and in different sections of France. Pouilly Fumé (also known as Pouilly-Blanc-Fumé), made from Sauvignon Blanc or Blanc-Fumé grapes, is produced around the village of Pouilly-sur-Loire. Pouilly Fuissé, from Chardonnay grapes is produced in four small *communes* in southern Burgundy.

Can wine be drunk with "hot" foods such as curry and chili? Broadly speaking, no, although there is one exception—Alsatian wines. These dry white wines, full-bodied, fresh and smooth, clean and fruity, go exceptionally well, the Alsace Wine Information Bureau tells us, "with fish, shellfish, and poultry, and are among the very few wines that go beautifully with 'hot' foods." Named after the variety of grape from which they are made (Sylvaner, Riesling, Gewürztraminer), unique among French wines, they are never blends and, contrary to most other fine wines, are ready to drink from the time of bottling, although they will keep longer than other white wines of the same type. Easily identified by the green, long-necked "flute" bottle of the Moselle wine, which since 1955 has been legally designated as the Alsatian wine bottle.

What is a Vin Blanc Cassis? White wine with a dash of black currant liqueur. *Cassis* is the French for black currant.

What is Lillet? A French apéritif vermouth, made with either white or red wine and, like vermouth, blended with herbs. Michael Aaron, a young New York oenophile, suggests adding a twist of orange peel to emphasize the subtle orange flavor.

What is a vin rosé? In *News From the Vineyard,* published by Almadén, the editor says: "It's a special sort of intermediate wine that has become enormously popular in the past 25 years all over the world." The *rosés* have been produced in Europe for centuries but the first in the United States were made in the 1940s. Most *rosés* are still wines, although some today are sparkling; and most are dry but, again, today we have some sweet. The *rosés* are modest wines (there are no great *rosés*) that, within reasonable limits, go with almost everything. When you buy, choose the youngest, never lay them away, and always serve well chilled.

What is Kir? An apéritif named in honor of the Mayor of Dijon who died in 1968 at the age of 92, after almost half a lifetime as mayor. To make it, add a little Crème de Cassis to a glass of chilled white wine and, if you like, a splash of soda water.

Are porto and port the same thing? No. *Porto* (or *vinho do porto*) is the legally protected name for wines from the Douro Valley in Portugal, made from grapes grown in this valley to which brandy, also made from grapes grown in the same region, is added. Because of new government regulations, "port" will be used henceforth to designate dessert wines produced in the United States with the label clearly stating the place of origin: California, New York State, or America. If you want to buy imported wine, ask for porto; if domestic, ask for port.

Is there a white port? Yes, made from white grapes. "Generally," Alexis Lichine writes in his *Encyclopedia of Wines and Spirits*, "it is a little sweeter than red port, but there is a growing tendency to manufacture a dry white port which is served as an apéritif in Portugal and is beginning to be known and appreciated abroad." White port is also made in California.

What does "D.O.M." mean on the Benedictine bottle? In 1510 Dom Bernardo Vincelli, one of the monks at the Benedictine monastery at Fécamp, France, discovered that a mixture of certain herbs and plants, when distilled with brandy, produced a delicious new liqueur, distinctly different from all other spirits. It came to be known as Benedictine, and its discovery was dedicated by the monks to God. "D.O.M." stands for *Deo Optimo Maximo*, the Latin for "To God most good, most great."

Are sherry and Madeira alike? In this sense only, they are both fortified wines which means that brandies or liqueurs have been added, thus boosting the alcoholic content above that of table wines. The occasions for drinking these wines are similar. Like sherry, Madeira is not drunk with a meal. The various types of Madeira divide themselves between apéritif and dessert, although the driest is sometimes served with soup. The dessert Madeiras, besides going with sweets, make a pleasant after-dinner drink. Madeira is frequently used in recipes. The four basic types of Madeira wine are: Sercial, a dry wine made from grapes grown on the highest slopes; Verdelho, medium dry but not as rich as Sercial; Bual and Malmsey, the two dessert wines. All Madeiras are matured for at least 4 years before being exported. England, we are told, is one of the largest consumers of Madeira wine in the world.

What is a pichet?   It actually means a jug or pitcher, traditionally used in France to serve wine. The modern version is a 16-ounce bottle of wine, usually Beaujolais.

Can a dark rum be light?   Although it sounds like a contradiction, it can. The trend today in all spirits is to make them lighter in color with a lower proof. The color of rums which are colorless after distillation is determined by the type of casks in which they are aged, the aging time, and the amount of caramel used by the distiller to color them. Caramel is not added for flavor but primarily to maintain uniform color, bottle for bottle. Labeled white or gold, 78% of all light-type rums are Puerto Rican. In the case of Virgin Island rums, you may run into some that are light in color although labeled dark. All Jamaica-type rums are dark, taste "rummy" (that's the molasses coming out) and are generally preferred by cooks for flavoring in cooking.

What should you drink with oysters?   In America, anything from beer to champagne; in France, a dry white wine, such as a chablis; in England, ale. So you have a wide choice.

What is malt liquor?   According to *Beverage Executive,* "Every brewmaster has his own conception as to what is actually meant by the term malt liquor. Some claim that it is blander than beer, but stronger. But all of the identification revolves around taste sensations. For the record, however, the products that are now on the market are more full-bodied but less 'hoppy' than beer. So much so, that you wonder if they are 'hopped' at all." Apparently, women like malt liquor because it lacks any taste of the bitterness traditionally found in beer. The price, it must be noted, is higher than regular beer.

What is ginger brandy?   A brandy flavored with ginger. Like ginger ale, ginger beer, and ginger wine, bruised ginger roots are used to give it its flavor. However, as you would assume, it is considerably stronger than any of these light drinks, although bottled at a lower proof than straight brandies. Like a cordial, which it really is, it is served after dinner. Used in combination with crystallized ginger over ice cream, or mixed with whipped cream and served over fresh gingerbread, it makes a delicious sauce. Next time you feel a cold coming on, use ginger brandy to make a hot toddy. It is as effective as any pill.

Is there such a thing as Napoleon Brandy?   We, in turn, might ask you which Napoleon you are talking about. Actually, only two Napoleons ever ruled France and the third, Napoleon III, was deposed in 1870. Assuming you were able to uncover a bottle of cognac going back to Napoleon III, it would be absolutely unpalatable to taste, let alone to drink, since cognac does not age in the bottle.

A number of cognac firms use the name Napoleon in advertising their brands, primarily, we assume, because of the romance, adventure, and intrigue associated especially with Napoleon I. But they know, and they expect you to know, that the cognac could not possibly date from Napoleon's time.

What are Pimm's Cups?   *The Dictionary of Food and Cookery & Menu Translator,* by Henry Smith, describes Pimms Cups (his spelling) in the following way: "Name of four well-known cups. No. 1 has gin as its base; No. 2, whisky; No. 3, brandy; No. 4, rum." A hundred-odd years ago the proprietor of Pimm's, a London restaurant, served a popular drink called a Gin Sling which eventually came to be known as Pimm's Cup No. 1. In addition to the original four, there are now two more: Canadian Whiskey (No. 5) and Vodka (No. 6). All, by the way, are 67% proof. To serve Pimm's Cups (any one), pour a jigger into a glass, add ice and soda or any other mixer you like. The original garnish was a slice of cucumber.

Are Pernod and pastis the same?   They are both apéritifs but Pernod is an apéritif flavored with anise and pastis is flavored with, among other things, licorice, which is somewhat less distinct in taste than anise. These and other apéritifs were developed as a substitute for absinthe, an extremely potent liquor of spirits infused with herbs, anise, and wormwood, which because of its potency has been banned in most Western countries. It is not banned in Spain, however, where it is the most popular of all the cordials, sold under the name of *anís*. When water is combined with any of these liqueurs, they turn cloudy. In her book, *Spices, Salt and Aromatics in the English Kitchen* (Penguin), Elizabeth David says, "A drop of this liqueur does wonderful things for the flavor of certain fish sauces and soups."

What does sack mean? The term used in Elizabethan England for sherry. Dry Sack, however, is a brand of sherry currently available.

Is Sekt the same thing as sack? Literally translated, *Sekt,* from the German, means dry wine or champagne, but since 1815 it has specifically meant German champagne-type or sparkling wines. About that time, a Berlin actor, playing Falstaff in Shakespeare's *Henry IV,* invented a popular joke by calling for his *Sekt* (sack is the early English name for sherry) and from then on used the same term in restaurants when calling for his favorite drink, which happened to be champagne. Another story says that the translators, who rendered *Henry IV* into German, changed sack to *Sekt.* Whatever, *Sekt* is now the generic name in Germany for all sparkling wines.

Is granité the same thing as sorbet? Yes. Both are water ices related to sherbet (see page 86), actually a fruit-flavored drink. *Granités* or *sorbets* are sometimes served in France at the midpoint of an extensive banquet to refresh the guests' taste buds. *Granité, sorbets,* or sherbets make a delicious climax to a summer lunch or dinner.

Where did the word booze come from? During the presidential campaign of 1840, bottles in the shape of log cabins were designed in Glassboro, N.J., to symbolize the home of William Henry Harrison, ninth President of the United States. A very alert distiller by the name of E. C. Booz filled the bottles with suitable spirits, and they came to be known as "booz bottles." Over the years, liquor became known in the vernacular as booze.

Birds

How long does it take to thaw poultry?

Poultry	Weight (ready to cook)	In the Refrigerator
Roasting	3 to 8 pounds	1 to 2 days
	8 to 12 pounds	1 to 2 days
	12 to 20 pounds	2 to 3 days
Frying Chicken, cut up	about 2 pounds	4 hours

Should a poached bird be cooled in the broth? For the best flavor, it certainly should, uncovered in the refrigerator. And this is important: Refrigerate it immediately after it is taken off the stove. To speed the cooling-off process, give the broth a stir when you think of it. The reason for this prompt cooling is that any poultry (chicken, turkey, duck, etc.) will deteriorate very quickly at too warm a temperature and you can end up by having it turn sour. Disaster! Cover when cold.

Obviously, if it's going to be served hot, you follow recipe directions.

Can you partially cook, then store poultry? Definitely not! It should be cooked thoroughly all at one time, never partially cooked. Remember, poultry (any kind) can develop botulism when undercooked and/or cooked at too low a temperature (300° is the minimum for oven cookery). So, beware! Take care! See page 60.

Can frozen raw or cooked poultry, once thawed, be refrozen? The U.S. Department of Agriculture says yes, if (make a note of the "ifs") the poultry still contains ice crystals; if it is still cold (about 40°); or if it has been held no longer than one or two days at refrigerator temperature after thawing. Make another note: Thawing and refreezing may lower eating quality.

What is the difference between poule, poulet, and poularde? *Poule* is French for the female of the common domestic fowl (*coq*, of course, is cock); *poulet* is a young chicken (the diminutive of *poule*); and *poularde* is a fattened chicken—much like our capon. *Poussins* (also called *petits poulets*) are little chickens or what we in this country call squab chickens, which weigh in at about a pound or slightly better. *Poulailler*, French for henhouse, for poulterer, and for theater gallery is also the name of a New York restaurant—Le Poulailler. Roger Fessaguet, one of the partners and *chef de cuisine* at La Caravelle, one of New York's few four-star restaurants, is your guarantee of high culinary standards.

What are roasting hens? When chickens (hens or roosters) are raised to an eviscerated weight of 3 to 4 pounds they are known and sold as broiler-fryers. But when the females (hens) are raised to 4½ pounds or larger, which takes several weeks longer, they are called roasting hens.

What does chicken cacciatore mean? It's the name of an Italian chicken dish, cooked in a casserole, well flavored with onion and garlic and served with a rich tomato sauce.

What is a peep? *Webster's International Dictionary* says, "A newly hatched chicken." It also means, to quote both *Webster's* and the *Oxford English Dictionary*, "a species of sandpiper and the Meadowpipit." To continue, we speak of a "gaggle of geese," meaning a flock of geese on the water and hence, opprobriously, a company of women; a brace of pheasants (this term is particularly applied to game and its meaning is, obviously, two taken together); a covey is a brood or hatch of wild birds, especially partridge and related birds.

Now we come to flock, and again we quote *Webster's*. To wit: flock, herd, drove, pack, bevy, covey, flight. Flock (used chiefly of sheep, goats, and geese); herd (cattle or larger animals gathered in a body); drove (cattle or swine driven in a body); pack (chiefly of hounds and wolves); bevy (quails, roes, larks); covey (of partridges); flight (various birds).

How much chicken do you allow per person? About ¾ pound for broiling, roasting, frying, barbecuing, poaching; ½ cup *cooked* boned chicken (salad or curry, for example); ½ chicken breast. One 3-pound broiler-fryer serves 4 and yields 2½ cups cooked diced chicken and, if poached, 2½ cups chicken broth. A 2-pound bird serves two with light appetites.

POACHED CHICKEN WITH LEMON SAUCE

1 5- to 6-pound stewing chicken	6 stalks (approximately) parsley
Chicken neck	1 bay leaf
2 onions, skin on, split, stuck with 4 cloves	6 to 8 peppercorns
1 large carrot, coarsely chopped	1 tablespoon salt
3 ribs celery with leaves, coarsely chopped	1 teaspoon thyme

Truss the chicken if the butcher has not already done it. Place, breast side down, in the kettle, with all ingredients except the thyme. Cover with cold water and bring to a boil slowly. Skim off with a large metal spoon any scum that rises to the surface. Reduce heat to simmer and add the thyme. Cover and cook very slowly until a drumstick is soft when squeezed and the skin just begins to shrink from the tip of the leg. The length of time will depend on the size of the bird and its age. Count on 1½ to 2 hours. Do not overcook. Meat should *not* fall from the bones.

Once the chicken has been removed from the broth, place the kettle back over a high heat and reduce until there are about 5 to 6 cups of concentrated broth left. Strain. Any you are not using immediately should be refrigerated in pint jars or frozen for future use.

If the chicken is not to be used at once, refrigerate immediately in the broth, uncovered. Give broth an occasional stir to help cool it off as quickly as possible so it won't turn sour. Cover when stone cold.

To present poached chicken: Lift from the broth by sticking a long wooden spoon into the cavity. Allow any broth to drain back into the kettle. Place on a warm serving platter and spoon some of the Lemon Sauce (see below) over it. Tuck a parsley bouquet in the tail.

Carve as you would roast chicken. Serve more Lemon Sauce in a warm sauceboat. Serves 5 to 6.

Another way: Carve the chicken in the kitchen in rather large pieces. Arrange on a heated serving platter. Spoon Lemon Sauce all over the chicken pieces. Serve any extra sauce in a warm sauceboat.

LEMON SAUCE

3 egg yolks
2 teaspoons arrowroot
Salt
White pepper, freshly ground

2 cups chicken broth, strained
Juice 1 lemon *
8 to 10 parsley sprigs, minced

Combine yolks, arrowroot, and salt and pepper to taste in the top of a double boiler. Whip together with a wire whisk until well combined. Add the chicken broth gradually, whipping constantly. Cook over simmering water, whipping vigorously, until the sauce will coat a spoon. *Can be prepared to this point in advance, sealed with Saran Wrap, and set aside.*

Sauce can be heated up over simmering water, whipping constantly with a wire whip. It must not be allowed to boil or it will curdle. Just before serving stir in the lemon juice and parsley.

* Boil the lemon a couple of minutes and it will yield more juice.

Does pink flesh indicate a chicken is undercooked? Not necessarily. Slight pinkness of the meat or miniature clots sometimes found in the legs or thighs of roasted birds are perfectly normal. You will find, too, that the bones of young birds are often discolored. A good sign, actually, because it is one of the best indications of a young bird. Other color variations in meat may be similarly deceiving. The "rainbow" that occurs occasionally in sliced hams is caused by the refraction of light on the ends of the muscle fibers, the U.S. Department of Agriculture tells us, and does not mean, as some people think, that the meat is not fully cooked. Even fresh pork, veal, or turkey will occasionally remain pink when properly cooked, due to a lack of fat that prevents a chemical reaction. If whatever tests you use for doneness indicate the meat is cooked and it is still pink, you may assume the chemical changes described by the U.S.D.A. scientists have taken place. So, sit down and have a good dinner.

What are the dark or greenish spots sometimes found on chicken livers? They are caused by the bile sack that rested on the liver before cleaning—harmless but unattractive. Just cut them out.

PAUL STEINDLER'S FINE TERRINE OF CHICKEN LIVERS

½ pound pork belly
¼ cup (½ stick) butter, softened
1 medium onion, coarsely chopped
1 bay leaf, crushed
Pinch thyme
Salt

White pepper, freshly ground
½ pound chicken livers
1 jigger (1½ ounces) cognac
1 small canned truffle, finely chopped (optional)

Cut the pork into small pieces, and boil in salted water to cover for half an hour. Then drain.

Meanwhile, melt *about 2 tablespoons of the butter* in a skillet and sauté the onion until lightly touched with gold but not browned. Add the bay leaf, thyme, salt, pepper, and chicken livers. Sauté lightly, taking care not to overcook. Livers should still be pink inside. While pork pieces are still hot, combine with the chicken liver mixture, softened butter, and the cognac. Spoon, a small amount at a time, into the electric blender and blend at medium speed until you have a smooth purée. Stir in the chopped truffle and spoon into a 3-cup terrine. Refrigerate.

To serve: Using a spoon dipped in hot water, scoop the pâté into a chilled serving dish, garnish wth chopped hard-cooked eggs or chopped aspic. Serve with toast triangles.

N O T E : Because this pâté is not cooked, it may curdle when first chilled. If this happens, bring it together again by whipping vigorously with a wire whisk.

What are the minutes per pound for roasting turkey? Authorities no longer gauge roasting time on minutes per pound but rather on number of hours based on the turkey's weight. The turkey is fully cooked if juices run clear yellow when the leg is pricked deeply with a fork, or a meat thermometer inserted between the thigh and the body reads 175° to 180°. When using a thermometer (the most accurate are those that register from 0° to 220°), make sure it does not touch any bone.

For a *completely thawed* turkey to be roasted in a preheated 350°

oven, here is a short timetable that should be used as a guide only. Always make the doneness test, or depend on a good thermometer (see pages 17–18).

Weight (ready to cook)	Roasting Time (unstuffed)	Roasting Time (stuffed)
8 pounds	2 hours, 10 minutes	2 hours, 50 minutes
10 pounds	2 hours, 30 minutes	3 hours, 40 minutes
12 pounds	3 hours	4 hours
14 pounds	3 hours, 30 minutes	4 hours, 40 minutes
16 pounds	4 hours	5 hours, 20 minutes
20 pounds	5 hours	6 hours, 40 minutes

Must you thaw frozen turkey in the refrigerator? Turkey specialists of the Agricultural Research Service of the U.S. Department of Agriculture say "no" if the thawing turkey is kept in its original plastic wrap and placed in a paper bag large enough to encompass it completely. Handled thus, the turkey can be allowed to thaw at room temperature because the atmosphere inside the bag will be only slightly warmer than that in the refrigerator. Therefore, the bird can be thawed completely without exposing the surface to temperatures higher than 55°, when bacteria can begin to multiply. Large turkeys of 20 to 25 pounds take about 15 hours to thaw; smaller ones, eight to twelve pounds, about twelve hours. After thawing, giblets should be removed immediately from the cavity and refrigerated, and the turkey should be wiped dry, inside and out, with paper toweling. It, too, must be refrigerated immediately and cooked within one to three hours after thawing. *This method should not be used for any poultry other than turkey.*

To thaw in the refrigerator, leave the turkey sealed in its original wrap and place the turkey on a tray. Allow 1 to 3 days, depending on size. *Another way:* Place the turkey still tightly sealed in its original package, under cold running water. Small birds will thaw in 3 to 4 hours; larger ones in 6 to 7 hours.

Is it true turkeys can be cooked overnight? Low-temperature cooking (200°), which is what this amounts to, is dangerous. By scientific tests, it has been determined that if turkeys are cooked at such a low temperature, regardless of the length of time, the bacterial count jumps dramatically and salmonella bacteria (which cause a serious food poisoning) multiply at a fantastic rate. So the answer is no! Turkeys, stuffed or unstuffed, should *never* be cooked at less than 300°.

What is a yearling turkey? It's a mature turkey which is less tender than a young one but can be used for poaching, soups, or salads.

Are hen turkeys more tender than toms? No. Once, when it took eight to twelve months to raise a turkey for the table, this may have been true, but today practically all turkeys in the market, whether girls or boys, are young—from three to six months old. The U.S. Department of Agriculture publishes a useful little leaflet, "How to Buy Poultry," which you may find helpful in buying all kinds of birds. Write for "Home and Garden Bulletin #157" to Superintendent of Documents, U.S. Government Printing Office, Washington, D.C. 20402, enclosing five cents in coin. Do not send stamps.

What exactly is foie gras? *Foie* means liver and *gras* means fat. Together, the two words translate into fat liver which is, in a sense, meaningless. However, gastronomically, *foie gras* is the liver of a goose or duck monstrously fattened. Although the French are generally credited with "inventing" *foie gras,* there are frescoes on the tomb of Ti, a royal official of the Fifth Dynasty in Egypt, depicting geese being force-fed. That was 4500 years ago. Homer, Herodotus, Cato, Pliny the Elder, Horace, and Apicius (he is credited with having written the first cookbook) all referred to *foie gras,* sometimes with truffles. So it is apparent it was known to Greek and Roman gastronomy. The Gauls followed in the steps of these pioneers, fattening their geese on figs just as the Romans did. As a matter of interest, *foie* derives from the Latin *ficatum,* meaning the liver of an animal fattened on figs. Today the geese are force-fed on maize (Indian corn).

What do the foie gras labels mean? *Foie gras* (see above) is pure fresh goose liver with the addition of seasonings, generally available in France and becoming more so in the United States in fine food stores. Expensive, and worth every bite. Not canned, but wrapped in foil. *Foie gras truffe* (or *aux truffes*) is pure goose liver with the addition of truffles—at least 5%—usually in a "ribbon" down the center; *foie gras naturel* is pure goose liver—and the best part of the liver—without truffles, used primarily as an ingredient in cooking; *pâté de foie gras* (also known as *bloc, purée, mousse, rouleau,* or *roulade de foie gras*) contains at least 75% pure goose liver and up to 25% other livers, with or without truffles; *pâté de foie d'oie* has somewhat less pure goose liver (only 50%) and the remainder is made up of other livers, usually pork. It is worth noting that all canned *foie gras* ages like wine and can be kept indefinitely. Fresh *foie gras* will keep about a month, refrigerated; canned, once opened, about ten days.

How do you serve foie gras? First of all, the unopened can should be refrigerated for several hours. However, do not freeze. It should then be unmolded with care to keep its shape (sometimes it's necessary to dip the can in hot water for a couple of seconds so the goose liver will slide out smoothly). Cut with a sharp thin knife dipped in hot water after each slice to avoid sticking. Present the *foie gras* on a dish garnished with lettuce leaves, bouquets of watercress, or chopped aspic. Serve with plain, unbuttered toast.

What is pressed duck? An old and famous recipe, made more famous by the Tour d'Argent, a three-star Paris restaurant, in which the duck is actually prepared at the table before the guests. In brief, according to Mr. Claude Terrail, owner of the Tour d'Argent, this is what goes on: A 2-pound duck is roasted at a high heat for about 20 minutes. It is then taken to the table with the sautéed, puréed duck liver. The legs are removed (sometimes they are sent back to the kitchen to be grilled). The breast, carved in thin slivers, is placed in a warm chafing dish. Juices and blood are extracted from the carcass in the duck press, warmed with the liver, finished with brandy, Madeira, and salt and pepper, and poured over the sliced breast. It should be served immediately.

**Breads, Cakes,
Cookies, and Pastries**

Why aren't the ingredients listed on bread labels? Because the recipe for 1- and 2-pound loaves is standardized by the U.S. Government, listing of the ingredients is not required by law. *Today's Food Market,* of the Extension Service of Kansas State University, also tells us there are now more than 70 varieties of breads available in this country, exclusive of homemade. You can buy bread as a mix, in frozen form, in brown-and-serve form, as well as ready for the table.

What is shortening? Fat, such as solidified vegetable oils (cottonseed and soybean oil), lard, butter, margarine, rendered poultry or beef fat, drippings from bacon fat, salt pork, ham, beef, or lamb. Generally applied to fats used in making breads, cakes, pastries.

What is presifted flour? All flour is sifted many times at the mill before packaging but until recently most recipes—and particularly recipes for cakes—called for sifting at home prior to making up the recipe. However, the big millers no longer recommend sifting although it has been our experience that cooks "conditioned" to sifting continue to do so. General Mills recommends spooning the flour straight from the bag, then leveling it off with the straight edge of knife; Robin Hood, on the other hand, recommends measuring in the same way, then removing one tablespoon of flour, leveled, from each cup of flour called for in the recipe.

Is it necessary to sift flour in cake baking?   First of all, all flours are sifted innumerable times before they are packaged but recently all the milling companies have determined by actual test that, broadly speaking, flour does not need further sifting. Hence, the message on flour bags, "presifted." However, if a recipe calls for sifting *before measuring* it is probably desirable to do so. Obviously, this is particularly true of cakes.

Is there an easy way to sift flour in quantity?   If you have more than 2 cups to sift, it is easier to sift it piecemeal, as it were—a cup or so at a time—because the flour goes through more quickly with less demand on one's muscles. This is particularly true of the hand "squeeze sifter." With the old-fashioned crank-type sifter, it doesn't matter because it can be turned with a minimum of effort and a maximum of efficiency.

What are the different types of flours?   *All-purpose,* suitable for all types of home baking and cooking except delicate cakes, such as angel; *instant,* granular, easily dissolved in liquids, does not need sifting, more expensive than all-purpose; *self-rising,* with a leavening agent and salt added, can be used in any recipe calling for baking powder and salt by omitting these ingredients from the recipe; *cake,* fine-textured and the most expensive of all flours, made specifically for delicate cakes.

Why does the amount of flour vary in bread making?   The all-purpose flour called for in bread making is made from hard wheat. Because it contains more gluten-forming proteins than soft wheat, which is milled to make cake flour, hard wheat gives more structure and elasticity to the dough, stretching it to form the framework that holds the gas bubbles produced by the yeast. Flours vary from one locale to another and even from one batch to another. Thus, in making bread, the balance of liquid to flour cannot ever be exact and is the reason for the range given in recipes. As you make bread, you will learn to know your dough by feel and know, too, when to add additional flour.

What exactly is yeast?   A living plant, yeast is the leavening used in breads and rolls that makes them rise and makes them light. The two types available are: active dry yeast and compressed yeast.

Active dry yeast comes in individual air-tight and moisture-proof packages or in 4-ounce vacuum-packed jars. Will stay fresh, when kept on cool, dry shelves, until the expiration date on the package.

N O T E : If dry yeast picks up moisture it will lose its stability. Compressed yeast, available in ¾-ounce, 1-ounce and 2-ounce cakes, is highly perishable and must be refrigerated (its life is only several weeks). The two yeasts can be used interchangeably.

Can I convert old-fashioned yeast recipes to the new, no-dissolve method? Yes, 1) measure ingredients including any water usually used to dissolve the yeast; 2) thoroughly mix the undissolved yeast (you can use active-dry yeast or cake yeast, crumbled) with ⅓ of the flour and all other dry ingredients; 3) heat liquids with the butter or margarine over low heat until *warm* (the fat does not need to melt); 4) add to the dry ingredients and beat for 2 minutes at medium speed in the electric mixer, scraping bowl occasionally; 5) stir in additional flour called for in recipe and proceed with preparation, following recipe directions.

How do you knead bread by hand? Kneading is simply blending by hand dough that is too stiff to mix in any other way except, of course, with the dough hook in the electric mixer (see below). First, remove any dangly jewelry and rings, except a plain wedding band. Turn the dough out on a floured board. Flour your hands and flatten the dough, then pick up the edge of dough farthest from you and fold it in half toward you. Now, using the heels of your hands, press down two or three times, pushing the dough away from you with a rolling motion. Turn the dough a quarter of the way around, fold it, press, and push again. Repeat this turning, folding, pressing, and pushing motion until the dough becomes satiny smooth and elastic. When bread has been kneaded 10 minutes, shape into a neat ball, place in a greased bowl, cover with a fresh towel, and put in a warm place (see page 66) free from drafts. At this point fermentation starts. When enough gas has been produced, it will puff the dough up to double its original size.

Can bread be kneaded by machine? Yes. The electric mixer with a dough hook attachment eliminates hand kneading entirely. We should point out that many a cook gets rid of her frustrations by hand kneading, and as a wag once pointed out, "It is good exercise for both of you." Be that as it may, with the dough hook, bread can be kneaded in about 3 to 4 minutes as against 8 to 10 when done by hand.

How do you make bread by the conventional method? Measure the amount of warm water (105° to 115°) designated by the recipe into a large bowl. Sprinkle in the yeast and stir until dissolved. Add lukewarm milk or other liquid called for in the recipe. Add butter or margarine. Stir in dry ingredients and knead (see page 65); allow to rise; and bake as directed.

N O T E : If liquid other than water is called for, substitute ¼ cup of water for ¼ cup of the other liquid and dissolve yeast as indicated above.

How warm is a warm place? Doughs that should rise in the conventional way (see "CoolRise" below), need an even temperature of about 80° to 85°. You can achieve this temperature in several ways: (1) set the bowl with the dough in an unheated oven with a large pan of hot water on the rack below (this is the method preferred by professionals); (2) before putting the dough into the rising bowl, warm the bowl by filling it with hot water, then empty, dry thoroughly, and grease; (3) fill a large pan two-thirds full of hot water, place a wire rack on top and the bowl of dough on the rack; (4) set the bowl in a deep pan of warm water (warm water, that is, *not hot*); (5) place the bowl out of drafts near, *not on*, the stove or radiator.

What does "CoolRise" mean in bread making? A method developed by the makers of Robin Hood flour, it simply means that the dough is mixed, kneaded, and shaped in a single operation. Once the loaves are in the pans they are then refrigerated for at least 2 hours or up to 24 hours. Thus, bread can be baked whenever it is convenient.

N O T E W E L L : Do not freeze.

Can you explain the One-Bowl method of making bread? By this method the butter or margarine is placed on top of the dry ingredients, then hot water, *right from the tap*, is added. See recipe below for Robin Hood's CoolRise Sweet Rolls.

COOLRISE SWEET ROLLS
(One-Bowl Method)

5 to 6 cups all-purpose flour
2 packages active dry yeast
½ cup sugar
1½ teaspoons salt

½ cup (1 stick) butter, softened
1½ cups hot tap water
2 eggs
Vegetable oil

Spoon the flour into a dry measuring cup and level off with the edge of a knife. It is convenient to pour it onto waxed paper. Combine 2 cups of the flour, the yeast, sugar, and salt in a large bowl. Mix very well. Place the butter on top. Pour the water over all. Beat with an electric mixer at medium speed for 2 minutes. Scrape bowl occasionally. Add the eggs and 1 cup more of flour. Beat this time at high speed for 1 minute until thick and elastic. Now, with a wooden spoon, gradually stir in *enough* of the remaining flour to make a soft dough that will leave the sides of the bowl. Turn out onto a lightly floured board.

Knead (see page 65) until dough is smooth and elastic. Five to 10 minutes. Cover lightly with a piece of Saran Wrap, then a fresh dish towel. Allow dough to rest for 20 minutes. Then punch down. Divide, shape into 12 rolls to fit into a greased 9 x 13-inch pan. Brush lightly with oil. Cover lightly with Saran Wrap. Refrigerate for 2 hours or up to 24 hours. Before baking allow the rolls to stand 10 minutes. Then bake in a preheated 375° oven for 20 to 30 minutes or until done. Turn out of pans immediately onto racks to cool. Brush the tops with butter or frosting.

Frosting: Combine ½ cup confectioners' sugar, grated rind, and juice of ½ lemon. Mix well. Brush the rolls while still warm.

What is Rapidmix? Also known as One-Bowl, it is a method of making bread and basic sweet doughs without dissolving the yeast. Developed by Fleischmann's.

FLEISCHMANN'S WHITE BREAD
(Rapidmix Method)

5½ to 6½ cups unsifted all-purpose flour
3 tablespoons sugar
2 teaspoons salt

1 package active dry yeast
1½ cups water
½ cup milk
3 tablespoons butter or margarine

In a large bowl thoroughly mix 2 cups of the flour, the sugar, salt, and yeast. Combine water, milk, and butter or margarine in a saucepan. Heat over low heat until liquids are warm (the butter or margarine does not need to melt). Gradually add to the dry ingredients and beat 2 minutes at medium speed in the electric mixer, scraping the bowl occasionally. Add ¾ cup of flour or enough flour to make a thick batter. Beat at high speed 2 minutes, again scraping the bowl occasionally. Now stir in enough additional flour to make a soft dough.

Turn out onto a lightly floured board or pastry cloth and knead (see page 65) until smooth and elastic—about 8 to 10 minutes. Place in a greased bowl, turning to grease all over. Cover, let rise in a warm place (see page 66), free from drafts, until doubled in bulk—about 1 hour.

Punch dough down, turn out onto a lightly floured board. Cover and allow to rest 15 minutes. Divide dough in half and shape into loaves. Place in 2 greased 8½ x 4½ x 2½-inch loaf pans. Cover and allow to rise a second time in a warm place, free from drafts, until doubled in bulk— about 1 hour.

Bake on the lower rack in a preheated 400° oven for 25 to 30 minutes or until the bread sounds hollow when thumped with your knuckles. Turn out of pans and cool on wire racks.

What's the best place to store bread?   In its original wrapper in the breadbox because bread keeps its freshness longer at room temperature. However, when hot, humid weather rolls around it fares better in the refrigerator because the coldness inhibits mold.

What exactly are fresh breadcrumbs?   Crumbs that have been freshly made, as against dried crumbs. (The term "soft" is sometimes used for fresh.) Recipes should and usually do specify the type of crumbs to be used. Fresh crumbs are best made from a firm-textured bread and most easily in the electric blender. Dried crumbs, seasoned and unseasoned, are available commercially. To make your own, simply dry bread in a low oven or use bread that has already dried out. Here, too, the electric blender works like a charm.

What exactly is a crouton?   The *Dictionnaire de l'Académie des Gastronomes* describes it as "a little piece of prepared bread." Adding, "it is the diminutive of *croûte*." Croutons, rounds, or triangles of bread, sautéed in butter, are used as a base for canapés or as a garnish for steaks, chops, small birds, stews, game, and so on. When cut into small dice, they are usually served with puréed soups, scrambled eggs, etc. The small commercial croutons on the market come both plain and seasoned. *Croûtes,* on the other hand, are small toasted bread cases, which are then filled with various mixtures such as cheese, ham, mushrooms, chicken livers, etc.

How do you make perfect croutons? Take firm bread, preferably day-old, and cut into shapes such as small cubes, triangles, rounds, etc. *One way*: Fry in butter and vegetable oil, half and half, or clarified butter, until golden all over. As they brown, lift out of the fat with a slotted spoon onto paper toweling. *Another way*: Butter the bread generously, cut into the shapes you want, then bake in a preheated 275° oven until crisp and golden—30 minutes or so. Or bake the shapes unbuttered, if you want dry croutons.

What does baguette mean in the kitchen? The French for baton, *baguette* is an apt name for a thin (about 2½ inches in diameter), 26-inch loaf of bread; a *flûte*, which is fatter (about 4 inches in diameter) is approximately the same length; a *ficelle*, the skinniest of the three (1½ inches in diameter) is somewhat longer than the *flûte*. The pleasure of these breads lies in their crustiness.

What is Anadama Bread? A cornmeal-and-molasses bread that originated over a hundred years ago in Rockport, Massachusetts. It seems a fisherman, sick and tired of the steamed cornmeal-mush-and-molasses dinner his lazy wife served him without end, one day seized the mixture, added flour and yeast, and baked it, saying, "Anna, damn her." Thus, Anadama bread. José Wilson, who has a house in Rockport, says the Anadama bread available there is absolutely wonderful.

What is lefse? A Norwegian bread. There are as many recipes as there are dialects in Norway. Although the recipe was originally made with freshly cooked potatoes it has been adapted to instant potatoes. In addition, it calls for heavy sweet cream, shortening, flour, salt, etc. The paper-thin *lefse* are cooked in a skillet, on a griddle, or in a *lefse* baker.

What is pappadam? Also spelled pappadum, it is an Indian "bread" much like a very thin pancake that is fried in oil until it becomes crisp. It is available in 6-ounce boxes, imported from India, in stores specializing in Indian foods.

What does panettone mean? A spiced yeast bread, apparently of Milanese origin, made with raisins, in every size from a small bun to a big loaf, the latter being a traditional Christmas gift. Usually available in this country in Italian food stores during the holidays. But it also means (here our authority is Frank Giambelli, *patron* of Giambelli restaurant, one of New York's fine Italian restaurants) an entrée made with veal, prosciutto ham, and mozzarella cheese.

Can pan sizes be switched in baking cakes? Certain cake pan sizes are ideal for particular cakes and they are, of course, the pans called for in recipes. "Sometimes," as is pointed out in *All About Baking* by General Foods Kitchens (Random House), "a cake will bake in other pans with, if not equally good results, *almost* as good results." This chart, adapted from this useful little book, gives suggested pan substitutes.

If a cake bakes in	*It will also bake*
2 8-inch layers	2 thin 8 x 8 x 2 squares; 18 to 24 2½-inch cupcakes
3 8-inch layers	2 9 x 9 x 2 squares
2 9-inch-layers	2 8 x 8 x 2 squares; 3 thin 8-inch layers; 1 15 x 10 x 1 rectangle; 30 2½-inch cupcakes
1 8 x 8 x 2 square	1 9-inch layer
2 8 x 8 x 2 squares	2 9-inch layers; 1 13 x 9 x 2 rectangle
1 9 x 9 x 2 square	2 thin 8-inch layers
2 9 x 9 x 2 squares	3 8-inch layers
1 13 x 9 x 2 rectangle	2 9-inch layers; 2 8 x 8 x 2 squares
1 12 x 8 x 2 rectangle	2 8-inch layers
1 9 x 5 x 3 loaf	1 9 x 9 x 2 square; 24 to 30 2½-inch cupcakes
1 8 x 4 x 3 loaf	1 8 x 8 x 2 square
1 9 x 3½ tube	2 9-inch layers; 24 to 30 2½-inch cupcakes
1 10 x 4 tube	2 9 x 5 x 3 loaves; 1 13 x 9 x 2 rectangle; 2 15x 10 x 1 rectangles

What size do tube cake pans come in? Eight, nine, and ten inches. Aluminum. You measure a pan at the top—that is, the diameter from one side to another.

Should a cake pan be greased with butter or with vegetable shortening? Modern cookbooks claim that butter—especially salted butter

—will burn. This has not been our experience. If you are apprehensive, brush the pan with a light coating of vegetable oil or grease it with vegetable shortening. Whatever you use, be thorough about it, so the pan—sides and bottom, curves and tube, if any—are all completely covered, following, of course, recipe instructions.

Why do you coat raisins with flour before adding to cake batter?   Not only raisins but currants and other dried fruits—to keep them from falling to the bottom of the cake when baked. Use a small amount of the flour called for in the recipe—just enough to coat the fruit lightly.

Where in the oven should cakes be placed for baking?   Layer cakes at the middle position, as near the center of the rack as possible, but diagonally opposite each other to allow heat to circulate freely. Pans should be at least a good inch from oven walls. If a second rack is used, stagger the cakes on the bottom rack so cakes do not "sit" on top of each other. All "air" cakes (angel, sponge, etc.) and fruit cakes should be baked at the lower-rack position—the rack below the center. All other cakes are baked at center position.

PASSOVER SPONGE CAKE

6 eggs, separated	2 tablespoons matzo meal
1 cup sugar	Good pinch salt
½ cup plus 2 tablespoons potato flour	Grated rind of 1 lemon
	Juice ½ lemon

'Line the bottom of a 9-inch-square pan with baking parchment or waxed paper.

Beat the yolks with a rotary or electric beater until thick and pale yellow. Then gradually begin to add the sugar, beating hard and constantly until the mixture makes "ribbons." Stir in the flour, matzo meal, salt, lemon rind, and lemon juice very thoroughly.

Beat the egg whites until they hold stiff shiny peaks when the beater is held straight up. Beat about a third of the whites into the batter vigorously, then fold in the remainder with a rubber spatula gently but completely. Pour into the prepared pan and bake in a preheated 325° oven for 1 hour or until a toothpick plunged into the center comes out dry—that is, without any batter clinging to it. Run a knife around the edge of the cake, then turn out on a cake rack. Peel off the paper, then reverse the cake so the top is topside. Once cool, wrap in Saran Wrap or foil.

What makes a cake fall in the middle?   Any one of a number of reasons, but probably because there was too much fat (butter, margarine, or oil).

Is it true that a real pound cake does not call for baking powder?
Yes. Pound cake, possibly adapted from the French *génoise* by
English cooks, although there is a great difference in the method of
preparation, was created long before baking powder was invented.
Baking powder appeared first in England about 1830—a primitive
version of the sophisticated ingredient we know today. The original
pound cake took its name from the fact that it was made with 1
pound each of butter, sugar, and flour, either 10 or 12 eggs, and
flavorings; no baking powder. In the 1896 and 1924 editions of *The
Boston Cooking-School Cook Book* (now known as *The Fannie
Farmer Cookbook*), the pound cake recipes are identical. No baking
powder. Early editions of *The Joy of Cooking* added cream of tartar,
a leavening agent that is part of the formula in modern baking
powders but the last edition of *The Joy* comes right out flatly and
calls for double-acting baking powder.

Since the true pound cake, like the *génoise*, is entirely dependent
on eggs to help it rise, it has undoubtedly posed serious problems
to many cooks. The addition of baking powder, although not traditional, certainly reduces the hazards against turning out a "sad" cake.
Some people, however, like "sad" cakes. Like Craig Claiborne, like
Helen McCully.

Why do pound cakes sometimes crack?   The American Institute of
Baking tells us there are three possible reasons: 1) the oven temperature is too high; 2) the baking-powder reaction is too slow;
3) the cake is overmixed. They add: "If the batter is properly for-
mulated, then a longer bake at a lower temperature ought to produce
a crack-free surface."

Can chocolate cakes be frozen?   Almost any cake can be frozen. If
it is frosted, you might have some trouble there. Best, we suggest,
to freeze the cake, then frost once it has thawed and come to room
temperature. The recipe that follows which is frosted or glazed
freezes like a dream and is a dream of a cake.

FRENCH CHOCOLATE CAKE
WITH CHOCOLATE GLAZE

½ cup (1 stick) butter, softened
1 cup almonds or filberts, skin on
¾ cup semisweet chocolate pieces
    or 4 1-ounce squares semisweet
    chocolate

⅔ cup sugar
3 eggs
Grated rind 1 large orange
¼ cup very fine bread crumbs

Butter the bottom and sides of an 8-inch round cake pan thoroughly, then line the bottom with baking parchment. Set aside.

Grind the almonds as fine as possible in an electric blender and set aside. Melt the chocolate in the top of a double boiler over hot, *not boiling,* water.

Work or cream the remaining butter with your hands, an electric beater, or in an electric mixer, until very soft and light. Very gradually add the sugar, beating constantly. When all the sugar is in, add the eggs, one at a time, beating hard after each addition. The batter at this point will look curdled, but don't be alarmed. Stir in the melted chocolate, ground nuts, orange rind, and bread crumbs thoroughly with a rubber spatula.

Pour into the prepared pan and bake in a preheated 375° oven for 25 minutes. Allow the cake to cool on a rack for about 30 minutes, then run a metal spatula around the edge and turn out onto a cake rack. If cake doesn't drop out easily, give the pan a bang with your hand. Very gently lift off the lining paper. Cool completely before glazing.

The center of the cake will not seem thoroughly cooked, hence its soft texture and exceptionally delicious flavor.

Glaze:

2 1-ounce squares unsweetened
    chocolate
2 1-ounce squares semisweet
    chocolate or ¼ cup semisweet
    chocolate pieces

¼ cup (½ stick) butter, softened
    and cut up
2 teaspoons honey
Toasted slivered almonds or whole
    filberts

Combine the two chocolates, butter, and honey in the top of a double boiler and melt over hot water. Remove from heat and beat until cold but still "pourable"—in other words, until it begins to thicken.

Place the cake on the rack on a piece of waxed paper and pour the glaze over all. Tip the cake so the glaze runs evenly over the top and down the sides. Smooth sides, if necessary, with a metal spatula. Garland the rim of the cake with toasted slivered almonds or filberts, placing them fairly close together.

This cake freezes very successfully if wrapped and sealed securely. Bring to room temperature before serving.

What is Spotted Dick? According to *The Art of British Cooking* by Theodora Fitzgibbon and her authority, Simpson's-on-the-Strand, London, where Spotted Dick has been served for nearly one hundred years, it is a roll of sweet dough mixed with raisins, then steamed. Served with jam or syrup.

What are crumpets? Originally, apparently, crumpets were made with yeast, potatoes, water, salt, and flour but the modern version is made with flour, eggs, milk, and baking powder. They are baked on a griddle in little crumpet rings and these days are usually made in a bakery. Reminiscent of, but far better in our opinion than, our English muffins. There is, possibly, nothing better than a perfect little crumpet, toasted, soaked in butter along with a good "cuppa" which translates into—a freshly made cup of hot tea. Other good things the British serve at teatime (and tea is as important to an Englishman as coffee to an American) include gingerbread, sponge cake, Eccles cakes (little turnovers made with short dough, filled with currants), Dundee cake, and assorted sandwiches such as watercress, smoked salmon, and sliced chicken between slices of white bread. Very elegant.

Where does the word cookie come from? Probably from the Dutch, *koekje*, the diminutive of *koek*, meaning cake. In Scotland where the word cookie is also used, it means a flat bun. In this country, of course, it is both a term of endearment and a short sweet pastry served with tea or to accompany desserts.

Are fortune cookies really Chinese? The fortune cookie, unknown in China, seems to be Western-inspired, although its origins are obscure. Apparently they were invented by Chinese restaurateurs but on the wrong side of the Pacific.

What are buñuelos? Buñuelo means "fritter" and as Philip Brown has written, "they are crisp, wonderful, deep-fried 'cookies' that it is almost impossible to stop eating." In Los Angeles you can buy them already made but the recipe is not at all difficult.

PHILIP BROWN'S BUÑUELOS

1½ cups all-purpose flour	1 egg
¾ teaspoon salt	Ice water
1½ teaspoons baking powder	Vegetable oil
2 tablespoons lard or shortening	Cinnamon sugar

Sift flour, salt, and baking powder together into a deep bowl. With a pastry blender or two forks, work lard or shortening into the mixture until mealy. Make a well in the center, add the whole egg and mix it in thoroughly with a fork. Add 2 or 3 tablespoons of ice water, working it in until all the flour is incorporated. Dough should be stiff.

Divide the dough into thirds and roll paper-thin on a lightly floured pastry cloth with floured pin. Cut into squares, diamonds, or any shape with a sharp knife.

Drop a few at a time into oil heated to 400° and deep fry until puffed and golden brown. Drain on paper towels. Sprinkle with cinnamon sugar (allow 2 tablespoons cinnamon to 1 cup sugar) or mixture of sugar and ground cloves. Serve as you would any cookie.

Are bagels Jewish? No. Although most people think of bagels as Jewish food (it's true Polish and Austrian Jews brought them to the United States), it was a Viennese baker who first conceived the idea of baking a local bread in the shape of a stirrup. Bagels are water doughnuts which first-class bakers make by hand; others, by machine. Once, it was said they could be made properly, only by hand and good bakers still do. A mixture of yeast, eggs, flour, salt, water, and oil, they are called *bublik* or *bublitchky* (the diminutive) in Russian; *buegel* or *bugel*, meaning stirrup, in Germany. From this, obviously, we get bagel and the doughnut shape.

What are cigarettes russe? A delicate, very rich, sweet biscuit rolled, while still warm, around a pencil-thick tube to give them the shape of a cigarette. No one seems to know quite why *russe* is attached to them unless it's because they resemble, in thickness and size, hand-rolled cigarettes such as Russians visiting France once made for themselves. Familiar to most Europeans since the early 1800s, there are now domestic *cigarettes russe* made by the same formula as those available in Belgium. Elegant, beautifully packaged, you will find them in all good food stores and supermarkets straight across the country. Delicious with a cup of hot tea or served with ice cream or an ice.

What is a gaufrette iron?   *Gaufres* are light pastries cooked in a mold; *gaufrette,* the diminutive, means small wafer or waffle (from the Dutch *wafel*). A *gaufrette* iron is the mold used to do the cooking.

What sizes do pie plates come in?   Until now, pie plates were 8½ inches and 9½ inches, inside top diameter. Now they have been standardized to 9 and 10 inches, inside top diameter. The former will hold about 4 cups and the latter almost 7 cups.

What is pastry flour?   Flour that is usually made of soft wheats, finely milled, although not as fine as cake flour. It is designed for making pastries and is used chiefly by bakers and biscuit manufacturers. It is difficult to find in the open market. Possibly available in health food stores.

What is the purpose in using a flan ring to bake a pie shell?   The most important reason is that the pastry, especially the bottom, bakes through better. Although pie pans can be used, Paula Peck says in her book. *The Art of Fine Baking,* "Flan rings give the best and most attractive results." Flan rings are available in rectangular, square, and round shapes. Essentially a metal hoop, with no top or bottom, usually about an inch high, flans are placed on a cookie sheet, then lined with the pastry. All shops specializing in fine cooking equipment carry flan rings in various sizes and shapes.

Can you explain the term "roll out"?   It simply means to take dough (biscuits, pastry, etc.) and roll flat, on a lightly floured board or pastry cloth, with a floured rolling pin, to the thickness indicated in the recipe.

How do you roll pastry properly?   Dust the cloth and stocking or board and pin, as the case may be, lightly with flour. The technique in rolling any pastry is to roll it lightly. With the exception of puff pastry which, in the preparation stages, is always rolled in a long strip, the ball of dough is placed on the floured surface, flattened (if it has been refrigerated, it will be firm), then rolled lightly from the center out to the edge in all directions, to make a circle of the desired size. Always lift the rolling pin as it nears the edge of the circle to keep the pastry from splitting or making it too thin. If the edge splits or cracks, pinch together or patch; if it sticks, loosen gently with a metal spatula, then lift and again flour the surface lightly.

What exactly is a pastry cloth? A large piece of canvas on which to roll pastry, cookies, doughnuts, noodles, ravioli, bread, etc. Because it is treated, the canvas will not absorb grease or moisture. It is always accompanied by a rolling pin sleeve that looks like a knitted stocking. Using the pastry cloth any dough can be rolled very thin and even the softest dough can be rolled without sticking. It's a marvelous piece of equipment available in the housewares department of department stores or stores specializing in fine cooking equipment.

How long can you store unbaked pastry? Roll the pastry into a ball, place in a plastic bag, all air squeezed out, securely tied; or wrap in Saran Wrap or foil, again securely. Refrigerate about eight to ten days or freeze (see below).

Can you freeze pastry? Yes. Roll into a ball, freeze, then wrap securely in suitable freezer wrappings. Thaw at room temperature. Pie shells, tarts, *bouchées* can all be made, frozen, then wrapped and stored in freezer. It has a fairly long freezer life. Thaw at room temperature, then follow baking instructions.

Are phyllo and strudel the same pastry? Essentially. Phyllo calls for somewhat more butter than strudel in the basic dough and is infinitely more delicious in making the various delicacies. The technique for making the two pastries is exactly the same and they both must be made by hand. There is no shortcut. Hence we recommend buying it already made. Phyllo is Greek, and strudel is Austrian. The leaves (or sheets), frozen, can be bought in many stores specializing in fine foods. Approximately 20 to 22 sheets to the pound, measuring 14 inches by 17 inches.

What flour is used for pâte feuilletée? Cookbooks on the whole are not consistent in designating the type of flour to use in making puff pastry (*pâte feuilletée*). Bread flour, pastry flour, enriched flour, all-purpose flour, and instant-blending flour are all called for in one book or another. Both bread and pastry flour are used chiefly by industrial bakers and are not readily available to the consumer. Enriched flour is any white flour to which vitamins and minerals have been added so, in a sense, it is meaningless terminology. Both all-purpose flour, also known as general-purpose, and instant-blending, also an all-purpose flour, are usually enriched. Although the modern all-purpose flours no longer need sifting before measuring, their structure is quite different from that of instant-blending which, because of its microscopically fine, sand-like texture, runs through a sifter like water and in water or liquid dissolves instantly—hence the name.

In testing *pâte feuilletée* we have used both all-purpose and Wondra,* General Mills' instant-blending all-purpose flour. Like Julia Child, co-author of *Mastering the Art of French Cooking*, and André Soltner, M.O.F., *Premier Cuisinier* (Executive Chef) at Lutèce, one of New York's great restaurants, we had extraordinary success with instant-blending flour. The dough is extremely flexible, rolls and turns easily, and the end result is a flaky, light-as-a-feather, tender crust.

* Wondra is available in 2- and 5-pound bags.

What is pâte à chou? A cream puff pastry that has innumerable uses. The dough can be made into cream puffs or éclairs, baked, filled with French pastry cream (vanilla, coffee, or chocolate), then frosted; or filled with mixtures such as lobster, crabmeat, or chicken to make hors d'oeuvre. The basic dough has many applications in cookery. Gnocchi *à la viennoise*, for example; in preparing potatoes *à la dauphine*, Duchess potatoes mixed with chou paste, shaped into balls, and deep fried.

PÂTE À CHOU

1 cup water	1 cup sifted all-purpose flour
½ cup (1 stick) sweet butter	4 whole eggs
Pinch salt	Crème pâtissière (see below)

Combine the water, butter, and salt in a heavy saucepan. Bring to a boil, take off the heat and stir in the flour all at once. Place back over very low heat and beat vigorously with a wooden spatula, until the dough leaves the sides of the pan and forms a ball. Take off the heat and beat in the eggs, one at a time, beating briskly after each addition until the dough is smooth. Makes 16 to 18 puffs or éclairs.

To make cream puffs: Drop by rounded tablespoons onto a greased baking sheet, leaving about 2 inches between puffs to allow for spreading.

To fill cream puffs: Fill a pastry bag, fitted with a small, plain tube, with crème pâtissière. Make a small, opening in the bottom of each puff with a paring knife. Insert the tube into the opening and fill the puff.

CRÈME PÂTISSIÈRE

2 cups milk	1 teaspoon vanilla
4 egg yolks	¼ cup cornstarch
¾ cup sugar	

Bring the milk to a boil over moderate heat in a heavy saucepan. Set aside.

Combine the yolks, sugar, and vanilla in a bowl and beat with a rotary or electric beater until the mixture makes "ribbons" and turns a pale yellow—3 to 4 minutes. Add the cornstarch and beat until smooth. Add the hot milk slowly, whipping constantly. Pour the mixture back into the saucepan, place over moderate heat, and bring to a boil, stirring constantly with a wooden spatula. Cook very slowly, stirring constantly, until the crème thickens almost to a paste. Place a piece of Saran Wrap flat on the surface so a skin won't form and refrigerate. Make about 3 cups.

NOTE: *Crème pâtissière* is a basic cream that can be used to fill cream puffs, éclairs, cakes, or as a base for sweet soufflés. If you wish to flavor it with liqueur such as cognac or kirsch or other flavors such as coffee or almond (if you use almond do not use vanilla in the basic recipe) add the flavoring when the crème is cold.

**Desserts
and Ice Creams**

Where does the word dessert come from? It derives from the French *desservir* which, according to the *Oxford French Dictionary*, means "to clear away, to remove dishes and plates from a table." Obviously, it has come to mean a course of fruits or sweets served after the entrée or main course.

What's the caloric count of ice cream, sherbet, ice milk? One half cup of ice cream gives 145 calories; sherbet, 130; and ice milk, 140. For dedicated calorie counters there is a dietary frozen dessert, artificially sweetened with saccharin, calcium cyclamate, or sodium cyclamate. However, *Today's Food Market* (Kansas State University) informs us: "This dessert is intended for use by diabetics only, under medical advice."

How long can you store ice cream in a freezer? A carton can be stored for 2 to 3 weeks in the freezing compartment of the refrigerator/ freezer combination, Consumer Education of Cornell University (New York City) tells us, or for one month in a home freezer that maintains a constant temperature of 0° or less. Ice cream should not be allowed to melt partially and then be refrozen because the result is a coarse, icy consistency.

Should ice cream be softened before serving? It isn't a case of should or shouldn't. If the ice cream is frozen hard, it is difficult to extricate from the carton and to serve attractively. We suggest "softening" it a bit by taking the carton from the freezer and placing it in the refrigerator for no longer than 30 minutes. The time, obviously, depends on the size of the carton. See below.

What is meant by "tempering" ice cream?   This simply means to hold the ice cream at room temperature for about 10 minutes before serving, or in the refrigerator for half an hour. Chocolate, fruit, and nut ice creams have a slightly higher sugar content and a lower melting point, so they can be served at freezer temperature.

Are there any special rules for making ice cream?   Yes. There are eight basic rules. 1) It is best to use two-day-old heavy cream for a finer-grained ice cream; 2) whenever possible, the mixture should be made a day ahead and refrigerated—this helps to make a smoother ice cream and to increase the volume; 3) the ice cream mixture should always be chilled before freezing, regardless of when it is to be frozen; 4) the container should be filled only to three fourths of its depth to allow for expansion during freezing; 5) sugar should be dissolved in liquid over heat before combining with the other ingredients; 6) texture and flavor are improved if the cream is scalded (this simply means to heat to the boiling point or until a film wrinkles over the top); 7) fruits should be added to the mixture when frozen but before it has ripened; 8) once the ice cream has reached the right consistency, which is when it looks like very heavy whipped cream, it should be allowed to "ripen," which simply means to mellow.

How do you freeze ice cream in an electric freezer?   You follow the manufacturer's instructions exactly. However, the freezing time is much shorter than by hand and, obviously, the time depends on the size of the freezer.

How do you freeze ice cream by hand?   You start by turning the crank slowly at first, until you begin to feel a slight pull. When it becomes difficult to turn, the ice cream will have reached the right consistency.

How do you pack an ice cream freezer?   Whether it's a hand or electric freezer it is done exactly the same way. Correct ratio of ice to salt is essential. Allow 4 to 6 parts chopped ice to 1 part coarse rock salt (also known as ice cream salt). After the ice cream container has been placed in the tub or pail, the crank secure on top, fill the tub one third full of ice before adding any salt; then add the ice and salt in alternate layers around the container until the tub is full.

What is meant by "ripening" in terms of ice cream? It simply means to mellow and here's how you "ripen" ice cream made in the hand freezer: Once the ice cream has reached the right consistency, pour off all the salt water from the tub. Wipe the lid carefully to make sure no salt drips into the container, then remove the lid, lift out the dasher, scrape it, and pack the ice cream down. Place double layers of foil over the top of the container, put the cork in the lid, and place the lid back on the container. Repack the tub with additional salt and ice, covering the top generously. Cover with several layers of newspapers or some heavy material; in the old days, cooks used the bag in which they cracked the ice. To "ripen" ice cream made in the electric freezer, place the container, standing up, in the freezer, which must maintain zero temperature.

How can you keep ice cream fresh longer? The U.S. Department of Agriculture tells us that if the carton in which the ice cream is packed is wrapped securely in heavy-duty foil, it will keep its quality a lot longer. This, of course, only in a freezer that maintains zero temperature or below.

Can you forestall fresh fruits from freezing in homemade ice cream? Yes. Completely cover prepared fruits with spirits such as cognac, rum, kirsch, etc., and allow to stand for several hours, before combining with ice cream mixture. The addition of the alcohol, which won't freeze, helps to solve the problem. Use the leftover liqueur to flavor some other sweet dish.

Can you freeze ice cream in the refrigerator? Yes. Pour the mixture into the ice cube trays. If the refrigerator does not have a separate freezer compartment maintaining zero temperature, set the temperature at the coldest point. When the ice cream has a one-inch border of thick frozen mush around the edge, transfer the mixture to a large, chilled bowl and beat it hard with a rotary or electric beater until smooth and creamy. Return ice cream to trays and freeze until firm.

VANILLA ICE CREAM

1½ cups light cream	4 egg yolks
½ cup sugar	2 teaspoons vanilla
¼ teaspoon salt	2 cups two-day-old heavy cream

Mechanical freezer method (see page 82): Heat the light cream in the top of a double boiler until a film shines on top. Stir in the sugar and salt until dissolved. Remove from heat.

Beat the egg yolks slightly; add a little of the hot cream, stirring constantly. Pour egg mixture into the remaining hot cream slowly, stirring constantly. Place back over simmering water and cook, stirring all the time, until the custard coats a spoon. Take off the heat. Cool. When cold, stir in the vanilla and the heavy cream. Freeze according to basic instructions. Makes about 1½ quarts, but this recipe can be doubled successfully.

Refrigerator method (see page 83): Follow same directions until you come to the heavy cream, which should be whipped before combining with the cold custard. Freeze according to basic instructions.

CHOCOLATE ICE CREAM

Mechanical freezer method (see page 82): Make up the Vanilla Ice Cream, according to the directions, adding 2 1-ounce squares unsweetened chocolate to the light cream when you make the custard. Follow basic freezing instructions.

Refrigerator method (see page 83): Make up the Vanilla Ice Cream according to directions, adding 2 1-ounce squares unsweetened chocolate to the light cream when you make the custard. Whip the heavy cream before combining with cold custard. Follow basic freezing instructions.

COFFEE ICE CREAM

Mechanical freezer method (see page 82): Make up the Vanilla Ice Cream, according to the directions, omitting the vanilla. Add 2 tablespoons powdered instant coffee to the light cream when you make the custard. Follow basic freezing instructions.

Refrigerator method (see page 83): Make up the Vanilla Ice Cream, according to directions, omitting the vanilla. Add 2 tablespoons powdered instant coffee to the light cream when you make the custard. Whip the heavy cream before mixing with cold custard. Follow basic freezing instructions.

CHOCOLATE CREAM SAUCE

3 1-ounce squares unsweetened chocolate
½ cup sugar
Dash salt

⅛ teaspoon cinnamon
½ teaspoon vanilla
½ cup heavy cream

Melt the chocolate squares over hot, not boiling, water. Take off the heat and cool.

Mix the sugar with ½ cup water, bring to a boil and cook for 5 minutes. Cool at room temperature. Stir in melted chocolate thoroughly. Add salt, cinnamon, vanilla, and cream. Serve hot over ice cream. Makes 1½ cups.

If sauce proves to be too thick, stir in a little extra cream.

GINGER SAUCE FOR ICE CREAM

1 cup water
¾ cup sugar
Juice ½ lemon

3 tablespoons finely chopped candied ginger

Combine the water, sugar, and lemon juice in a saucepan. Bring to a boil, reduce heat, and cook until mixture registers 230° on a candy thermometer or the syrup makes long gossamer threads when dripped from the tip of a spoon. Take off the heat and stir in the ginger. Bring to a boil again. Makes 1 cup.

Can be served hot or cold and if made in a quantity keeps perfectly, refrigerated.

MAPLE WALNUT SAUCE FOR ICE CREAM

Bring about 1½ cups real maple syrup to the boiling point. Then cook a few minutes to thicken slightly. Take off the heat and stir in ½ cup or so coarsely chopped walnuts. Allow sauce to cool. Keeps well refrigerated.

HONEY NUT SAUCE FOR ICE CREAM

Heat ½ cup liquid honey to the boiling point only, then stir in ½ cup coarsely chopped walnuts, blanched almonds, or filberts.

Is it true sherbets are of Turkish origin? Yes. The Turkish spelling is *serbet,* the Arabic, *sharbah,* and the Persian, *sharbat.* Actually, it is a drink, and in the days of the sultans, sherbets made of fresh fruits such as black cherries or strawberries, sweetened with sugar or honey and diluted with cold water, were served to honored guests in exquisite sherbet glasses. Many of these lovely glasses from the old palaces are now on exhibition in Turkish museums. The slender graceful glasses are still made in Turkey (the ones available to us are evidently adapted from the original designs), and *serbets* are still drunk. However, sherbet, as we make it in the West, is really an ice— a cool and refreshing climax to a splendid dinner.

How do you freeze sherbets? Exactly as ice cream. See page 82.

LEMON CREAM SHERBET

Grated rind 3 lemons
1½ cups lemon juice * (about 7 lemons), strained
1¼ cups sugar

Dash salt
3 cups milk
1 cup heavy cream

Mix lemon rind, lemon juice, sugar, and salt together. Add milk and cream gradually, stirring until sugar has dissolved. Freeze in mechanical freezer or refrigerator according to basic ice cream directions. Makes about 2 quarts.

* Boil the lemons a couple of minutes and they will yield more juice.

TANGERINE SHERBET

5 tangerines
2 cups sugar
¼ cup Grand Marnier or Curaçao

4 egg whites
Pinch salt

Cut the tangerines in half and squeeze on a reamer to extract the juice. Strain and set aside. Sliver the rinds from 3 of the tangerines. Drop in boiling water for 1 minute, then rinse under cold water. Place in a heavy saucepan with *1½ cups of the sugar* and *1½ cups of water*. Bring to a boil over moderate heat, stirring constantly. Boil, without stirring, for 4 minutes or until thermometer reaches 200° to 210°. Cool. Combine the syrup, Grand Marnier, and juice.

Pour into the container of an electric freezer packed with layers of crushed ice and coarse salt. Freeze for 15 to 20 minutes or until sherbet is *almost* firm. Meanwhile, combine the remaining sugar (½ cup) with ¼ *cup of hot water* in a heavy saucepan. Stir over moderate heat until the syrup comes to a boil. Boil gently, without stirring, for 8 to 10 minutes. Do not allow the mixture to brown.

While syrup is cooking, beat the egg whites with the salt in the electric mixer until whites hold firm, shiny peaks when the beater is held straight up. Begin to add the syrup in a steady, slow stream, beating constantly. When all the syrup is in, continue beating another 5 to 6 minutes. Stir the meringue into the tangerine mixture and freeze another 15 minutes. Can be turned into a mold and frozen, or not, as you like. Serves 10, but remember that like all "water" ices it melts fast.

Is a copper bowl essential for whipping egg whites?   In the opinion of many fine cooks, it is. The theory of these cooks and many chefs is that in an *unlined* copper bowl, whites "mount" more smoothly and you get a larger volume. It is our unsupported opinion that the copper bowl and big balloon whip (also considered essential) are a hangover from another era when cooks had nothing more efficient to beat with. In this electric age, we have found the big electric mixer and electric beater give us extremely satisfactory results.

Why do meringue shells sometimes stick?   High humidity is probably the reason. The same thing can happen to macaroons which are also made with egg whites. The Poultry and Egg National Board recommends covering baking sheets with heavy brown paper or baking parchment, spooning or piping the meringue on the paper, then baking in a preheated 225° oven for about 70 minutes. When properly cooked, the meringues (or macaroons) can be lifted off the paper easily. No sticking. If the humidity is extremely high, bake the meringues a few minutes longer. It is perhaps worth noting that the French bake meringues at 200° for 2½ to 3 hours which makes a very dry meringue. We ourselves prefer them softer and somewhat chewy, which results when they are cooked for a shorter time.

MERINGUES

4 egg whites	Good pinch of salt
1 cup granulated sugar	

Cover two baking sheets with either heavy brown paper or baking parchment. Do not grease. Do not flour. Do not wet the paper. Set aside.

Beat the egg whites in a medium-size bowl with an electric or rotary beater until the eggs begin to hold a shape. Sprinkle with salt. Begin adding the sugar gradually, beating hard and constantly. The finished meringue should be very shiny and stiff enough to stand in peaks when the beater is held straight.

Spoon onto the prepared baking sheets and bake in a preheated 225° oven for about 70 minutes. If the humidity is very high you may need to bake them a bit longer. At this point, you can lift the meringues from the sheets with your hands. Look, no spatula! Cool on wire racks. This makes a rather soft, chewy meringue. Makes 18 to 20 meringues.

To serve, whip 1 cup heavy cream with a dash of vanilla. Place one meringue on each dessert plate, cover with a good spoonful of the whipped cream and place a second meringue on top.

Variations: Purée a cup or so of ripe strawberries, sweeten to taste, and mix with the whipped cream; or fill meringues with ice cream instead of whipped cream.

N O T E : Meringues will keep well in a well-sealed tin container.

MERINGUES COOKED IN THE FRENCH MANNER

The French like a hard meringue in contrast to the chewy (see above).

Make the meringues as indicated above. Spoon the mixture into a pastry bag fitted with a No. 7 tube and press out oval shells about 1½ inches wide and 4 inches long on the paper-lined baking sheets (see above). Sprinkle with sifted confectioners' sugar. Bake in a preheated 200° oven for 2½ to 3 hours. Correctly, the baked shells should be pure white but if your oven isn't constant, they may turn a pale yellow. Lift from the baking sheets at once and cool on wire racks.

To serve, whip 2 cups heavy cream with a dash of vanilla until it begins to hold a shape. Then gradually add ¼ cup sifted confectioners' sugar, beating constantly. Continue beating until the cream is stiff. Spoon the cream into a pastry bag and press about 3 tablespoons onto the flat side of the meringue. Place another shell on top and sprinkle the top with a little shower of cocoa or sifted confectioners' sugar.

What is a vacherin? A French *entremets* made with meringue filled with *crème Chantilly* or ice cream; if the latter, it is garnished with *crème Chantilly* and candied violets.

What is Mont-Blanc? A cold *entremets* made with chestnuts. Essentially it is a dome of *crème Chantilly* (sweetened whipped cream) and sweetened chestnut purée—the general effect being, in a sense, a mountain. Hence the name *Mont-Blanc.* The Viennese call it *Kastanienreis;* the Hungarians, *Gestenyepure.*

How do you test baked custards for doneness? The test for custards that are to be served cold is somewhat different from the one for those that are to be served hot. *For cold baked custards,* insert the blade of a knife one inch from the *outside edge* of the baking dish. If the blade comes out clean—that is, without any of the mixture clinging to it—the custard will be firm all the way through when cooled. If, in error, you should test the center of the custard and find it thoroughly cooked, *immediately* place the dish in a pan of ice water to stop further cooking. *For hot baked custards (quiche Lorraine,* for example), insert the blade of a knife *one inch from the center* of the custard. Again, if perfectly baked, the knife will come out clean. The point to remember, in both instances, is that the custard continues to cook for several minutes after it comes from the oven. In the case of a hot custard, it will be firm by the time it is served.

What is custard royale? An unsweetened, baked custard, cut into shapes such as cubes, slices, diamonds; used as a garnish in a hot consommé; hence, *Consommé royale.*

What is a torte? A type of rich cake made with eggs, ground nuts or breadcrumbs, sugar, butter, and flavorings, but without flour. Finished with a rich frosting. Apparently Austrian.

PAUL STEINDLER'S SACHER TORTE

Since Paul had a tour of duty as a chef at the famous Sacher Hotel in Vienna, this recipe comes, in a sense, right "from the horse's mouth." Currently, he serves it at his Duck Joint, one of New York's more interesting restaurants.

4 tablespoons (½ stick) sweet
   butter
½ cup sugar
6 eggs, separated
3 1-ounce squares unsweetened
   chocolate
¼ cup almonds, skin on

½ cup instant-blending flour plus 1
   tablespoon
Grated rind 1 lemon
1 teaspoon vanilla
Apricot glaze
Chocolate glaze
Whipped cream

Take an 8-inch spring-form pan. Cut a piece of baking parchment to fit the bottom. Dab the bottom with a bit of butter to make it hold. Butter the sides well. Refrigerate.

Place the butter, sugar, and egg yolks in the electric mixer and beat for 10 minutes at high speed. Meanwhile, grate the chocolate in the blender until very fine; also grate the almonds in the blender very fine. Finally, grate the lemon rind.

When the butter mixture has been sufficiently beaten, stir in the chocolate, almonds, flour, lemon rind, and vanilla thoroughly. Beat the egg whites until they hold firm shiny peaks when the beater is held straight up. Beat a third of the whites into the batter vigorously with a wire whisk. Fold in the remainder with a rubber spatula gently but thoroughly. Pour into the prepared pan and bake in a preheated 300° oven for 1 hour or until a toothpick inserted in the center comes out dry. Immediately, once it's cooked, release the spring form and turn the cake out on to a cake rack. Lift off the bottom of the pan and the parchment paper. Allow the cake to cool completely.

To complete the torte: Cut the cold cake in half, across. Spread a layer of apricot glaze * over the cut half. Replace the top. (*Note:* You'll have some extra glaze which can be used to advantage over ice cream or puddings.) Place the rack on which the cake sits on a large piece of waxed paper. Pour the warm melted chocolate glaze † over the top of the cake and tip the rack back and forth so the glaze runs down the sides. Smooth the sides with a small spatula. Do *not* touch the top or you'll ruin the shiny surface. Allow the cake to stand until the glaze is firm to the touch. Serve with whipped cream.

Important: When the glaze is firm but not hard, mark the slices (about 12) so that when it's cut the glaze won't crack.

* *Apricot glaze:* Heat the contents of a 12-ounce jar of apricot jam with ½ cup of sugar and ½ cup of water. Cook, over moderate heat, stirring constantly, for 5 minutes. Strain through a fine sieve. Cool completely. Stir in Cognac, Grand Marnier, or kirsch to taste.

† *Chocolate glaze:* Melt 3 1-ounce squares unsweetened chocolate and 2 1-ounce squares semisweet chocolate over simmering water.

SOUR CREAM TORTE

3 cups sifted all-purpose flour	1 cup (2 sticks) sweet butter, cut up
¾ cup sugar	1 egg

Filling:

3 cups (3 8-ounce cans) shelled walnuts

3 cups commercial sour cream

2 cups sifted confectioners' sugar

1½ teaspoons vanilla

Mix the flour and sugar together in a bowl. Work in the butter with a pastry blender or two knives until the mixture looks mealy. Stir in the unbeaten egg and mix with your hands until the dough holds together. Divide the dough into seven equal parts. Roll each part into a 9-inch circle on a lightly floured cookie sheet (use a 9-inch cake pan as your guide). Bake 10 to 12 minutes in a preheated 350° oven until the edges begin to brown lightly. You'll undoubtedly have to bake the layers in two or three batches. Cool and lift from the cookie sheet with a spatula to cake racks.

To make the filling: Chop the walnuts very fine (do not use a blender) and mix with the sour cream, confectioners' sugar, and vanilla. Spread a layer of filling between each layer, arranging the layers on top of each other, one after another. Finish the top layer with a sifting of confectioners' sugar. Allow the torte to mellow in the refrigerator for about 5 hours or longer, if there's time. Delicious.

What's an easy way to make macaroon crumbs? The easiest way we know is to buy the Italian macaroons, *amaretti* they're called, and pulverize them in the electric blender.

What is Deacon Porter's Hat? Ask any Mount Holyoke College student, or alumna, and she is likely to reply, "It's a steamed spicy pudding and delicious." It is named after Deacon Andrew W. Porter, who, in 1837, supervised the construction of the first building on the campus, the oldest women's college in this country. Apparently, the recipe still appears on the college menu. Here is the recipe:

DEACON PORTER'S HAT

½ cup shortening

1 cup molasses

1 cup buttermilk

2 cups all-purpose flour

½ teaspoon baking soda

½ teaspoon cinnamon

½ teaspoon ground cloves

½ teaspoon freshly grated nutmeg

¼ cup raisins

Sift the flour with the baking soda and spices; melt the shortening and stir in the molasses and buttermilk. Combine the two mixtures. Then stir in the raisins. Correctly, the batter should be stiff. If not, add more flour. Turn into 2 1-quart molds (1-pound coffee cans can be used), filling them about half full. Cover tightly. Lacking a lid, use heavy-duty foil, tied down securely. Place the molds on a rack in a large kettle. Add boiling water to the kettle to reach to half the depths of the molds. Steam over moderate heat for 2 hours.

Serve hot with hard sauce. Serves 6 to 8.

Eggs, Cheese, and
Other Dairy Products

How many calories are there in 1 large egg?   77.

How fresh are the eggs in our markets?   This is a real believe-it-or-not. Today, with modern processing and marketing methods, eggs are often so fresh that when cooked they are difficult to peel. You must have run into this problem in your own kitchen. After they've been washed eggs are sprayed with a fine mist of an odorless and tasteless mineral oil that retards aging by plugging the thousands of microscopic pores in the shell through which an egg normally "breathes." Like people, eggs take in oxygen and expel carbon dioxide; it is this breathing process that thins the egg white and ages the egg.

Should eggs be washed after purchase?   No, no, no! A thousand times no. See above about the mineral oil that is sprayed on the washed egg to keep it fresh.

What are the blood spots sometimes found in eggs?   First of all, they are absolutely harmless and it would be our recommendation that you completely ignore any you come across. However, for your information, blood spots are caused by a ruptured blood vessel on the yolk surface during the formation of the egg or by a similar accident in the wall of the oviduct of the hen. Only about 1% of all eggs produced have blood spots and only a very small percentage of these escape the eyes of the graders.

Are egg size and quality related?   No. The size of an egg has nothing whatever to do with its quality. If it's a grade-A egg, it's grade A all the way from small to jumbo. You will find, however, a slight difference in the thickness of the shell. The smaller the egg, the sturdier the shell because these eggs come from younger hens. Extra-large eggs are somewhat more fragile and should be handled with more care.

Can you substitute small eggs for large?   Yes, if of the same quality. If a recipe calls for one large egg, you can always substitute two small ones.

Is a small egg ever a better buy than a large one?   The size of eggs is based on minimum weight per dozen following standards established by the U.S. Department of Agriculture: large, which weigh 24 ounces; medium, 21 ounces; and small, 18 ounces. When buying eggs, smaller ones are a better buy if the price difference per dozen is more than 7 cents for the next larger size of the same grade. If, for example, a dozen medium-size eggs cost 60 cents and a dozen large cost *more than* 67 cents, the medium-size eggs are the better buy. This situation is more likely to exist in the late summer or fall when small and medium eggs are plentiful.

Is it true refrigerated eggs separate more easily than those at room temperature?   Yes, and don't ask me why. Take my word for it, they do.

Why do boiled eggs sometimes crack?   Probably because they were cold when plunged into boiling water. Eggs should be at room temperature before cooking. Allow about half an hour after they come from the refrigerator.

Is there an easy way to shell hard-cooked eggs?   The Poultry and Egg National Board says: "Immerse the hard-cooked eggs in cold water immediately. Crackle the shell. Roll egg between hands to loosen shell, then start peeling at the large end of the egg. Dipping in a bowl of water also helps to ease the shell off."

Why do my hard-cooked eggs sometimes have green discolorations between the white and yolk?   Whites have sulfur in them and the yolks, iron. When the two meet, you get that reaction. It's perfectly harmless but not inviting. You can help to prevent it by cooking eggs at a low temperature, never overcooking, and cooling promptly in cold water.

How can you poach an egg and keep it shapely?   The Poultry and Egg National Board tells us that if you dip the egg in boiling water for *exactly* 8 seconds (count), then break the egg into a saucer and slip it into simmering water, it will emerge from the water as shapely as a Powers model. Easy?

Are pasteurized eggs available to consumers?   No, but the way things are going they probably will be some day. Eggs are pasteurized to destroy pathogenic (disease-causing) organisms; this is mandatory in all processing plants that are government inspected.

What can you do about mold on cheese?   Cheeses such as Cheddar, Swiss, Parmesan, etc., all develop mold if not used. If the mold has not penetrated too deeply, you simply scrape it or cut it out and use the remaining cheese.

How can you use up odds and ends of cheese?   All of us, at one time or another, are confronted with bits of cheese that are not sufficiently presentable to serve. What to do? Combine all the cheeses, regardless of types, chop coarsely, and place in the top of the double boiler. Then sprinkle lightly with baking soda. Melt the lot over simmering water, then cool. Once cold, you have an excellent, inexpensive cheese spread. Here's a way to use up a tag end of blue cheese or Roquefort: Mix it with the same amount (by weight) of sweet, softened butter, then add a good dollop of cognac. In both instances, place in a jar, cover securely, and refrigerate.

What is the best way to cut blue cheese?   Since it is inclined to be crumbly and, like all cheeses, should be served at room temperature, it is best to use a sharp, thin knife dipped into cold water before slicing. You will remember, of course, to take off the coating or paper, if any.

Can you dice feta cheese?   Yes, if it's firm, not crumbly.

How can you keep feta cheese from drying out? If covered with a brine and refrigerated, it will keep fresh and firm about two weeks. Boil enough water to completely immerse the cheese. For every two cups add ¼ cup salt. Cool. Place the feta cheese in a deep bowl and cover completely with the brine. Seal with foil or Saran Wrap. Feta dries out very quickly and loses both taste and texture if not protected in this way. Feta imported from Greece—which travels packed in a milk-and-water brine and is sealed in cans—is made of sheep's milk, not the classic goat's milk because, interestingly, there is a shortage of goat's milk in Greece.

What is braided or string cheese? Edward Edelman of Ideal Cheese Shop (New York) tells us it is a Syrian-type cheese, somewhat like a mild mozzarella, that is made in the United States. Interestingly enough, it looks like strings or braids. It is used only for hors d'oeuvre and cannot be used for cooking.

What is fondue? A famous Swiss dish composed of grated natural Swiss cheese (either Gruyère or Emmenthal or a combination of both), a whisper of garlic, pepper, dry white wine, and kirsch. The fondue is cooked in an earthenware or glazed iron casserole, then set on the table over a heating element. Hard-crust French or Italian bread, cut in bite-sized cubes, is speared on a fork (preferably long), then dipped into the bubbling mixture. Good hot tea with an occasional sip of kirsch always accompanies a fondue in a Swiss home. The American version of this classic dish is an uninspired casserole consisting of milk, bread crumbs, grated cheese, whole eggs, and seasonings, baked in the oven.

By what legerdemain beef fondue, sometimes called *fondue bourguignonne,* got into the picture remains a mystery, since *fondue* (from *fondre*) means "melted." The one common denominator is that you eat it as you do fondue. Thus, spear cubes of raw beef on a long fork and cook it to your taste at the table, in bubbling oil. It is served with condiments such as chili sauce, mayonnaise, or mustard. But there is also *fondue orientale,* which calls for four different meats cooked in a rich broth; *fondue aux fruits de mer,* which is a fish fondue, and finally, there is a *fondue chocolate,* invented by Konrad Egli, patron of New York's well-known Châlet Suisse. *Fondue au fromage,* a Brillat-Savarin recipe, is a dish of scrambled eggs made with cheese, which seems to us stretching the point. Finally, *fondue* is also used to describe vegetables cooked in butter or a mixture of butter and oil for a very long time until reduced to a pulp, i.e., until they become *fondues* or melted—*Fondue de tomates,* for example.

CLASSIC CHEESE FONDUE

1 pound Switzerland Swiss cheese, grated	Salt
1 clove garlic, peeled and split	Pepper, freshly ground
2 cups dry white wine	Nutmeg, freshly ground
1 teaspoon cornstarch	Crusty French or Italian bread, cut
3 tablespoons kirsch	into bite-sized pieces

Rub an earthenware flameproof casserole with the garlic. Add the wine and place over a low heat. When the wine just reaches a bubble but is *not boiling,* add the cheese, a handful at a time, stirring constantly with a fork. Stop between additions of the cheese so the first lot is melted before you add the second.

Combine the cornstarch and kirsch and mix until smooth. Stir into the cheese mixture and continue stirring until the mixture begins to bubble—about 2 or 3 minutes. Season to taste with salt, pepper, and a dash of nutmeg. Serves 4.

Lift the casserole from the stove to a heating unit on the table. To eat fondue in the traditional way, spear the bread (preferably on long forks) and dip it into the fondue, stirring as you do. By stirring you help to capture some of the fondue on your bread, but it also helps the fondue to maintain a proper consistency. It is important to keep the fondue bubbling, so you must regulate the heat to that end. If it becomes too thick, stir in a little more wine, heated.

At the very end, and every fondue aficionado anticipates this point, the fondue forms a crust on the bottom. At this point turn off the heat and share this delicacy with everybody. It is customary in Switzerland if your bread drops off your fork to forfeit a bottle of wine to the host or hostess.

What is raclette? From *racler,* to grate, it is a Swiss cheese fondue, a specialty of the canton of Valais. The cheese is melted by placing it in front of an open fire, and the softened part is scraped off as it melts. Traditionally, the scrapings are served hot with potatoes and gherkins, and accompanied by a dry white wine. A small portable electric *raclette* stove, now imported into this country, greatly simplifies the preparation of this interesting dish.

What is Liptauer cheese?   Classically, a soft, rather oily Hungarian cheese to which any number of condiments are added. A very good adaptation can be made with cream cheese, butter, sour cream, chopped chives, chopped onions, and paprika.

What is Petit-Suisse?   A delicate double crème, one of the richest of all fresh French cheese. New York's Ideal Cheese Shop tells us it is now flown in fresh every week. It comes six little "roll mops" packed to a box. Absolutely delicious served with sugar and strawberries or preserves.

What is tête de moine?   Meaning "Monk's Head," it is also known as Bellelay cheese and has been produced for centuries in the Abbey of Bellelay, founded in the 12th century, northwest of the Lake of Bienne, Switzerland. Made of whole milk, *tête de moine* derives its appearance after the rind has been removed, making the cheese resemble a monk with a tonsure. Even in Switzerland, this interesting cheese is not readily available, since it is produced locally and in limited quantities.

How can butter be bought these days?   More ways than you think. The American Dairy Association writes us as follows: "The most common package is the pound carton containing four quarters, but cartons containing one pound solid and parchment-wrapped pounds are also available in some markets. There are also tubs containing either eight ounces or one pound, and tubs are frequently used for whipped butter."

How long can butter be frozen?   The U.S. Department of Agriculture tells us that it will maintain its quality for about 2 months. Daily supplies of butter should be stored in the regular section of the refrigerator but taken out 10 to 15 minutes before using so it will spread more readily.

What is margarine?   "A food fat, generally made by blending selected fats and oils (soybean, cottonseed, corn, and safflower) with some form of milk or cream (which gives its flavor) and other ingredients to produce the desired flavor, consistency, and composition," Cornell University's Consumer Education Program, New York City) tells us. By Federal law, margarine (once called oleomargarine) must contain

80° fat. All margarine is fortified with a prescribed amount of vitamin A; some margarines also have vitamin D added. Coloring is also added.

How many types of margarine are there? There are six: regular, whipped, soft, premium, unsalted, and the low-calorie or diet spreads. *Regular* margarines, all-purpose, usually cost less than other types since they are generally made from soybean or cottonseed, the least expensive oils. *Whipped* margarine has inert gases injected into it to increase its volume 50%. Softer than regular margarine, it is easier to spread. Use as you would regular. It is packed six sticks to a one-pound package. *Soft* margarine has a much softer consistency than regular because of its higher liquid oil content. This is also why soft margarines have a higher proportion of polyunsaturated fats. This extra softness increases its spreadability and blendability. Packaged in 2 ½-pound tubs. *Premium* margarines, made from more expensive oils, have a delicate flavor, cost more than regular. Use as you would regular. *Unsalted* margarines are especially for people on sodium-restricted diets and those who prefer an unsalted table spread. Use as you would regular. *Regular, premium,* and *unsalted* margarines are all available in one-pound packages (4 ¼-pound sticks). *Low-calorie* or *diet spreads* are imitation margarines because they contain about half the fat content of regular. Not recommended for baking and special precautions must be taken for pan-frying because of high water content. Available in 2 ½-pound tubs.

How can you tell when butter has reached the right temperature for browning meats and vegetables? As butter begins to get hot, it foams up, the foam diminishing when the butter is properly hot. The food should be browned at this point before the butter begins to brown, unless you are using clarified butter. A little oil combined with unclarified butter helps to prevent butter from burning at high heat.

What are beurres composés? "Composed butters," to translate from the French, applies to butters that are mixed with one or more ingredients and used as an addition to certain sauces or dishes or as an accompaniment to fish, meat, or vegetable dishes. Under *Cold Flavored Butters (Beurres Composés),* the authors of *Mastering the Art of French Cooking* say, "Butter can be put to a variety of appetizing uses when it has been creamed with herbs, wines, mustard, egg yolks, shellfish meat, or other flavorings." Mustard butter, for example, and lemon, anchovy, garlic, tarragon, snail, shellfish, mushrooms, etc.

What is pasteurized milk?   Milk that has been heated sufficiently to kill disease-producing bacteria and diminish the number of other microorganisms. It's named after Louis Pasteur, the great French scientist. About 90% of all marketed milk is pasteurized. The U.S. Department of Agriculture recommends it, and in most large American cities it is mandatory.

What is filled or imitation milk?   A product made from non-fat dry-milk solids and vegetable oil, but without any butterfat included, *Today's Food Market* of Kansas State University informs us. Not yet nationally available, it can, however, be found in several major cities in New York State.

Can you stop milk from "catching" when heated?   This perennial problem confronts all cooks, big and little. We discussed it with Jean-Claude Szurdak, chef-owner of New York's fine Elysée Pastries. He tells us a heavy pan and low heat helps matters; that the addition of a couple of tablespoons of water to the milk may turn the trick; and finally, that stirring the milk every few minutes while it is heating sometimes forestalls sticking. Usually effective in these circumstances is the Flame Tamer, a double metal device made for both gas and electric stoves, that can be used in place of a double boiler because it distributes heat so evenly.

Can evaporated milk and condensed milk be used interchangeably? No. Evaporated milk is whole milk with about half the water removed; then the milk is homogenized to prevent separation, cooked, canned, and sterilized by heat. Sweetened condensed milk is also evaporated whole milk that has up to 40% sugar added, which preserves the milk without final heat sterilization. Evaporated milk can be used straight from the can as a substitute for cream; it can be whipped; or it can be reconstituted by the addition of equal amounts of water, then used as you would use whole fluid milk. Sweetened condensed milk, which is very thick and rich, is used to make ice cream and other frozen desserts, lemon and other pie fillings, cookies,

candies, etc. It has excellent keeping qualities but, as is true of evaporated milk, must be refrigerated once opened.

What is all-purpose cream?   A light whipping cream with 30% fat. Because of the lower fat content (heavy or whipping cream has a milk
fat content of at least 36%), it can be whipped but it takes longer and
does not become as thick as regular whipping cream.

What's the difference between light, coffee, and table cream?   None
whatsoever. It's cream with a milk fat content of about 18%.

What is half-and-half?   A mixture of milk and cream which contains
between 10% and 12% milk fat.

What is sterilized cream?   Whipping cream that has been sterilized
(280° to 300°) and will keep indefinitely under refrigeration. It is
sold in glass bottles in refrigerated dairy cases. Ordinary pasteurized
whipping cream (or heavy cream, as it's usually called) is pasteurized
at 165° to 180° and will keep in the refrigerator for from 10 to 15
days. To people who like "fresh" cream, sterilized cream tastes
"cooked." The U.S. Department of Agriculture tells us that sooner or
later it will be packaged in paper cartons.

Why won't my cream whip sometimes?   You can buy cream for various
uses, and if the cream does not contain enough butterfat, 36% to 40%
(known as heavy or whipping cream), it won't whip. "The cream
with the least butterfat," reports *Today's Food Market* of Kansas
State University, "has only 18% butterfat. Although labeled as cream,
the label won't tell you the butterfat content. But you will find this
information on the containers of coffee cream (30%) and light cream
(30% to 35%)." A lesson to all of us. Read labels, *all* labels, before you
put your money on the line.

At what point do you stop whipping before cream turns to butter?
You can't be specific, because so many factors are involved. The butterfat content; the age of the cream (two days old, at least, for the
best volume); the temperature of the cream, bowl, beater (all should
be thoroughly chilled). Assuming all those specifications are met, the
authors of *Mastering the Art of French Cooking* say, *for lightly
beaten:* "Beat the cream until the beater leaves light traces on the sur-

face of the cream and a bit of cream lifted and dropped on the surface will just retain its shape." *For cream that requires more body:* "Continue beating for a few seconds more or until cream is a little bit stiffer and forms soft peaks." Beyond that you are courting trouble, because the chances are the cream will turn to butter. *To hold beaten cream,* if necessary, beat in a little sugar. This stabilizes it somewhat.

What is cream in aerosol cans?   A cream packed under pressure in an aerosol container which causes the product to whip when pressed. In addition to cream, it may also contain sugar, flavoring, and a stabilizer.

What is buttermilk?   It's the product that remains when fat is removed from milk or cream, sweet or sour, in the process of churning. Actually, the buttermilk you buy today is cultured buttermilk made by coagulating pasteurized skim milk with lactic bacteria. In some instances you may find bits of butter in the milk which are added by the dairy to give that special flavor buttermilk drinkers love. Buttermilk has all the nutrition and the few calories of skim milk, but has added flavor. In cooking, buttermilk is used in making biscuits, rolls, corn bread, etc.

Is there a substitute for buttermilk?   If it is to be used for baking, you can "sour" milk by adding 1 tablespoon of white vinegar or lemon juice to 1 cup of fluid whole milk or you can use 1 cup of fluid whole milk mixed with 1¾ teaspoons of cream of tartar.

What is "imitation" sour cream?   There are products on the market under various fanciful names, such as sour dressing or cream dressing, made with vegetable fat, milk solids, and lactic acid. The latter is used in lieu of fermentation, and the vegetable fat replaces the animal fat found in real sour cream. Sometimes called imitation sour cream, it is not, nor should it be, considered a substitute for cultured sour cream. In addition, there is an acidified sour cream made with butter fat and milk solids in the same ratio as cultured sour cream, but without fermentation. Tasters tell us the flavor compares favorably with the commercial sour cream with which we are familiar.

What exactly is yogurt?   Also spelled yoghurt, yoghourt, and yohourt. In this country, it is made from low-fat milk to which lactic cultures are added, turning the milk from a liquid to a custard-like consistency with a smooth texture and a refreshing mildly acid flavor, faintly reminiscent of walnuts. In Bulgaria, where it is extremely popular, it is made from goat's and water buffalo's milk, making a mixture that is twice as rich in butterfat as cow's milk. Bulgarians, reputedly long-lived, eat yogurt from the cradle to the grave, at all meals. You can buy plain yogurt (Belgians mix it with grenadine syrup), or yogurt flavored with vanilla, coffee, strawberry, raspberry, boysenberry, blue-berry, mandarin orange, pear, peach, spiced apple, pineapple orange, prune, apricot, or Dutch apple. Weight watchers, take note: 1 cup *plain* yogurt averages only 130 to 140 calories.

What is coconut milk cream?   It is milk made from coconuts with the addition of sugar, sometimes pectin and coconut flavoring. Available in stores specializing in fine foreign foods, particularly Mexican foods.

Fish and Seafood

Are "white meat" tuna and "light meat" tuna the same thing? No. *Food for Us All,* the 1969 yearbook of the U.S. Department of Agriculture, says, "Tuna is packed from six species: albacore, bluefin, blackfin, skipjack, yellowfin, and little tuna." Albacore, with lighter meat than the others, is therefore the only tuna permitted to be labeled as "white meat." *Food for Us All,* a veritable gold mine of information, is in fact a popular encyclopedia of food for the consumer whether he lives in the country or the city. It can be obtained from the Superintendent of Documents, Washington, D.C. 20402, for $3.50.

Is all domestic tuna packed in oil? No. One brand, a fancy albacore solid-pack white tuna is packed in spring water. For weight-conscious people this is possibly important since there are about 100 less calories per can than in oil-packed tuna.

What is grated tuna? Usually referred to as flaked, it is, as you might think, small bits of tuna, in contrast to solid-pack or chunk-style. Less expensive than the other packs, it is ideal when you want to mix the tuna with mayonnaise or sour cream, etc., to make sandwiches, dips, and so on. The solid pack contains solid fillets of tuna, best used when you want large pieces of tuna on a cold platter, for example, or in salads. Chunk-style, which is broken into bite-sized pieces, is ideal in cooked dishes.

Is sole easy to broil? It couldn't be easier, as the following interesting recipe indicates. Note well, however, that you do not turn the fish (broiled or sautéed)—it is much too fragile and would break into pieces.

FILLET OF SOLE WITH BANANAS

1 firm banana per person	Lemon juice
Butter	Salt
½ pound fillet of sole per person	White pepper, freshly ground

Peel the bananas and cut on the bias in fairly large pieces. Butter generously a flat baking pan large enough to hold the fillets without overlapping. Add the fillets, top with banana slices, sprinkle with lemon, salt, and pepper, and dot all over with butter.

Broil 3 inches from the source of heat in a preheated 450° oven for 5 to 7 minutes or until the fish flakes easily when pierced with a fork. Baste once during the cooking time with melted butter. Do not attempt to turn the fish. Serve in a heated platter, garnished with a bouquet of parsley and with lemon butter on the side.

Lemon butter: Allow about 3 tablespoons of melted butter per person and add fresh lemon juice to taste.

Where do we get smoked salmon? The best and most expensive is imported from Scotland; but salmon imported from Nova Scotia, and smoked in Brooklyn, is known as Nova Scotia smoked salmon or "Nova." The *one* firm that smokes salmon in Nova Scotia does not export it to this country except on order.

JEAN-CLAUDE SZURDAK'S
MOUSSE DE SAUMON FUMÉ

1 pound Nova Scotia smoked salmon	Juice of 1 lemon, strained
	3 tablespoons sweet butter, melted
2 cups heavy cream	White pepper, freshly ground

Cut up the salmon into relatively small pieces, cutting out any discolored bits and eliminating any bones. Combine in the electric blender with the cream (it may be necessary to do a small quantity at a time) and purée until smooth. Stir in the lemon juice and butter thoroughly. Finally, add several twists of pepper from the peppermill. It should be quite spicy with pepper. Taste for salt.

You can, if you wish, make little lettuce cups and fill them with the mousse or you can spoon the mousse into a crystal bowl. Garnish with well-drained capers and serve with small toast triangles. Serves 12 to 15 easily.

COLD SALMON MOUSSE

1 tablespoon butter
3 tablespoons shallots or green onions, finely minced
2 cups clam juice (2 7-ounce bottles) or fish stock
¼ cup dry white wine or dry vermouth
2 envelopes unflavored gelatin

2 cups freshly cooked salmon, flaked and packed down well
2 tablespoons cognac
Salt
White pepper, freshly ground
Pinch of nutmeg
¾ cup heavy cream

Melt the butter in a heavy skillet, add the shallots and about ¼ *cup water*. Bring to a boil, then cook over moderate heat, until all water has evaporated—a matter of minutes. Meanwhile, combine clam juice or stock and wine in a saucepan and sprinkle the gelatin over them to soften. Bring to a boil over moderate heat and stir until gelatin has dissolved—about 3 to 5 minutes. Combine with the salmon, pour into the electric blender, and blend at top speed until you have a smooth purée. Place in a bowl, add cognac, salt, pepper, and nutmeg. Season more highly than you would normally, because the cream will dilute the seasonings. Cover, place in a refrigerator until *almost set*, giving it an occasional stir.

When the mixture has reached the right consistency, beat the cream until it holds a shape when you lift up the beater. Fold the cream into the salmon mixture thoroughly and pour into a 6-cup mold (if metal, it should be tin-lined, otherwise the mousse will discolor). Chill in the refrigerator until firm. Serves 6.

To serve, unmold on a cold platter. To help mousse drop out of the mold easily, hold bottom of mold in hot water a few seconds. Surround with small (inside) lettuce leaves filled with freshly cooked, cooled peas dressed lightly with sauce vinaigrette, and thinly sliced tomatoes or cherry tomatoes.

How do you poach whole fish?   Often cookbooks and cooks will use the word "boil." This is an error. If you boiled fish you would ruin it. Fish is already tender and unlike meat does not need to be cooked to tenderize it. So, correctly, fish is poached, which simply means it is simmered and by simmer I mean the liquid should shiver. In short, barely move. The french say *frémir*. Whether cooked in court bouillon (see below) or in salted water, whole or in a piece, tie up the fish in a cheesecloth, leaving long ends so that it can be lifted easily from the liquid. To poach fish *à point* measure it—use a ruler—at its thickest point, then poach it 10 minutes per inch. Let's say the fish measures 2 inches thick, you would cook it, all told, 20 minutes.

NOTE WELL : Fish should be at room temperature before cooking. So bring the court bouillon or water to a boil, add the fish, bring to a boil a second time, reduce heat to simmer, and cook according to these directions. Properly cooked, the fish will flake when probed with a fork. Lift from the broth immediately and keep warm, if it is to be served hot.

About the fish cooker: Whatever you use it is essential for the fish to be completely immersed in the liquid.

COURT BOUILLON

3 quarts water	2 ribs celery, coarsely chopped
2 cups dry white wine	1 bay leaf
3 onions, each stuck with 3 cloves	1 teaspoon dried thyme
4 carrots, washed, coarsely chopped	1 or 2 stalks parsley with sprigs
	1 tablespoon salt

Combine all ingredients in the cooker, bring to a boil, then reduce to simmer and cook for 1 hour. Then add the fish, as described above.

What's red snapper like? It is a marvelous fish, beautiful to look at, with juicy, white meat and a delicious flavor. Most red snapper is caught in the Gulf of Mexico and it is available year round. Can be broiled, baked, steamed, or poached. A treat whatever way it is prepared.

RED SNAPPER WITH SAUCE RÉMOULADE

1 4-pound red snapper	2 ribs celery, chopped, with leaves
Few stalks parsley	1 tablespoon salt
1 onion, skin on, split	1 teaspoon cayenne

Have the fish man clean the fish, leaving the head and tail intact. Choose a fish cooker or baking pan large enough to hold the fish comfortably. Fill with water and add all remaining ingredients except the fish. Bring to a boil, then simmer 30 minutes. Wrap the fish in a large piece of cheesecloth, leaving long ends so you can remove the fish easily when cooked. Place the fish in the pan, turn heat to high, and bring to a boil a second time. Reduce heat to simmer and cook 10 minutes to the inch. *Do not cook by weight.* Measure the fish at the thickest point. If, for example, the fish measures 3 inches thick, cook for 30 minutes. Lift the fish to a platter and remove the cheesecloth with care. Allow to cool at room temperature if it is to be served that day. Otherwise, refrigerate and bring to room temperature before serving.

Sauce rémoulade: To 1½ cups homemade mayonnaise (see page 180), add 1 generous teaspoon Dijon mustard, 2 tablespoons each of chopped gherkins, well-drained capers, parsley, fresh tarragon or chervil (if available), and a "whisper" of anchovy paste. Allow the sauce to stand for a couple of hours to mellow. Equally good with sliced, hard-cooked eggs, shellfish, or cold meats.

What are fish 'n' chips?   Fillets of fish, dipped in batter, then deep-fat fried; the chips are sliced potatoes fried in oil to a crisp, golden brown (in the United States we know these as "French fries"). Best eaten immediately with a sprinkling of salt and malt vinegar. ("No pepper," as any Englishman will tell you.) Fish and potatoes have probably been eaten in one form or another in England forever, but fish and chips in tandem, as it were, date from about 1860 when a vendor mounted a small stove on a two-wheeled cart and began hawking the combination in the streets, delivering his "goods" wrapped in newspaper. Now, fish 'n' chips shops are popping up all over the United States and you can walk out from any one of them with this good English fare (we speak with familiarity) wrapped up in a facsimile of an English newspaper.

N O T E : In England, chips is used in the singular, not plural (chips).

Are fish 'n' chips available frozen?   Yes. In your supermarket. English-style fish 'n' chips in 5-ounce, 7-ounce, 1-pound, and 2-pound packages. You simply heat them up—and they heat up perfectly—in your oven. And if you've yet to eat fish and chips, piping hot with vinegar and salt, you're in for a delicious surprise.

What is mullet? One of the few fishes that can be found throughout the entire world. Very popular in the American South, its Spanish name is Lisa. Like mackerel, although it is smaller, it is a fat fish, so it lends itself to broiling, deep-fat frying, oven frying, or baking. Smoked mullet is popular in Florida. Marinated in an oil and vinegar mixture, and seasoned, it lends itself to outdoor grilling.

Is catfish a salt- or fresh-water fish? Fresh-water. Extremely popular in the southeastern and midwestern parts of the United States. And because it is so popular it is now being raised in pond "farms" as far west as California.

What are groupers like? A very delicate, sweet fish that has been called the chicken of the sea. Found in great abundance on the Gulf coast and along the Southern Atlantic coast. Both red and black groupers have been reported from Woods Hole (Massachusetts). Groupers are sold whole, or as steaks or fillets, and are usually fried or broiled, or the fillets can be baked in a sauce. Available the year round.

How is cod available nowadays? Frozen (portions or sticks, crumbed, ready-to-cook) and as fillets or steaks. But you can still buy dried salted cod and if there's anything better than codfish cakes on a Sunday morning with homemade apple sauce, we've yet to taste it.

FISH CAKES

¾ cup salted codfish	2 tablespoons cream
1 cup mashed potatoes	Butter
1 egg, well beaten	

Soak the fish several hours in cold water. Drain, shred, add fresh water and heat to the boiling point. Repeat until the fish tastes fresh. Mix with all remaining ingredients except the butter. Then beat with a wooden spatula until fluffy. Shape into small flat cakes. Heat a good lump of butter in a heavy frying pan and sauté until brown on one side; turn and sauté the second side. As you cook the cakes, place on paper towels on a platter in a warm (120°) oven. Serves about 4.

What does mahimahi mean? Dolphin, from the Hawaiian. It is also a dish composed of fillets of dolphin, coated with a flavorful mixture including soy sauce, chopped scallions, sesame seeds, vegetable oil, etc. Then sautéed in butter.

What are matjes? Herring, spiced and sugar-cured. In Scandinavian countries, presented as a first course with chopped chives, sour cream, and hot boiled potatoes, dressed with chopped fresh dill feathers. Matjes are available canned or by the piece in Jewish delicatessens.

What is a kipper? A herring that has been cured and smoked. It is also the term used to describe the method—that is, "to kipper." Further, kipper is used to define a male salmon during the spawning season. Although kippers are available canned, there is nothing to match kippers bought at the fish market, heated in the oven just long enough to puff up, served with a good homemade bread, sweet butter, and a cup of good hot tea.

What kind of fish is a sardine? Oddly and interestingly, there is no such fish as a true sardine. This comes to us straight from the authoritative *U.S.D.A. Food and Home Notes.* They say, "Sardine is a collective word for a variety of soft-boned herring caught in many waters and packed in many ways." Sardines are canned everywhere they are caught and the first records of their being caught date to about A.D. 495, off Yarmouth, England. All U.S. sardines are packed in the state of Maine, which is probably why Americans say "Maine sardines."

Is Boston bluefish a true bluefish? No. It isn't even in the same family. Dubbed Boston bluefish by the New Englanders probably because the uncooked fish, much like true bluefish, is dark. The flesh, however, turns white when cooked. Boston bluefish is actually pollock, a close cousin of both haddock and cod, and of special interest now because we are running out of haddock (once the economic mainstay of the New England fishing industry), due to overfishing for the last several years. Whether you call it pollock or Boston bluefish (we think its name should be changed legally), it is well flavored, with a good texture that holds up well under freezing. The fresh fish can be prepared as you would haddock or cod. We refer you to *James Beard's Fish Cookery,* an excellent authoritative source for good fish recipes. For frozen steaks and fillets, follow package directions. The Bureau of Commercial Fisheries tells us that frozen breaded stick fillets are in the near future.

Are king mackerel and Spanish mackerel the same? Let us say they're cousins. The king (also known as kingfish) takes top rank among game fish and is equally valued as food fish. It cruises off the coast of Florida and as far south as Brazil. It has a superb flavor, with few bones, and ranges in weight from 5 to 30 pounds. Available from November to March. The smaller fish are usually cooked whole while the larger ones are cut into steaks. The Spanish, an equally gamey fighter, was described in 1815 by an ichthyologist as "A fine and beautiful fish; comes in July." Actually, Spanish mackerel is available almost all year round since it's caught off Northern waters in the summer and off Florida from November through March. They average about 1½ pounds and are sold whole or filleted.

Where does the word caviar come from? Probably from the Turkish, *khavyar* (the Russian name is *ikra*)—in all likelihood because the Turks and Persians were the first to export these marvelous "black berries." It might be well to point out right here that caviar ranges in color from black to gray, dark brown to golden yellow ("the caviar of the Czars"), the latter being rather rare but sometimes available.

What is the best caviar? Color has nothing to do with quality. All caviar is the roe of sturgeon, and although we are inclined to think of whole-grain Beluga, which is certainly the most expensive, as the finest, the caviar from the Sevruga (also spelled Sevriouga or Chivrouga) and the Ossetrina (meaning sturgeon), also spelled Ossetrova (meaning roe), and Ocetrina (meaning meat), can be very good indeed, if the roe was treated in the proper manner. As is true of all caviar, the quality of these caviars depends entirely on the amount of salt with which they were packed and the care with which they were handled.

Are fresh and salted caviars different? No. All caviar must be salted to preserve it. Otherwise it would turn into a tasteless mush. Caviar imported into this country must, by U.S. Government regulations, be either processed (canned) or preserved whole in salt.

What is Beluga malosol? Malosol simply means "little salt." It is not, as some people mistakenly think, a brand of caviar, but a means by which a buyer can distinguish a lightly salted—the most desirable— caviar from a heavily salted one. The most important characteristics of first-quality caviar are that the "berry" must be whole, uncrushed, and well coated with its glistening fat.

How does pasteurized caviar compare with fresh? First-quality pasteurized caviar is so good that few, if any, experts can tell the difference. The great advantage is that it calls for very little salt—a most desirable feature.

What is pressed caviar? When caviar is graded, the smaller eggs are sieved out. The result, defined as lightly pressed or compressed, is a caviar in which the grains do not separate distinctly as they do in first-quality caviar. It is usually packed with 10% salt. Actually, Russian Russians, who eat caviar almost as casually as Americans eat potato chips, prefer pressed caviar. On a cost basis, the price of pressed caviar in the United States is about one third that of a great Beluga.

What is tamara? Carp or cod roe, available in stores specializing in Greek foods.

LEON LIANIDES' TAMAROSALATA

1 8-ounce jar tamara	1 cup light olive oil
8 slices firm, white bread	Juice of 3 lemons, strained
1 medium onion, peeled and grated fine	Greek black olives
	Lemon slices
1 clove garlic, peeled and grated fine	½ cup raw pistachio nuts, chopped fine
6 to 8 sprigs parsley, minced	

Pour the tamara into a big bowl. Soak the bread in cold water, then squeeze out all the water and add to the roe. Add the onion, garlic, and parsley. Using an electric beater, begin to combine the mixture, alternately dribbling in the olive oil and lemon juice, beating constantly. Continue beating until you have a smooth, pink-colored mixture. Place in a suitable serving dish and chill for at least one hour. Then garnish with Greek black olives and thin slices of lemon. Sprinkle with chopped pistachios. Keep refrigerated until serving time. This is a perfectly delicious dip accompanied by fresh toast points.

NOTE : Tamarosalata should not be kept more than two or three days because it tends to lose flavor.

What are sea urchins?   Round, pillow-shaped sea creatures, known in France as *oursins*, whose quill-like exteriors (hence their being known as sea hedgehogs in some places) have a tender, sweet roe inside that is eaten like an egg with a garnish of lemon. This, perhaps, explains why they are sometimes called sea eggs. According to *Larousse Gastromique*, the best are green, black, and purple. However, Mr. Joseph Enea, the knowledgeable owner of New York's splendid fish shop, Pisacane, tells us he has never seen black in this country and that those available to us (the green ones) come from Maine.

What are the types of American oysters?   We have only three species: Eastern, which encompasses all oysters found along the East Coast from Maine to the Gulf of Mexico; Olympia, native to the West Coast; and the large Pacific or Japanese oyster, also called "Immigrant" oyster, because it was introduced to Pacific estuaries from Japan. Eastern oysters are further categorized by the areas in which they are found. Thus, Bluepoints and Fireplace come from Long Island waters; Chesapeake from Chesapeake Bay or its tributaries; Mobjack, grown in Mobjack Bay; Lynnhaven, grown in tidal creeks near Virginia Beach; Tangier, produced in Tangier Sound; Seaside and Chincoteague, from the bays off the Atlantic on the eastern side of the Delmarva Peninsula; and Bon Séjour, taken from a bay of the same name which is an estuary of Mobile Bay.

How long can you keep oysters, once opened?   Oysters are at their best when opened and eaten at once. However, they should not—never (*jamais, jamais, jamais*)—be kept longer than 24 hours, completely covered and refrigerated.

What are "Fried New York Counts"?   The Fishery Council tells us that the term stems from the days when it was possible to buy 140 oysters to a gallon—big frying oysters. (Today you get something like 175 to 200.) So, it was the count per gallon in New York that gave the oyster dish its name.

What is geoduck? Pronounced "gooeyduck," it is also spelled "goe-duck," "goeyduc," "gooeyduck," or "gweduc" (apparently a corruption of an Indian term that could mean "earth duck" or even "big clam"). It's a giant clam that has nothing whatsoever to do with duck. It abounds in Puget Sound and it is said to be the gastronomic rival of any mollusk or crustacean. People familiar with it compare it to abalone, one of the West Coast's great delicacies, adding, "But it's better!"

Washington State restaurants prepare geoduck steaks much like abalone, breading it, then sautéeing over a high heat. East Coasters will probably have to go to the West Coast to enjoy geoduck.

What is Potage Billi-Bi? Also sometimes spelled Billy-Bi (but always pronounced *billy-bee*), it is an incredibly subtle and rich cream-and-mussel broth created in 1925 by Louis Barthe, then the chef at famous Ciro's in Paris, and later at Maxim's. The story goes that a certain William Brand who frequented Ciro's asked chef Barthe to serve only the broth to some American guests rather than, as was customary, with the mussels. Thus, a new soup was born; dubbed Billy Brand's, it became, in true French fashion, Potage Billi-Bi. Usually served cold with a sprinkling of minced chives, it is very good hot, too. The cooked mussels, mixed with *sauce Gribiche,* can be served cold as a first course for lunch or dinner.

How are scallops sold? In New England, by the quart; otherwise, by the pound. If frozen, they are always sold by the pound everywhere.

What exactly are Coquilles Saint-Jacques? Although the French *co-quille* means scallop, when it's followed by Saint-Jacques it seems to be an all-encompassing name for scallops served in a scallop shell with innumerable variations, such as: *à la crème,* with white wine, cream, egg yolks, cayenne, and lemon juice; *au gratin,* with white wine, mushrooms, and breadcrumbs; *Mornay* is similar except that the dish is glazed with a Mornay (cheese) sauce; *à la parisienne,* with white wine, mushrooms, and truffles, and a piping of Duchess potatoes around the edge of the shell. In some recipes, oysters, mussels, and/or shrimp are used as a garnish. The name originated centuries ago. In the Middle Ages, *coquilles* were found only along the banks of Spain's Galice River. Monks making pilgrimages to Saint-Jacques-Compostelle tied shells to their girdles or hats as proof of their journeys.

How much shrimp should you buy per person?   It's hard to say since appetites vary so. For a first course, 1 pound medium-size would probably serve about four people but if the shrimp is to be served as a main course in a big sauce (see recipe for Curried Shrimp for a Party below), 3 pounds will serve about 8.

CURRIED SHRIMP FOR A PARTY

3 pounds shrimp, defrosted and shelled
6 tablespoons (¾ stick) butter
2 large onions, peeled and minced
2 large apples, cored, chopped fine
3 to 4 tablespoons curry
½ cup all-purpose flour

3 cans (10½-ounce size) condensed chicken broth or 4 cups homemade, heated
1 cup heavy cream
Salt
Freshly ground pepper
Fresh lemon juice

Melt the butter in a large, heavy enameled saucepan. Add the onion and apple, 1½ cups water, and cook over moderate heat until all the water has boiled away and both onion and apple are soft. If necessary, add more water.

Stir in the curry and cook for 2 minutes. Next stir in the flour until smooth. Cook 3 minutes longer. Next stir in the hot broth, bring to a boil, and then simmer for 10 to 15 minutes, giving the mixture an occasional stir. *The sauce can be cooked to this point, sealed with Saran Wrap, and refrigerated.*

Finally, stir in the cream, salt, pepper, and lemon juice to taste. Add the shrimp and bring to a boil. Simmer for about 2 minutes, no longer. To serve, spoon into a large heated bowl or handsome tureen.

Condiments: Chutney is a classic accompaniment to curry; the other possibilities include (you can serve as many as you wish) sliced bananas (sprinkled with lemon juice to keep them from darkening), freshly grated or commercial flaked coconut, crisp bacon pieces, peanuts or sliced toasted almonds, chopped chives or scallions, raisins plumped in cognac. Each should be presented in a small dish (it's attractive if the dishes all match and they are presented together on a tray) with a spoon so each guest can serve himself.

How is canned shrimp available?   Deveined, or what is known as the standard pack, which is not deveined. Deveining, we must emphasize, is a luxury not a necessity. Canned shrimp are graded from tiny all the way to colossal. A 4½-ounce can, net weight, will yield approximately 1 cup of shrimp. It is important to emphasize that you must not cook canned shrimp. They should be heated only; otherwise, both flavor and texture are destroyed.

Are freeze-dried shrimp available?   Not to people like us. Only to restaurants but hopefully they will be one day since they are a superior product.

How do you cook frozen, breaded, uncooked shrimp?   Fry, from the frozen state, in vegetable oil heated to 375° on the thermometer for 3 to 4 minutes or until shrimp turn golden. Drain on paper towels. Or thaw and sauté in hot butter and vegetable oil (half and half)—just enough fat to make a film over the bottom of the pan—until golden on both sides. Three to four minutes.

What are Maine shrimp?   A species of shrimp (*Pandalus borealis*), Northern shrimp, that it once was thought could only be caught in Scandinavian waters. It is a remarkable fish, looking somewhat like our Eastern lobster, in miniature, without the big claws, and when properly cooked, tasting like it, too. Experts tell us they are even more delicious and delicate than those caught off Sweden. They are now available cooked frozen, heads on; cooked peeled and frozen; peeled, cooked ready to use frozen I.Q.F. (individually quick frozen—a great advantage in that you use only what you need and return the remainder to the freezer); frozen in solid blocks which are good in prepared dishes; frozen, shrimp meat; finally, breaded. All packages give recipes. It is important to emphasize that Maine shrimp are in no way (taste or appearance) like the familiar Gulf shrimp. It is an entirely different animal. The Scandinavians eat them with toast and butter accompanied by beer or Aquavit. No sauce. We think they taste good, with a little sauce, such as Good Sauce for Shellfish (see page 118).

GOOD SAUCE FOR SHELLFISH

4 tablespoons mild prepared
mustard
4 tablespoons sugar
6 tablespoons vinegar
Salt

Freshly ground pepper
1 cup vegetable oil
Juice ½ lemon
Few sprigs dill, minced

Mix mustard, sugar, vinegar, salt, and pepper together. Dribble in the oil, beating hard and constantly wtih a wire whisk. When it has the consistency of a light mayonnaise (it takes only a couple of minutes), stir in lemon juice and dill. Delicious.

What are soft-shell crabs? They are not, as many people think, a species of crab, but rather the blue crabs found along the Atlantic and Gulf coasts. Crabs shed their shells many times before reaching maturity, and the soft-shell crab is one caught just after it has emerged from its latest shell. In season from April to October, weather permitting. So-called hard-shell crabs once had soft shells, which have hardened.

Why are the green Atlantic crabs called blue? There seems to be no logical explanation, since the body of the crab is a greenish color. The claws, however, *are* blue and white.

What is lump crab? Crab meat comes from two areas of the blue crab's body: the claws and the body. Back-fin lumps are large chunks of crab meat from the back portion of the body. Since only two lumps are obtained from each crab, it is the most expensive but the most desirable when appearance is important. The remaining meat from the body, called regular or "flake," less expensive than lump, is the most popular. Meat from the claws, sweet but dark in color, is the least expensive and generally used in dishes where appearance does not have to be taken into consideration.

CRAB LOUIS DRESSING FOR 4

2 cups homemade mayonnaise
(page 180)
½ cup finely chopped green onions
(scallions)
½ cup seeded, minced sweet
green pepper

½ cup chili sauce
Handful parsley sprigs, minced
Dash cayenne pepper
Salt to taste
Lemon juice to taste
½ cup heavy cream, whipped

Combine all the ingredients together. Arrange the crab meat (allow about 1 pound cooked for 4) on a bed of lettuce on individual salad plates. Coat with Louis dressing and garnish with crab legs (if available), ripe tomato slices, and sliced hard-cooked eggs.

What kind of crab meat comes in cans?   The blue, Dungeness, and king crabs, usually packed in water but sometimes, depending on packer, in acidulated water. Available in 6½ to 7½-ounce cans. (Our answers on crab cooking are based on information from experts at the U.S. Bureau of Commercial fisheries.) See also snow crab, page 120.

Why are there bits of shell and cartilage in freshly cooked and canned crab meat?   Because the meat must be picked by hand from the body and from between cartilage, and it is inevitable that tiny pieces elude the picker. Obviously, it is not a serious problem, but it does require that the homemaker pick over the meat before using.

What are she-crabs?   As you might assume, female crabs. Southerners have made a specialty of she-crab soup, which calls for roe, the tiny eggs of the crab. But as Craig Claiborne, the distinguished food authority has pointed out, "This is mostly theoretical, since most of these soups are made indiscriminately with crabs of no matter what sex, and they rarely contain the roe."

How is freshly cooked blue crab meat available?   In three packs: back-fin lump, regular or "flake," and the claw meat, in 8-ounce, 12-ounce, and 16-ounce vacuum pry-open cans; sometimes, in large markets, in four-ounce cans. Unlike pasteurized crab meat, it can be found only close to the source. Its refrigerator life is no more than two or three days.

What is pasteurized crab meat?   A relatively new method of preserving freshly cooked blue crab meat. A breakthrough really, since it is now possible to keep this famous delicacy for several weeks. The crabs, straight from the ocean, are cooked, the meat is picked from the shell by hand, packed into special containers, and sealed. It is then pasteurized and immediately refrigerated. During tests, tasters were unable to distinguish between the pasteurized crab meat and freshly cooked. Thus, for the first time, freshly cooked crab meat is available on a national basis. Available in three standard packs: back-fin lump, regular or "flake," and claw meat. In 8-ounce, 12-ounce, and 16-ounce containers.

Are Dungeness, king, and tanner crabs all the same animal? No. Dungeness, a magnificent species indigenous to the Pacific Coast, yields white meat from the body and reddish from the legs. On the Coast, they are available whole in the shell, freshly cooked; the body and claw meat, out of the shell, is available by the pound, freshly cooked, ready to eat. Nationally, the Dungeness is available whole, frozen, in the shell. King crabs from Alaska, whose meat comes only from the legs, are available frozen, ready to eat, in 6-ounce and 12-ounce packages. The tanner crab (see snow crab below), also from Alaska, is smaller than the king, and the leg meat is a little darker. The legs, frozen, ready to eat, are available by the pound.

How do you prepare Dungeness crabs? Pull up the tail (the crab should be alive, remember) and, using the tail as a lever, pry off the back shell and lift out the eyes. Rinse out crab under running water and fish out the lungs. Pull off the legs and pull the body (the center part) out of the shell. Crack legs and claws and cut the big chunk of meat into five or six pieces. Cook following recipe instructions.

Are the queen crab and snow crab identical? Yes, known as queen crab or Atlantic queen crab in Canada (in Quebec, *crabe des neiges*) and snow crab in the United States, but tanner crab in Japan. After February 15, 1971, any of this family (*chionecetes*) sold in the United States must be labeled Snow Crabmeat. A perfectly delicious, snow-white meat with a vivid red surface, the snow crab is relatively new on the market. The snow crab packed in the United States is both canned and frozen but that imported from Canada or Japan may be either frozen or canned.

What is cioppino? A kind of seafood dish (fish and shellfish, especially crab) with Italian overtones. In Jack Shelton's *Private Guide to Restaurants,* which covers West Coast restaurants exclusively, he writes, "Cioppino is not an Italian dish at all; it is strictly a San Francisco creation. In fact the word itself is not an Italian word and is not directly translatable. For that matter, even its origin is dubious but a plausible theory is that it is an Italianization of the English word 'chop' with the 'ino' suffix being the Italian diminutive. Thus, cioppino turns out to mean "little chopped-up pieces."

What is Lobster Thermidor? According to Julia Child, "The French

Chef" of TV fame, it was created on January 24, 1894, at Chez Maire, a Paris restaurant on Les Grands Boulevards, to celebrate the opening of Victorien Sardou's play, *Thermidor*. The dish is composed of boiled lobster combined with butter, minced shallots, seasonings, cognac, and mushrooms, in a rich, creamy sauce, the whole baked in the lobster shell.

What is Florida crawfish?   Crawfish or crayfish is a diminutive freshwater lobster. So, in all likelihood, Florida crawfish is the spiny lobster that's caught off the coast of Florida.

What is abalone?   It's a shellfish, classified, Jack Shelton writes in his *Private Guide to Restaurants*, as a snail, which cannot be bought outside of California. It is, however, available in cans. Abalone can be prepared in many ways although the most popular seems to be as steak.

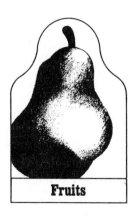

Fruits

What fruits originated in the Western Hemisphere? Avocado (Colombia); cranberry (North America); guava (tropical America); pineapple (Paraguay and southern Brazil); red raspberry, blackberry, and huckleberry (North America); papaya (possibly the West Indies, Central America, or Mexico).

Is there any way to keep ripe fresh fruit from decaying? You can inhibit decay for about a week or ten days with activated charcoal, a gas-absorbent charcoal used, incidentally, in Tareyton cigarettes, which not only helps to keep fresh fruit longer, but also prevents other foodstuffs from picking up unwanted tastes. When strawberries, peaches, raspberries, blueberries, cherries, and plums are available in the market, you will discover how effective activated charcoal filters are when used in the hydrator of your refrigerator with fresh fruits, in the main section to remove odors, and in your silver drawer to help prevent tarnishing.

How do you store dried fruits? In tightly covered containers at room temperature—that is, not above 70°. When the weather is warm and humid, they should be refrigerated.

How do you grate an apple or a pear? Apples and pears are both grated the same way. Place a medium-coarse or coarse grater (depending on the recipe) on a piece of waxed paper. Then rub the fruit, skin on, working around and around down to the core, which is discarded.

How do you prepare apples for salad?   Core, using an apple corer. Peel or not, whatever the recipe calls for. Cut into circles about ¼ inch thick. Pile the circles on top of each other, then slice across both ways. This method gives you more or less precise shapes.

How do you peel, core, slice, and chop apples?   To peel, hold the apple in one hand and work around and around the fruit with a vegetable peeler (which is the easiest) or a sharp paring knife; then remove the core with an apple corer. To cut into wedges, slice into whatever size the recipe indicates. To slice into rings, peel or not as recipe calls for, core, using an apple corer, then slice across to the thickness wanted. To chop or dice: Peel or not, as directed, then core with an apple corer, and cut in half. Lay one piece, cut side down, and make parallel cuts the length of the piece. Then, holding the pieces together with one hand, cut across down the full length to the size wanted.

APPLE SLICES BAKED IN BUTTER

4 to 5 all-purpose apples	Juice 1 lemon
Salt	Butter
Sugar	

Pare, core, and slice the apples very thin. Arrange in neat rows, overlapping slightly, in a flat baking dish that can go to the table. Sprinkle lightly with salt, fairly generously with sugar, add the lemon juice, and pour the melted butter (about 4 tablespoons) over all.

Place in a preheated 300° oven and bake, basting occasionally, for about 25 minutes or until apple slices are tender. This can be done ahead of time. Just before serving, sprinkle with a little more sugar, dot all over with butter, and slide under the broiler until the edges of the apples turn golden.

Serve immediately with pork, goose, duck, or game, or as a dessert with heavy cream.

How do you keep apples from turning dark?   Marinate the fruit in fresh lemon juice, which adds flavor; or make a bath with 1 cup of water and the juice of 1 lemon; or simply place them in salted water. Orange juice is just as effective as lemon juice, we are told, and even the juice drained from canned peaches, apricots, pears, etc., can help to inhibit browning. And of course there are the commercial products (Fruit-fresh and Fruit-save). Both protect apples as well as bananas, cantaloupes, melons, peaches, pears, etc., from darkening.

What are Granny Smith apples?   A perfectly charming apple with a bright green skin and very white crisp flesh, good for both eating and cooking, that comes to us from New Zealand. Because their seasons are the reverse of ours, their apples mature in February and March, arrive in the United States as early as May and usually last through our summer.

MINTED APPLES

½ cup firmly packed brown sugar	¼ teaspoon ground cloves
¼ cup granulated sugar	2 tablespoons chopped fresh mint
¼ cup soft butter	4 cups peeled, sliced Granny Smith
¼ teaspoon ground cinnamon	apples

Combine brown sugar, granulated sugar, butter, cinnamon, cloves, and fresh mint. Arrange a layer of apples in a one-quart baking dish. Dot with sugar mixture. Repeat layers, ending with sugar mixture. Cover dish with aluminum foil. Bake in preheated 350° oven for 1 hour. Serve warm. Makes about 6 servings.

What are controlled-atmosphere apples?   All fruits and vegetables, like people, begin aging the minute they are "born." If, after apples reach maturity, and have been harvested, the aging process is allowed to continue, they reach a point at which they are no longer edible. Cold temperature retards the aging process so that apples can be kept in prime condition for many months. Controlled-atmosphere storage (a refinement of conventional storage techniques) or "CA" as it is known to professionals, makes it possible for us to have prime-quality apples as long as nine months after they have been picked. Obviously, you can't do this at home.

How are canned apples available?   One pound and 1 pound, 4 ounces.

How is applesauce available?   The regular from 8½ ounces, in tin, to 1 pound, 9 ounces, in glass; unsweetened or artificially sweetened from 8 ounces to 1 pound; apple-cranberry sauce, in glass, 1 pound, 9 ounces.

Are zest and rind the same thing?   Zest is the oil derived from the rind of a lemon or an orange. Rind is the skin of citrus fruits which in the case of the lemon or orange can be grated to use as a flavoring agent in innumerable dishes. However, zest is also used to describe a piece of peel or a twist of these fruits when added to a drink. The metal zesters now on the market for scoring or peeling citrus fruits are extremely useful.

Is a green-tinged orange ripe?   Regreening, as it's known by growers, is a phenomenon of nature that seems to be particularly true of Valencias, the great juice orange. Even a fully ripe, bright Valencia orange will turn slightly green at the stem end while still on the tree. So the answer is yes. Valencias from California and Arizona are in the market from May through October; those from Florida from February to July.

How do you store oranges?   They should be stored in the hydrator of the refrigerator. Cut fruit should have the surface sealed with Saran Wrap or foil, and peeled fruit should be wrapped securely in either Saran Wrap or foil to prevent its drying out. Use, however, as soon as possible.

How are canned grapefruit and orange sections available?   In syrup, from 8 ounces to 1 pound; in water or artificially sweetened, in 8-ounce cans. Grapefruit and orange sections, mixed, are available in the same sizes.

Does a lemon heated in hot water yield more juice?   A real believe-it-or-not—it really does. This little trick came right out of *The Blue Sea Cookbook* by Sarah D. Albertson, but it is supported by the Florida citrus canners, who always place fruit briefly in hot water before processing. By actual measure, a lemon allowed to stand in very hot water about 2 minutes yielded 2 tablespoons more juice than one of the same size that had not been heated. The same technique can be applied to all citrus fruits.

How can you protect a lemon, once it's grated? The best way we know is to squeeze the fruit immediately, pour the juice into an individual plastic ice-cube container, and freeze it. Grated lemons—in fact, any grated citrus fruit—will dry out or mildew in the hydrator even if protected by a wrap of some kind. Freezing seems to us a happy solution and, presto, lemon juice when you want it.

Other than fresh, how is lemon juice available? In lemon-shaped plastic containers, canned, bottled, and frozen. You may be mildly interested to know that today almost half the California lemon crop is bottled, canned, or frozen. Bottled and frozen cost about the same and are the least expensive; canned is slightly higher; fresh juice and the juice packed in plastic "lemons" are the most expensive, with fresh somewhat lower than the plastic lemons.

Can you squeeze the juice from a tangerine? Yes. Just cut it in half and squeeze as you would a lemon or orange.

How can you choose ripe peaches? We're told by the experts that the real clue to ripeness is the soft creamy-to-gold undercolor of the yellow part of the skin; that red color is not a sign of ripeness; that a very pale peach can be riper and sweeter than one with deep-red cheeks. Blush depends on variety. If you examine a peach you'll notice along the crease that one cheek is slightly rounder at this line which indicates the peach was picked at the proper time. Avoid peaked or wrinkled cheeks and peaches with even a hint of green at the stem end. If a peach with all these qualities is still firm, it tells you the peach was firm-ripe when shipped so needs to soften at room temperature. Peaches are ready to eat when they feel *barely* soft. Always refrigerate full-ripe peaches and remember to bring them to room temperature, when they taste their best, before serving. Medium to large peaches are usually the best buy for flavor and quality.

PÊCHES EN CRÈME BRÛLÉE

8 very ripe peaches, peeled	Light brown sugar
Superfine sugar or kirsch	Commercial sour cream

Arrange the sliced peaches in a 1-quart baking dish (a soufflé mold is excellent). If not sufficiently sweet, sprinkle lightly with superfine sugar, or dribble a few tablespoons of kirsch over all. Spoon a thick layer of sour cream over the peaches, reaching almost to the top of the dish. Cover with a ½-inch layer of sifted brown sugar. Slide under a preheated broiler, 4 to 5 inches from the source of the heat, just long enough to caramelize the sugar. Watch sharply to make sure the sugar doesn't burn. Don't even close the oven door.

Can you describe the peaches available in today's market? Peaches can be white-fleshed or yellow-fleshed; freestone or cling; red-skinned or yellow-skinned; with a faint blush or no blush at all. All peaches grown commercially today are defuzzed, if they are not naturally fuzzless—and many are—then they are washed, before shipping.

How do freestone and clingstone peaches differ? With freestone peaches, the ripe flesh separates very readily from the pit when the peach is cut; with clingstones, commonly called "clings," the flesh is inclined to cling tenaciously to the pit (see below), sometimes making it difficult to separate them cleanly. Fresh clingstones are available very early in the peach season and are best eaten out of hand.

When is the fresh peach season? Fresh peaches are being picked somewhere in the United States (33 states produce them) from May through October. The first to come into the market (in May and June) are generally clingstones; the later ones are freestones. So, all told, fresh peaches are available five months of the year with July and August the peak season.

How can you prevent peaches from darkening? Sprinkle with lemon juice, then cover with ice and refrigerate. Or cover with orange, lemon, or pineapple juice or bottled lemon or orange drink concentrate. Drain before using.

Should peaches be peeled before eating? Not if you are going to eat them out of hand. In some instances, obviously, they should be peeled; it depends on how they are going to be used. To peel, simply let them stand in boiling water for a few minutes and the skin will slip off easily.

Will peaches ripen on the windowsill? Definitely not. In fact, no fruit will ripen on the sill or in strong sunlight. All this will accomplish will be to shrivel the skin and encourage decay. See how to ripen tomatoes, pages 218–219.

How are canned peaches available? Peaches and pears are packed the same way: in extra heavy and heavy syrup, from 8¾ ounces to 1 pound, 14 ounces; in light syrup from 8½ ounces to 1 pound, 13 ounces; in water or artificially sweetened, from 8 ounces to 1 pound, 12 ounces.

How do you "stone" cling peaches? In preparing cling peaches for slicing or canning, cut entirely around the pit starting at the blossom end (opposite from stem), then twist gently and you will have two perfect halves. The pit can be removed from the one half easily with a spoon. We suggest the pit can also be removed by whacking a heavy knife into it, then twisting to lift it out.

What are those little specks on banana skins? They're good signs. They mean the banana is sweet and ripe. Actually, they're sugar spots. Another way to tell if a banana is ripe is to look at the tip. If it's green and just turning to yellow it indicates the banana is ripe and sweet enough to eat. Don't buy bananas with wrinkled skin; it means they are dry.

How can you judge a cantaloupe? A mature cantaloupe has a smooth, green indentation at the stem end. If the stem is attached, it is immature. And good-flavored flesh is indicated on the outside by a light beige or yellowish background, a high, even cork-like net.

Should you refrigerate ripe cantaloupes? Unless they are very ripe, it is best to leave them out of the refrigerator. Store in as cool a place as possible and eat within 2 or 3 days. Melons, like all fruit, taste best at room temperature. If you refrigerate them, do not cover.

Should the seeds be left in a cut melon? Yes. Remove the seeds only from the piece of the melon you are going to eat. Seeds act as a shield to keep the flesh moist and fresh. Seal the entire piece, of course, with Saran Wrap or foil, especially the cut sides.

Is it true there are seedless watermelons? Yes. Seedless watermelons are sometimes available but mostly in the Midwest and in very, very limited supply, the reason being that they are so costly to produce. To give you an example, the seeds cost about $150 a pound as against $2.50 for regular melon seeds. If you run into them, you'll find the flesh very red, crisp, and sweet, but don't you think we're all going to miss the seeds?

What's a honey ball? It's similar to the honeydew melon except that it is much smaller, very round, and slightly and irregularly netted over the surface.

What is a prune? Prunes (*prune* is French for a fresh plum, and *pruneau* for dried) are a special variety of tree-ripened royal purple plums that are washed and then dehydrated. This turns them into prunes. One further step, prior to packaging, is a steam treatment that makes them moist, tender, ready to eat. Available pitted and unpitted.

JAMES A. BEARD'S PRUNE WHIP

Butter	1 teaspoon vanilla
1¼ cups pitted prunes	½ cup coarsely chopped walnuts
¼ cup sugar	5 egg whites

Butter a 2-quart baking dish or casserole generously. Add a couple of tablespoons of sugar and tip the dish back and forth (best done over the sink) to coat the sides and bottom lightly with sugar. Turn upside down and dump out any excess. Set aside.

Cover prunes with water in a saucepan and cook until tender when pierced with a fork. Drain and chop very fine. You should have 1 cupful. Mix with the sugar, vanilla, and chopped nuts. Beat the egg whites until they hold firm, shiny peaks when the beater is held straight up. Beat about a third of the whites into the mixture with a wire whisk. Then fold in the remainder with a rubber spatula.

Pour into the prepared dish and bake in a preheated 375° oven for 20 to 25 minutes or until lightly browned. Serve warm (not hot) with whipped cream. Serves 6.

Why bother pitting prunes when you can buy them without pits? The California Prune Advisory Board tells us that prunes with pits, like meat with bones, have more flavor. They recommend them for fruit dishes. In cooking, however, tender, sweet, pitted prunes simplify life greatly.

What is lekvar? A thick purée of prunes used as a filling for cakes and pastries. Of Hungarian origin. Available in stores specializing in Hungarian delicacies.

When do plums come on the market? July, and they last into September. Although we are all more or less inclined to think of plums in terms of green and purple, actually, the color is only "skin deep." Plums come in shades of green, purple, blue, yellow, and red, and it is well worth noting that they come on the market fully ripe. Of the many varieties, the Santa Rosa comes on the market earliest and lasts the longest and there are more Santa Rosas than any other variety. Plums can be used to make sherbets, kuchens, jam, salads, and of course, they are flawless eaten out of hand.

SANTA ROSA ALMOND PLUM BUTTER

5 pounds ripe plums   Sugar
½ cup water   Almond extract

Choose fully ripe, but not overripe plums. Wash fruit and remove stems. Combine the plums and water in a heavy kettle. Cook over low heat (simmer, actually) until the plums burst, juice flows freely and pulp separates from pits. Shake kettle frequently to prevent sticking. Note, a Flame Tamer * works well under these circumstances. Push fruit through a sieve to make a purée. If too thin—and remember, this is a jam—put back over very low heat and continue to cook until the purée is thick enough to mound on a spoon.

For each cup of purée, add ¾ cup of sugar, stirring it in well. Heat to the boiling point and boil vigorously, stirring constantly. When the mixture forms 2 drops on the edge of a metal spoon—this is known as sheeting —it is cooked. This should take about 30 minutes. At this point stir in 2½ teaspoons almond extract. Pour immediately into hot, sterilized jars. Seal. Makes about 8 half pints.

* Flame Tamers are available from stores specializing in fine cooking equipment and can be used as a substitute for double boilers because they distribute the heat so evenly.

How are canned plums packed?   Purple, greengage, and all others, in extra heavy and heavy syrup from 8¾ ounces to 1 pound, 14 ounces. In glass, 1 pound and 1 pound, 13 ounces; in light syrup, from 8½ ounces to 1 pound, 13 ounces; in water or artificially sweetened from 8 ounces to 1 pound, 12 ounces.

How are canned apricots available?   In extra heavy syrup or heavy syrup from 8¾ ounces to 1 pound, 14 ounces; in light syrup, from 1 pound to 1 pound, 13 ounces; in slightly sweetened water, in 1 pound, 12-ounce cans; artificially sweetened, from 8 ounces to 1 pound, 12 ounces.

What is a cactus pear like?   Once known as the prickly pear, with justification, because the entire surface is covered with little needles. Happily, the modern cactus pear is denuded of its prickles before it goes to market. It is pear-shaped, with a dull-brown rough skin, off-set by the most glorious, bright-red flesh. Very juicy, but also very "seedy," it is beloved by Italians, who peel the fruit and eat it out of hand, seeds and all. In Boston, New York, Pittsburgh, Chicago, and other cities where there is a concentrated Italian-American population, you can find the cactus pear in season, starting in September and going through the winter.

What are winter pears?   They come on the market in November and last through June: the chunky Anjou, green or greenish yellow; the Bosco, with the long, tapering neck, green or brown to golden russet; and the Comice, famous for its great size and beauty, greenish yellow to yellow with red splashings.

   N O T E : If the pears are to be cooked, they should be very firm. Always peel pears to eat out of hand in order to savor them at their most delicious, and always serve at room temperature.

POACHED FRESH PEARS

2 cups sugar	1 vanilla bean
3 cups water	8 fresh pears
Whole rind of 1 lemon	

   Combine all the ingredients except the pears in a heavy saucepan just

large enough to hold the pears comfortably. Bring to a boil. Reduce heat
and simmer 5 minutes. Cool.

Leaving the stems on, peel the pears, one by one, and add immediately
to the syrup to keep them from discoloring. Place over a low heat and
bring slowly to a boil. When the syrup reaches the boiling point, take off
the heat. In order to forestall darkening it is important for the pears to be
completely covered with syrup. Seal with Saran Wrap and refrigerate
overnight.

N O T E : Any extra syrup, after the pears have been served, can be
refrigerated in a covered jar and used to poach other fruits at some future
time.

How do you ripen winter pears?　The pear experts recommend buying
firm pears and ripening them at home. Keep the pears in a bowl at
room temperature until the flesh yields to gentle pressure in the palm
of your hand. You'll note that pears, whatever the color or variety,
begin to ripen at the stem end, and it usually takes from 3 to 5 days
for them to reach just the right stage of ripeness to eat out of hand.
After they are fully ripe, store in the refrigerator. Never refrigerate
unripened pears. In some food stores you may find "conditioned"
pears, which simply means they are ready for immediate use.

N O T E : Pears should never be frozen.

When are red currants in season?　So short a time they are hardly
here before they're gone—from about the 4th of July until the 24th.
Most, if not all, red currants come from nearby gardens since they,
like gooseberries, carry a blight for white pine trees and state laws
prohibit their being planted.

What are the marks of good red currants?　They should be bright
colored and firm. If any of the currants are soft and breaking away
from the stem, the fruit is too mature. The berries, washed in cool
water, stripped from the stems, then crushed and mixed with superfine sugar, weight for weight, can be frozen most successfully.

ELLEN-ANN DUNHAM'S ROTE GRÜTZE

This is a German dessert usually made with raspberries and red currants although other berries may be used. It is awfully good served cold
with cream, vanilla sauce, or whipped cream.

4 pint boxes ripe red currants   Pinch salt
2 pint boxes fresh ripe raspberries   2 scant cups sugar
⅞ cup quick-cooking tapioca

Wash the currants and pull the berries off the stems. Pick over the raspberries and discard any that are overripe. Combine both raspberries and currants with 4 cups of water in a heavy saucepan. Bring to a boil, then simmer for about 10 minutes. Strain through a fine sieve lined with several layers of dampened cheesecloth. Return the purée to the saucepan. Add the remaining ingredients, place over a very low heat, and stir until dissolved. Take off the heat and allow to stand until cold. Makes a little over 2 quarts. Keep well refrigerated. Serve with plain or whipped cream.

KATHLEEN FISHER'S SPICED RED CURRANTS

5 pints red currants   ¼ cup cider vinegar
1 teaspoon ground cloves   7½ cups sugar
1 teaspoon cinnamon   ½ bottle liquid fruit pectin

Wash the currants and strip off stems. Place in a large, heavy kettle, stir in the cloves, cinnamon, vinegar and ½ cup of water. Cook, over moderate heat, stirring constantly, until mixture comes to a boil. Turn down heat to simmer, cover, and cook slowly 10 minutes. Mix in the sugar thoroughly, increase the heat, and bring to a rolling boil. Boil 1 minute, stirring constantly. Take off the heat, stir in the pectin at once. Spoon off any foam that rises to the surface. Continue stirring and skimming for 5 minutes. While still hot, ladle into scalded 8-ounce tapered jars, leaving about ⅛ inch "headroom." Makes 10 to 12 jars. Seal according to directions.

Excellent with hot or cold chicken, turkey, ham, duck, goose, lamb, or veal.

What are juniper berries?   The berries of the juniper tree, a small evergreen shrub, used in flavoring gin. In Alexis Lichine's excellent *Encyclopedia of Wines and Spirits,* he writes: "The English words 'gin' and 'geneva' (nothing to do with the Swiss city) are corruptions of *jenever* and *genièvre* (French), both meaning juniper." Juniper berries are commonly used in that French classic, *choucroute à l'alsacienne;* in Sweden to make a conserve to accompany cold meat; and in Germany frequently to flavor sauerkraut. If the berries are not available, gin can be substituted.

How long will fresh sweet cherries keep? If placed in a plastic bag with a number of small holes punched into it with any small, sharp instrument, cherry experts tell us they will stay fresh, crisp, and delicious for 2 to 3 weeks under normal refrigerator temperatures. From the end of May through July is cherry time.

How are unpitted cherries available? *Pitted cherries and unpitted cherries are packed the same way in the same can size.* In extra-heavy or light syrup from 8¾ ounces to 1 pound, 14 ounces; in light syrup from 8½ ounces to 1 pound, 13 ounces; in water or artificially sweetened from 8 ounces to 1 pound, 12 ounces.

How are cranberries available today? Fresh, by the pound, nationally; frozen, by the pound, in certain areas; whole cranberry sauce, in 1-pound cans; jellied cranberry sauce in 8-ounce and 1-pound cans; cranberry-orange relish in 14-ounce glass jars; deluxe cranberry-raspberry sauce in 8-ounce and 1 pound cans; and these cranberry drinks: cranberry juice cocktail and cranberry apple juice (in 1 pint, 1 quart, and 48-ounce cans), and cran-prune drink in quart cans only.

What are lingonberries? A mountain berry that grows wild in Northern Europe, in Maine, and in Canada. Not unlike our familiar cranberries, although smaller, they are also known as lingenberries and lings. Available imported from Sweden in jars, cooked, in U.S. stores specializing in Scandinavian foods. Also imported from Canada, ready-to-cook, by the pound, most of the year.

How are canned blueberries available? In heavy and light syrup, 15-ounce cans.

Can you freeze fresh blueberries? Certainly. First, choose berries that are plump, fresh, clean, and uniform in size. Depending on the variety, they may have a "bloom," a natural waxy, protective coating. Pour into freezer containers just as they come from the box, leaving about ½-inch headroom between berries and lid. Seal and freeze. To use, rinse and treat exactly as you would fresh berries. So when cold, snowy January rolls around you can sit down to a breakfast of fresh blueberries, brown sugar, and cream. Nice?

When are gooseberries in season? In June and July only and the chances are they will come from nearby gardens, since they are not raised commercially. Like red currants, they carry the white pine blight, so they cannot be grown in states where this tree is important. In buying gooseberries, look for bright, firm berries free from moisture, dirt, and leaves. Wash, then "tip and tail" just before using. Gooseberries are always sold in quart boxes.

GOOSEBERRY FOOL

An old English dish that is perfectly delicious. There are many versions. Here's one we like.

1 quart green gooseberries	Juice 1 lemon *
1 cup sugar	1 cup heavy cream, whipped
Grated rind 1 lemon	

Top and tail the gooseberries. Combine with the sugar and 1 cup of water in a heavy saucepan. Bring to a boil, then simmer until the fruit bursts. While still hot, blend a small amount at a time in the electric blender. Stir in the lemon rind and juice. Cool. Just before serving, fold in the whipped cream. Serves about 6.

*Boil the lemon, *after* grating, for a couple of minutes and it will yield more juice.

How is canned fruit cocktail available? Fruit cocktail and fruits for salad are packed the same way. In extra-heavy and heavy syrup, from 8¾ ounces to 1 pound, 14 ounces; in light syrup from 8 ounces to 1 pound, 13 ounces; artificially sweetened from 8 ounces to 1 pound, 13 ounces.

What are black mission figs? Large, dark-purple figs that are one of many varieties that include: Calimyrna, large white; Adriatic, white; Kadota, smaller, also white. Our fresh-fig season runs from June to the end of September. Figs are highly perishable and should be bought for immediate use. Ripeness can be determined by the degree of softness to the touch. Overripeness is detectable by a sour odor, which is due to fermentation of the juice. Fresh figs imported from Greece come into our markets from the middle of October through Christmas.

What is cherimoya? Considered one of the three finest fruits in the world, the other two being the pineapple and the mangosteen (an Asiatic tropical fruit that is not grown in this country and which, despite its name, is not related to the mango). The flavor of cherimoya has been linked to a delicious sherbet or ice cream. When prepared as it is in the tropics—thoroughly chilled on ice—there are few desserts to equal it. Raised in California, it is usually only found in markets specializing in fine fruits. Probably introduced to California from Mexico about 1871. A hybrid cherimoya, called atemoya, raised in Florida, is more apt to be found in fine fruit markets. Available in the fall or winter.

How is canned pineapple packed? In extra heavy and heavy syrup from 8½ ounces to 1 pound, 14 ounces; in light syrup and juice from 8 ounces to 1 pound, 13 ounces; in water or artificially sweetened from 8-ounce to 1 pound, 4 ounce cans; in unsweetened juice (no sugar added) sliced, crushed, or in chunks in 15¼-ounce cans.

Is pineapple ever packed in its own juice? Yes. You can buy sliced and crushed pineapple and pineapple chunks in unsweetened pineapple juice (no sugar added), all in 15¼-ounce cans.

What are fuyu? An Oriental persimmon introduced some years ago by the U.S. Department of Agriculture, under the name "Fuyugaki." It has the exceptional characteristic of never being astringent. So, unlike other varieties, can be eaten while still firm, just like an apple. It is the only light-fleshed variety known that is non-astringent while the flesh is still firm. Raised in both Florida and California. Beautiful and delicious, it is available in the late fall or winter.

Can you eliminate the astringency in persimmons? Yes. Place the persimmons in a plastic bag with ripe (they must be ripe) apples, allowing two apples to four or five firm persimmons. Squeeze out all air and tie securely. Keep at room temperature. In about 3 to 4 days the persimmons should be soft and perfectly ripe and all astringency will have disappeared. Nice?

What is kiwi fruit? Known as Chinese gooseberries in New Zealand, from where we import them, they are oval-shaped, about the size of a large lemon, brown, hairy-skinned, and have a perfectly beautiful green flesh studded with soft black seeds. In the market from May to September. Kiwis will keep for weeks, refrigerated. To ripen, place in a plastic bag with a couple of overripe apples, with a few holes punched in the bag, for a few days or until they are soft to the touch. Incidentally, this is a good way to ripen any fruit.

How do you serve kiwi fruit?   Rub off the stiff brown hairs with a coarse cloth. Cut each kiwi in half, sprinkle with lemon or lime juice and eat with a spoon directly from the skin. Or peel, slice fairly thin, sprinkle with lemon juice, and coat lightly with a thin, "pouring" custard.

Meats

How long can you store meat in the refrigerator? Refrigerator temperatures are usually 36° to 40° but some very modern refrigerators have special meat storage areas where temperatures are lower (29° to 34°). Thus, the storage time can be extended.

Meat (LOOSELY COVERED)	Recommended Maximum Storage Time
Beef	
Standing Rib Roast	5 to 8 days
Steaks	3 to 5 days
Pot Roasts	5 to 6 days
Stew Meats	2 days
Ground Beef	1 to 2 days
Liver (sliced)	1 to 2 days
Heart	1 to 2 days
Pork	
Roasts	5 to 6 days
Chops	3 days
Spareribs	3 days
Pork Sausage	2 to 3 days

Cured and Smoked Meats

Hams, Picnics (whole, half, or slices)	7 days
Bacon	5 to 7 days
Dried Beef	10 to 12 days
Corned Beef	5 to 7 days
Tongue	6 to 7 days

Lamb

Roasts	5 days
Chops	3 days
Heart	1 to 2 days
Liver (sliced)	1 to 2 days

Veal

Roasts	5 to 6 days
Chops	4 days
Liver (sliced)	1 to 2 days
Sweetbreads (cooked)	2 days

Cooked Meats

Home-cooked Meats (tightly covered)	4 days
Hams, Picnics	7 days
Frankfurters	4 to 5 days
Meat Loaf (sliced)	3 to 4 days
Luncheon Meats (sliced)	3 days
Bologna Loaves (unsliced)	4 to 6 days
Dry and Semi-dry Sausage (unsliced)	2 to 3 weeks
Liver Sausage (sliced)	2 to 3 days
Liver Sausage (unsliced)	4 to 6 days

Poultry

Chicken (ready-to-cook, whole)	2 days
Chickens (cut up)	2 days
Turkeys (ready-to-cook)	2 days
Duckling (ready-to-cook, whole)	2 days
Cooked Poultry (tightly covered)	3 to 4 days

Can you thaw and refreeze meat?   According to the Research Department of the U.S. Department of Agriculture, you can. In a recent report they say: "Contrary to popular opinion, meat which has been frozen and thawed is no more perishable than meat which has never been frozen. In fact, our research has shown that some of the bacteria which are responsible for meat spoilage do not grow quite as well in thawed meat as they do in unfrozen meat. Further, experiments have shown that beef roasts which have been thawed and refrozen five times were considered just as good by an expert taste panel as roasts which had not been frozen at all." Remember this, however: Either fresh or frozen meat should always be kept as cold as possible.

What is meant by "Federally graded" meat?   Grades are reliable guides to meat quality—its tenderness, juiciness, and flavor. Meat grading is a voluntary service provided by the U.S. Department of Agriculture's Consumer and Marketing Service to meat packers and others who request it and pay a fee for the service. So not all meat is graded, although a large percentage of it is. The highly trained U.S.D.A graders rate only whole carcasses or wholesale cuts because quality differences are difficult, or impossible, to recognize in the smaller retail cuts. Once graded, the carcass is stamped with a purple, shield-shaped grade mark with the letters U.S.D.A. and the grade, such as Prime, Choice, or Good. Beef, lamb, and veal are all graded; only pork is federally inspected. Prime is the finest quality and most expensive; Choice, generally available in most retail markets, is considered the best buy on the basis of palatability and cost; Good, less desirable meat, is also considerably less expensive.

What is meant by "Federally inspected" meat?   It means the meat or poultry you put on your dinner table has been inspected for wholesomeness by U.S. Department of Agriculture meat inspectors who, in addition, supervise the cleanliness and operating procedures of packing plants to insure that the meat or poultry is not contaminated or adulterated. Those products that pass inspection are stamped with a round mark that bears the legend "U.S. INSP'D & P'S'D." On December 15, 1967, President Johnson signed the Wholesome Meat Act, which assures you that the meat or poultry you buy has been inspected by the Federal Government or by an adequate state program. Not true, heretofore, when meat was not sold across state lines.

Do you carve meat with or against the grain?   Against.

Can you cook two roasts, for example, at one time?   Yes, if you take into consideration any variance in weight.

Should meat be wiped before cooking?   It is not only unnecessary but ridiculous. Unless you can see the need for it, which is extremely doubtful in this day and age, it is a useless gesture.

What do you consider the best meat thermometer?   Taylor's Gourmet thermometer which registers from 0 to 220°. The dial, glass-covered so it can remain in the meat during the cooking period, is not much larger than a nickel and the shaft is about the size of a knitting needle. It is a flawless piece of equipment and comes equipped with tested roasting temperatures, thus, at last, taking the guesswork out of meat roasting. An absolutely essential piece of equipment in my opinion. Expensive but worth every penny. Rotisserie cooks should love it.

What is the right type of pan for roasting?   A low-sided roasting pan with a rack is ideal (it is not always necessary to use the rack; follow your recipe). A standing rib roast obviously does not need a rack since it stands on its own rack—the ribs. No cover is ever used.

How can you judge whether meat is spoiled or not?   Your nose will help but, further, there is usually a general change in the quality of the meat which includes loss of freshness and a color change from bright red in the case of beef or pale pink for pork or veal to a dull grayed color. An off-odor will certainly develop and if the meat has been kept in an unopened package, a slippery surface may appear. The best rule, of course, is, "When in doubt, throw it out."

How long can thawed meat be kept before cooking?   Meat which has been thawed but has not reached room temperature should be refrigerated and may be kept as long as fresh meat.

What can you do with frozen meats in case of a power failure?   Leave the freezer door closed as meats will usually stay frozen up to 8 hours.

If meats have completely thawed, but are still cold, cook and then refreeze—assuming the power has come on again.

What's the easiest way to marinate meat? With the plastic bag at hand, you've got it made. Now, anything can be marinated or macerated the easy way. Simply put the food in a bag large enough to hold it, add the marinade or maceration, squeeze out the air, and secure with a rubber band or tie band. Place in a bowl or pan just in case there's some leakage. Turn whenever you think of it so the food absorbs the flavors all over.

What does à la bourguignonne mean? Sometimes written without the "à la," it means in the Burgundy manner. That is, onions, mushrooms, and a red wine sauce served with meat, usually beef.

Are braising and cooking in liquid the same? No. See description of braising, below. Cooking in liquid is a method that is more usually applied when making meat soups or stews. As with braising, large, less tender cuts of meat are used.

Is pot-roasting the same as braising? The answer is no, although cooks are inclined to use the term "pot-roasting" to mean a method of cooking. Pot roast is the name applied to chunky cuts of meat (round or rump steak, brisket, chuck, shoulder, or arm—the less tender cuts that call for long, slow cooking) that are cooked by braising. The braising is done as follows: The meat is browned slowly on all sides in hot fat, seasoned with salt, pepper, herbs, and spices; then cooked, with the addition of a small amount of water, vegetable juice, or broth, tightly covered, either on the top of the stove or in a slow (300° to 325°) oven.

How do you lard meat? It's done with a larding needle, of which there are many types. The type used by French chefs is a hollow, tapered metal tube 8, 10, or 12 inches long, ⅛, ¼, or ⅜ inches in diameter at the top. The size of the piece of meat determines the size of the needle to use. One end of the needle is pointed for easy insertion into the meat; the other end is split so the metal can be squeezed. To lard, insert the "string" of larding fat into the split end of the needle as far as it will go. Push the needle into the meat up to the split.

Then squeeze the end together as tightly as possible to hold the lard as you pull the needle through with the pointed end. The type used by butchers, we were informed by David Adams of New York's Fitz Market, is a half-hollow metal cylinder with a wooden handle. It, too, comes in various lengths and sizes. To lard, you simply lay the larding fat in the hollow, push the needle into the meat, turn it over, and withdraw the needle. This type is very easy to use, especially when a recipe calls for larding the meat with nuts, garlic slivers, or other flavor makers. Whatever type you use, remember that practice makes perfect. Both types are available where fine cooking equipment is sold.

Should all broiling be done at the high broil point?   No. Broiling is fastest at that position, but unless the meat is all of the same thickness, there is a very real possibility of overcooking the thin part and undercooking the thick (chicken is a good example). Also, the surface can cook too quickly, and the inside of the meat may be quite raw (steak, for example). With gas, the broiling is done with the oven door closed, and in modern stoves there is a range of temperatures which the cook should learn to use as she uses the oven. The best guide is, obviously, the use-and-care book that comes with the stove, but common sense can play an important role, too. With electric stoves, the broiling is done with the door ajar. Here, the broiling pan must be moved up or down, as the case may be, to arrive at different temperatures. The manufacturers of electric ranges suggest 1 to 3 inches from the heating unit for rare meat; 3 to 5 for medium rare; and 6 inches for well done. All foods to be broiled should be brought to room temperature before broiling.

Is meat salted before or after roasting?   Cooks used to say that if meat was salted before roasting, it drew the blood out of the meat. Not true. Salt can penetrate no more than half an inch, if that. So you can season your roasts before (which chefs do), during, or after you cook them.

How long does it take to thaw meat?

Meat	Refrigerator	Room Temperature
Large Roast	4 to 7 hours per pound	2 to 3 hours per pound
Small Roast	3 to 5 hours per pound	1 to 2 hours per pound
1-inch Steak	12 to 14 hours	2 to 4 hours

How can you tell if frozen beef products are tender? You can't. Labels
do not give the grade of the cut from which the meat came. Cornell
University's Consumer Education Program (New York City) tells
us they have found that frozen beef steaks are sometimes described
"as chopped and shaped, with a range in price from 87 cents to $1.07
a pound; frozen minute steaks, as wafer-sliced, ranging in price from
$1.36 to $1.64 a pound." They advise consumers the only way to
judge products is by trying them. We suggest this could be rather
expensive.

Are London Broil and flank steak the same thing? Not necessarily.
London Broil (the name is said to have originated in a New York or,
possibly, a Philadelphia restaurant at least 40 years ago) is prepared
from several beef cuts, including flank, the National Livestock and
Meat Board informs us. Beef cut from the clod (shoulder or chuck)
or from the top round or from the sirloin tip (cut lengthwise with the
grain) or even from the muscle, once referred to as the "tail" of the
porterhouse (now removed by butchers), are all used.

How do you carve London Broil (flank steak)? With a fork, hold the
steak firmly on the platter or board (a board is practical because it
helps to keep the meat from slipping), and start slicing at the small
end of the steak almost parallel to the board with a long, thin, sharp
knife—in other words, on the bias. Slices should be very thin.

*What is the difference between hamburger, ground beef, ground chuck,
ground round, and ground sirloin?* The U.S. Department of Agriculture points out that each of these names on the label on a package of
ground meat has a distinct and different meaning. It is important to
note here, however, that nutritionally they all have the same amount
of protein, vitamins, and minerals.

   Hamburger can contain up to 30% fat, which may include the addition of beef fat over and above that attached to the meat being
ground. But it cannot be labeled as regular hamburger if it contains
extenders such as non-fat dry milk, soybean products, cereals, water,
etc. Ground beef can contain the same amount of fat, but usually re-
tailers will limit it to 20 to 25%, since only that fat which is normally
on the meat is used. It is illegal to add additional fat or extenders. You
get somewhat less shrinkage with ground beef than with hamburger,

but both are best used in meat loaves, casseroles, sauces, and in Italian and Mexican dishes calling for ground beef.

Ground chuck, meat from the shoulder or "chuck" of the animal, slightly leaner than hamburger or ground beef, 15 to 20% fat, is especially good for patties. Ground round, just what its name implies (round steak ground up), has a fat content of about 11%, and is therefore less desirable for grinding and making patties. It is excellent for people on low-fat diets. Broadly speaking, however, it is best used in combination with other ingredients. Ground sirloin, the best, comes from sirloin steak and definitely makes a "king" of a hamburger.

No matter what kind of ground beef you buy, look for the bluish-red color that indicates freshly ground meat. And remember, for tenderness and juicy results, cook only to the medium stage even if it is combined with other ingredients, and don't ever pound meat patties into shape; treat them tenderly, like a baby.

HAMBURGERS IN CREAM

6 tablespoons (¾ stick) butter
1 bunch (5 to 6) scallions (white part only) or 3 tablespoons, minced fine
3 pounds ground chuck
¼ cup condensed beef broth

1 cup heavy cream
¼ teaspoon nutmeg, freshly ground
Salt
Freshly ground pepper
1½ tablespoons flour

Heat 2 tablespoons of the butter in a heavy skillet. Add the scallions and ½ cup water. Cook until all the water has boiled away and the scallions are limp and transparent. If necessary add more water. Cool slightly.

Mix the scallions with the meat, using a light hand, and shape into 12 patties. Heat another 2 to 3 tablespoons of the butter in the skillet. Sauté the patties over a good heat about 3 minutes on each side. Add more butter as it is needed. As the patties are cooked, lift them to a heated platter and keep warm. Stir the broth into the pan juices, then the cream, nutmeg, and salt and pepper to taste.

Make a *roux* by working 1½ tablespoons of flour into 1½ tablespoons of butter. Drop by bits in the simmering sauce, whipping constantly with a wire whisk. Bring up to a simmer, whipping constantly, and cook just long enough for the sauce to thicken lightly. Pour over the patties to serve.

Serves about 6. Very good with sautéed or fried potatoes and fresh watercress.

Why do my pan-fried steaks and chops often look anemic? Chances are they were damp when you put them in the pan. Dry between layers of paper towels, but don't allow the meat to dry out. Just get rid of the surface moisture.

What exactly is Red Flannel Hash? It is the aftermath or end result of a boiled New England dinner, which as every American knows, or should, is corned beef served with cabbage, beets, turnips, carrots, and potatoes. Traditionally, the boiled dinner was served on Tuesday (ironing day in the old days) and the huge kettle could simmer thriftily on the back of the stove while the irons sat on the front. Then, Wednesday or Thursday was the time for Red Flannel Hash made from the leftovers. The corned beef was sliced cold, to go *with* the hash, *not to go in it.* The hash was made with the vegetables, and the beets are what give it the distinctive color. Traditional accompaniments are corn muffins and a fruity dessert such as baked apples. Followed by "lots of creamy coffee." However, Cecily Brownstone, Food Editor of the Associated Press and an authority on American cooking ways says, "In more recent times, meat was added to the hash, depending on the region." In Mrs. D. A. Lincoln's 1883 *Boston Cook Book* (she preceded Fannie Farmer at the Boston Cooking School), the recipe for vegetable hash is given as follows: "Equal parts of cabbage, beets, and white turnips, and as much potato as there is of all the other vegetables. Chop all very fine, add a little salt and pepper, put a spoonful of drippings in the pan and when hot, add the hash and cook slowly until warm through."

N O T E : The beets are not cooked with the corned beef but separately the day before and "pickled" overnight in vinegar.

What is Steak Diane? Created in 1923 by Nino (for twenty-five years *maître d'hôtel* in New York's Drake Hotel) when he worked at the famous La Plage in Ostende, Belgium. Essentially, it is steak that has been pounded very thin, then cooked in front of the guests in a mixture of dry mustard, butter, chives, coarsely ground pepper, and salt, then finished with lemon juice, Worcestershire sauce, fresh butter, and chopped parsley.

How do you sauté steaks?   Steaks up to 1½ inches are, in our opinion, better sautéed than broiled, a philosophy in which both the French and Italians concur. Place enough butter or vegetable oil or a combination of the two (about half and half) in a large, heavy skillet to make a good film over the bottom of the pan. When the fat is hot, add the steak (or steaks—don't crowd the pan) and sear the bottom. Reduce the heat and cook gently. Turn and sear the second side. Allow about 1 minute on each side for a ½-inch steak; 4 to 5 minutes on each side for a thicker, say 1½-inch steak, on each side. This timing is based on rare steak, which we prefer. The degree of doneness depends on how rare you like your steak.

How do you broil steaks?   Do not attempt to broil a steak thinner than 1½ inches or, better, 2 inches. It has been our experience that broiling under medium heat, whether with electricity or gas, gives a better final result. Slash the fat on the steak several times to prevent curling. Place on a *cold* broiling pan in a preheated broiler about 3 inches from the source of heat. Cook a 2-inch steak 4 to 5 minutes on the first side, then turn and cook another 4 to 5 minutes. At this point, test for doneness by cutting the steak near the bone (if any) or by cutting the actual steak. If it is too rare, broil a bit longer. For steaks thicker than 2 inches, sear on both sides over a high heat, then reduce the heat to finish it. Obviously, a thicker steak takes more time.

To serve the steak, lift to a heated platter, season with salt and freshly ground pepper, and coat with softened butter or serve with Sauce Béarnaise or Bercy (pages 176–177).

Is a standing rib roast a better buy than a rolled rib?   Possibly, and particularly if the boned rolled rib roast contains the less tender short rib section. A rolled standing rib roast contains the "eye" alone. There's one further point: The rolled roast is harder to carve because of skewers or, more likely, string, which must be there to hold the meat together.

N O T E : After carving the slices you need, turn a rolled roast back so it sits flat and retains the juices.

What is a chuck blade roast?   It comes from the chuck or shoulder section of the animal. If U.S. Department of Agriculture Prime or Choice, this cut can be oven roasted. If not, it's best to use it as a pot roast or in a stew.

How do I carve a standing rib of beef?   First of all you need a good, sharp carving knife. Buy at least a 3-rib roast. Place the roast, largest end down so it will "sit" firm on a large, heated platter. First, remove the suet which is used only to protect the meat while roasting. Steadying the roast with a fork, cut along the rib bone with the tip of the carving knife to separate the meat from the bone. Start slicing across the top of the roast toward the ribs. I prefer it sliced thin as it's done in France and England but in this country we are inclined to cut it somewhat thicker. Arrange individual servings on heated dinner plates and garnish with a sprig or two of watercress. Once you reach the point where you again have to separate the rib from the meat, remove the entire rib (the first). This, the carver usually considers his prerogative and puts aside for himself. Serve a tablespoon of the drippings or natural juice on each plate.

What are chicken steaks?   They are cut from the shoulder of the animal just under the shoulder blade. When properly prepared, the gristle is removed and the meat is cut into steaks much as a fillet of beef or the whole piece can be roasted. It is such a delicious piece of meat, unreliable markets have been known to sell it as fillet of beef.

What is a filet mignon?   First of all, let's discuss the tenderloin. The least-used muscle in the animal and therefore the most tender (some say the least flavorful, too) begins in the sirloin and ends at the rib end of the short loin. It is from the tenderloin, also called fillet of beef, that we get the following "steak" cuts: *châteaubriand,* a double tenderloin, cut out of the center or thick end, usually served to two; *petit filet, tournedos,* and *filet mignon,* the last coming from the tip or smallest end. Other than the *châteaubriand,* which is cut two inches thick, they are all cut about one inch thick and all are cooked the same way—either sautéed or broiled, usually served with a sauce. The tenderloin, larded, or barded, with fat, can be roasted at a high temperature. Currently one of the most popular recipes is *Boeuf Wellington,* the fillet of beef coated with *foie gras* or *duxelles,* wrapped in pastry, then baked. Customarily served with *sauce Périgueux* (Madeira and truffles). An overrated dish that belongs in the professional kitchen, in our opinion.

Is Beef Wellington English or French? You'll be as surprised as we were to discover it's Irish. In Theodora Fitzgibbon's book, *A Taste of Ireland,* it is called Wellington Steak but it is, in fact, the tenderloin or fillet of beef, enrobed in pastry and baked, and generally known as Boeuf Wellington. Apparently a great favorite of the Duke of Wellington, the "Iron Duke" who defeated Napoleon at Waterloo.

Is a porterhouse the same as a T-bone steak? It's like this: both come from what is known, commercially, as the short loin of beef. *Porterhouse,* considered by many the best of all steaks, cut from the large end of the short loin, includes a generous piece of the tenderloin; *strip,* or boneless loin (also known as New York cut in the West but not in New York) is a porterhouse with the tenderloin removed; *T-bone,* with a smaller amount of tenderloin, is also cut from the short loin; *shell steak* is a T-bone or porterhouse with the tenderloin removed; the fifth steak from this section, called a *club* or *Delmonico* (boneless club), has no tenderloin. But note that in some areas rib steaks, from the same section as the standing rib roast, are often sold as club steaks. All these steaks can be broiled or sautéed (also called pan-fried and pan-broiled).

JACQUES PÉPIN'S STEAK AU POIVRE

4 shell steaks, boned, about 8 ounces each
Salt
2½ tablespoons green peppercorns, drained
6 tablespoons (¾ stick) sweet butter

3 shallots or scallions, peeled and minced
2 tablespoons cognac
¼ cup red Burgundy
1½ cups canned brown beef gravy

Sprinkle both sides of the steak with salt. Crush the peppercorns into a smooth paste, then work into the paste about 2 tablespoons of the butter. Smear both sides of the steak with the pepper mixture.

Heat 2 tablespoons of the butter in a large, heavy skillet. When a rich brown, sauté the steaks 3 to 4 minutes on each side for medium rare. Lift the steaks from the pan to a warm platter and keep warm.

Add the shallots to the pan and sauté for one minute. Add the cognac and ignite. When the flames die out, add the wine and bring to a boil. Cook until reduced to about half. Add the beef gravy and bring to a boil again. Continue to boil for a few minutes. Stir in the remaining butter and pour the sauce over the steaks.

What is a sirloin tip? Let's look at the sirloin, which is the end of the loin section of the animal, as a whole. It is from this section that we get sirloin roasts and steaks. The steaks from this section are: pin-bone sirloin, flat-bone sirloin, wedge-bone sirloin, and boneless sirloin. The amount of bone varies greatly. To get the best, choose a steak with a good "marbling," and a moderate amount of surrounding fat. It is well to note here that the names of these steaks may vary from region to region, but if you keep in mind the section from which these steaks come you should be able to identify them to your butcher wherever you live. The sirloin steak is very large, making it a most desirable cut for a big-steak family or a party. Best to broil. The sirloin roast, the classic English roast of beef, is in the opinion of the British, better than a rib roast. Now we come to the sirloin tip. A boneless cut with very little waste, it is available as both a roast and a steak. Although not quite as tender as a true sirloin, prime or choice can be oven-roasted (other grades should be braised as a pot-roast), and steaks broiled, pan-broiled, or braised.

BOW'S SAUERBRATEN FOR 10

At Abraham & Straus, Brooklyn, New York, where they take the business of cooking seriously, Bow Ross was their gourmet consultant for many years.

4 pounds sirloin tip or chuck, tied	1 large Bermuda onion, peeled
Salt	and sliced
Freshly ground pepper	1 lemon, sliced
1 cup wine vinegar	1 cup dry red wine
1 bay leaf	Flour
6 juniper berries, crushed	2 tablespoons lard or vegetable oil
6 peppercorns	½ cup Madeira wine
6 whole cloves	¼ teaspoon ginger
2 tablespoons sugar	¼ teaspoon allspice
	6 gingersnaps, crumbled

Rub the meat with salt and pepper. Place in a large plastic bag. Combine vinegar, bay leaf, juniper berries, peppercorns, cloves, sugar, onion, lemon, and red wine with 1 cup of water in a saucepan. Bring up to a boil but do not boil. Pour over the meat. Squeeze out all air and tie the bag securely. Then place in a pan or bowl (in case of leakage) and refrigerate for two days, turning occasionally so the meat will be well soaked with the marinade.

Lift the meat from the marinade and pat dry with paper towels. Set the marinade aside for the moment. Coat the meat with flour, shaking off any excess. In a large, heavy, enameled casserole, heat the lard or oil until smoking. Brown the meat on all sides. Strain the marinade over the meat. Cover securely and cook in a preheated 350° oven for 2½ to 3 hours or until the meat is tender when pierced with a fork. When cooked, lift from the casserole to a heated platter and keep warm in a low oven (140°). Mix 3 tablespoons of flour with the Madeira wine until smooth. Stir into the liquid in the pan. Bring to a boil, then cook, whipping with a wire whisk, for about five minutes. Finally, stir in the ginger, allspice and crumbled gingersnaps. Bring to a boil again. If the sauce seems too thick to you, add a little boiling water, but take it easy.

To serve: Slice the meat and arrange on a hot platter so the slices overlap. Then coat lightly with the sauce. Pour remaining sauce into a heated sauceboat. Serve with noodles or potatoes.

Is steak and kidney pudding the same as steak and kidney pie? No, although both are made with steak and either lamb or ox kidneys (some pie recipes include oysters, too). The pudding, however, is finished with a suet crust, then steamed, and the pie with a flaky pastry, then baked. Both are English as the Union Jack and, when well prepared, perfectly delicious.

MAURICE MOORE-BETTY'S STEAK, KIDNEY, AND OYSTER PIE*

2 pounds top round steak, sliced thin
¾ pound beef kidney
1 cup flour
1 tablespoon salt

Several twists of the peppermill
2 dozen oysters with their liquor
Pastry for a 1-crust pie
1 egg yolk

* Adapted from a recipe in *Cooking for Occasions* by Maurice Moore-Betty (David White).

Cut the meat into pieces about 2 x 3 inches; wash the kidney thoroughly and cut into small pieces; combine the flour, salt, and pepper in a bag;

add the pieces of steak and kidney and shake until thoroughly coated with the mixture. Lift the meat from the bag. Reserve the flour. Cut the oysters in half, reserving the liquor. Wrap a piece of steak around each half oyster. Arrange a layer of the steak rolls in the bottom of a deep pie dish or 1½-quart casserole. Add a layer of kidney pieces. Repeat the layers, mounding them slightly in the center. Sprinkle with the remaining seasoned flour. Pour over the oyster liquor, adding enough water to reach to half the depth of the dish.

Roll the pastry about ¼-inch thick into a circle somewhat larger than the circumference of the baking dish. Roll up on the rolling pin, center over the dish and unroll. Trim the pastry with a sharp knife even with the edge of the dish. Cut a long narrow strip of pastry and place all around the edge of the pie. With the tines of a fork, make a design all around, pressing the pastry down firmly.

Beat the egg yolk with 1 tablespoon of water and brush the edge of the pastry well. Roll out any remaining pastry and cut into decorative leaf shapes. Make a small hole in the center of the pastry to allow steam to escape and arrange the pastry leaves around it. Now brush the entire surface of the pie with the beaten egg yolk.

Place in a preheated 350° oven and bake for 1½ hours. Very good served with a mélange of carrots, celery, and green beans, followed by a cool sherbet.

What is shepherd's pie?   Also called cottage pie, it is not, as Theodora Fitzgibbon points out in *The Art of British Cooking,* the most exciting of English dishes. Essentially it is ground beef, with onion and seasonings, topped with mashed potatoes, then baked and served with a rather sharp relish.

Does "gravy and beef" mean the same as "beef and gravy" on a can? No. In *Today's Food Market* (Kansas State University) they say that if the label on frozen or canned meat products reads "gravy and beef" it means you are buying more gravy than meat; but if, on the other hand, beef is first, and the label reads "beef and gravy" there will be more meat. A nice little tip that should teach us all to read labels starting at the left.

What is meat glaze?   The French term is *glace de viande.* It is beef stock that has been boiled down slowly to the consistency of syrup, which becomes a hard jelly when cold. Used to give a flavor boost to sauces and soups, it is so concentrated you use it only in very small quantities, such as half a teaspoon or so. Dissolved in hot water, meat glaze can be used in place of stock. Any good cookbook (*Mas-*

tering the Art of French Cooking, for example) will give a recipe and we should point out it is relatively easy to make. Lacking your own glaze, we have found Bovril a good substitute.

What is jerky?   Originally beef or other meat cut into long strips and dried in the sun. Actually a method of preserving meat used by the frontiersmen of the Old West. Today, however, we have the 20th-century version—strips of meat dried scientifically in sanitary plants. The taste is similar to dried beef with its salty, beefy flavor and, as *Today's Food Market* of Kansas State University wisely points out, "If you are a snacker, you might as well eat nutritious ones."

How did veal birds get their name?   Craig Claiborne, author of *The New York Times Cookbook* says: "The chef who first dubbed the dish may have been a Frenchman with a sense of humor. He called his meat rollups *oiseaux sans têtes* or 'headless birds.' The Italians turned the phrase and called them *uccellini* or *uccelleti scappati,* 'little birds that flew away.'" So, when the recipe reached these shores, the dish became, typically, plain veal birds. Whatever the language, they are basically the same: thin slices of meat (generally veal, although beef is frequently used), filled and rolled, then braised. A further note from Mr. Claiborne: "Some Italian menus call veal birds *bracioline and rollatine.*"

VEAL BIRDS, ITALIAN STYLE

¾ cup ham, finely chopped (about
   1 large slice)
1 clove garlic, peeled and minced
6 to 8 sprigs parsley, minced
Salt
Black pepper, freshly ground
1½ pounds veal scaloppine, cut
   into thin, even slices
Flour
3 tablespoons butter

3 tablespoons olive oil
¼ cup dry white wine
2 cups chicken broth, your own or
   canned
½ small onion, peeled and
   chopped fine
1 small carrot, peeled and sliced
   thin
1 rib celery, cubed
½ teaspoon rosemary

The slices of veal should be similar in size so that when the "birds" are finished, they will look more or less alike.

Combine the ham, garlic, parsley, salt, and pepper to taste. Spoon a little of the mixture onto the veal slices. Roll up and fasten securely with toothpicks. Dredge with flour. Now heat the butter and oil in a heavy skillet. Brown the "birds" on all sides. Add the wine and cook, over moderate heat, until almost all the wine has evaporated. Add the chicken stock and simmer for 10 minutes. Add the vegetables and rosemary and cook another 20 minutes. Serves 6.

Can veal be broiled?   No. It has too little fat to broil well.

Are piccate and scaloppine the same thing?   Yes, both mean small squares of veal (*piccata* is the singular), sliced very thin, then pounded, usually cut off the leg. *Escalope* is the French equivalent of the Italian scaloppine. The Oxford French Dictionary translates *escalope* thus: "Collop, veal cutlet." Collop, in English culinary terms, means a "small cut of meat" and cutlet a small cut of meat (usually mutton) cut off the ribs. In the United States, however, veal cutlet is the same cut as the top of the round of beef, the "eye," the bottom or the tip. Germans and Austrians call this cut *schnitzel*. Some people mistakenly call veal chops cutlets.

What is "spring" lamb?   Since lamb is now available the year round, the old familiar designations, "Spring" and "Genuine Spring Lamb" have correctly been abandoned since they are meaningless. The age of the lamb in U.S. markets averages less than 8 months, but the lamb can be as young as 5 months.

SAUTÉED BABY LAMB CHOPS

4 chops per person	Freshly ground pepper
Butter	Watercress garnish
Salt	

   This unusually delicious and succulent method of cooking lamb chops involves a discussion with your butcher. What you want and what you must insist on, is having him take the ribs and cut them in two, *right through the bone*. Some butchers do this by machine. At the same time have him cut off the bone ends, but not "French" the chops. This gives you small thin chops that cook in seconds or almost.
   Before you start cooking, have ready a platter warming in a low (140°) oven. This is important because lamb cools much more quickly than other meats. *To cook,* heat 3 to 4 tablespoons of butter in a large heavy skillet.

When hot, add only as many chops as will fit into the pan without crowding. Turn the chops once when you add them to the pan so they are buttered on both sides—best done with your fingers. Sauté over a high heat, a total of 3 minutes, turning once. They will take on only a little color and will be pink inside—the perfect way to serve lamb—any lamb. As the chops cook, lift to the heated platter and keep warm. Season with salt and freshly ground pepper and garnish with a bouquet of fresh watercress.

What is New Zealand lamb? Lamb (legs, shoulder, rib racks, and loins) imported into this country from New Zealand. All frozen and available nationally. It is "spring" lamb (see above) in the sense that it is young lamb about 4 to 6 months old. As is true of American lamb, it is inspected, not only by the New Zealand Department of Agriculture, but on arrival here, by the U.S. Department of Agriculture. The distinctive flavor is a result of the grasslands on which the ewes feed.

What are netted lamb roasts? A number of years ago the American Lamb Council originated netted boned lamb roasts (leg, shoulder, and breast). The cut surfaces are rubbed with powdered egg white which acts as a binder; the meat is then rolled and encased by machine in a tube of elastic netting. The meats can be roasted, after thawing, in their nets which are removed after roasting or they can be sliced to whatever thickness you like, then broiled or sautéed. Available in good food stores nationally.

What is "hothouse" lamb? Extremely young lamb that weighs, all told, about 15 pounds, dressed weight, and "baby" lambs are those that weigh in at 8 to 10 pounds. Both are sold in quarters only. The hind quarter, the meatiest, of a "hothouse" will serve 4 at most, while that of a "baby" will serve one trencherman or two more restrained eaters. Lamb that is more than 1½ to 2 years old (in short, sheep) is called mutton, a meat that is greatly underestimated by Americans, but in England and France a saddle of mutton is considered a great delicacy.

How do you make a paper frill (papillote)? These paper frills used to finish the bone of a lamb chop or a ham are made like this: Cut a long rectangle of baking parchment, approximately 25 inches long and 5 inches wide. Fold lengthwise. Along the folded side, cut strips one-fourth inch apart, down to about half the width of the paper.

Now unfold the paper and lay it flat on the table, then fold it the opposite way. Secure the two ends with a staple or a piece of Scotch tape. Roll the paper up on a pencil or the end of your finger. Secure with Scotch tape or a dab of glue. Frills can, of course, be bought ready made in some shops but they're not as pretty as those you can make yourself. Besides, they're rather fun to make.

What is the "fell" on lamb?   A paper-like covering that should be left on leg roasts but is removed by the butcher from steaks and chops.

Do fully cooked hams need further cooking?   Yes. To an internal temperature of 140° in a preheated 325° oven. Here is a chart from the National Livestock and Meat Board to guide you.

Type Ham	Weight	Baking Time (approx.)
Boneless	3 to 5 pounds	1½ to 1¾ hours
	7 to 10 pounds	2½ to 3 hours
	10 to 12 pounds	3 to 3½ hours
	12 to 14 pounds	3½ to 4 hours
Bone-in	10 to 13 pounds	3 to 3½ hours
	13 to 16 pounds	3½ to 4 hours
Semi-boneless	4 to 6½ pounds	1¾ to 2½ hours
	10 to 12 pounds	3 to 3½ hours
Picnic	4 to 8 pounds	1¾ to 2¾ hours
Canned Hams	1½ to 3 pounds	1 to 1½ hours
	3 to 7 pounds	1½ to 2 hours
	7 to 10 pounds	2 to 2½ hours
	10 to 13 pounds	2½ to 3 hours

How long should cook-before-eating hams be cooked?   They should be cooked to an internal temperature of 170° in a preheated 325° oven. Here is a chart to use as a guide.

Type Ham	Weight	Baking Time (approx.)
Boneless	8 to 11 pounds	2½ to 3¼ hours
	11 to 14 pounds	3¼ to 4 hours
Bone-in	5 to 7½ pounds	3 to 3¼ hours
	10 to 12 pounds	3½ to 4 hours
	12 to 15 pounds	4 to 4½ hours
	15 to 18 pounds	4½ to 5 hours
	18 to 22 pounds	5 to 6 hours
Picnic	4 to 8 pounds	2½ to 4 hours
Shoulder Roll	2 to 3 pounds	1½ to 2 hours

What does "water added" on a ham label mean? The U.S. Department of Agriculture tells us that it means the ham contains up to 10% added moisture after it has been cured and processed. Under Federal inspection regulations, if the added water goes beyond 10%, the product would have to be labeled "imitation ham."

What is the difference between a cured and a smoked ham? Cured ham, the upper part of a pig's hind leg, is ham that has been preserved by salting. The art of curing or "corning" involves either a liquid salt cure generally called brine or pickle cure, or a dry salt cure. The term "corned" comes from the Old Norse word, *korn* which refers to grain. Since grain or granulated salt is used, meats preserved in this manner are called "corned"—like corned beef. The methods of curing vary from place to place and country to country but regardless of the method, the meat is labeled fully cooked or ready-to-cook. A smoked ham is first cured (see above), then smoked over hard wood (hickory is the most common) for a given length of time, depending on the size and the processor. Like cured hams, they are labeled fully cooked or ready-to-cook.

What are smoked shoulder butts and picnic hams? Technically, they are not hams since they come from the shoulder, not the hind leg of the pig, but they have characteristics similar to ham. Smoked shoulder butts weighing from 2 to 3 pounds are boneless, can be baked, simmered in water, sliced and pan fried, or broiled. Picnics, also shoulder cuts, are available in two forms: cook-before-eating or fully cooked.

What precisely are country hams? Hams that have been given a dry salt cure, then smoked and aged and frequently labeled with such names as Smithfield, Tennessee, Georgia, Kentucky, etc., to indicate the area in which they were produced. Most of us are inclined to think of country hams as Virginia hams because hams were first cured and smoked in the United States in Smithfield, Virginia, 300 years ago. The razor-backed hogs used for these hams are raised on a diet of peanuts which gives the meat a unique quality and flavor. Actually, they are very rich and a little goes a long way.

How long do you cook pork? As you must be aware it is important to cook pork thoroughly but that does not mean cooked to death. Pork, one of the most delicious meats, has always carried the stigma of trichinosis. Now, with modern technology, it has been well established that once pork has reached an internal temperature of 137°, it is perfectly safe. However, it should be cooked to 165° to 170° to make it edible and succulent. The most reliable way to test roasted and braised meat for doneness is with a reliable meat thermometer (see page 142). Here is a roasting chart from the National Livestock and Meat Board for you to use as a guide.

ROASTING
(325° to 350° F. oven temperature)

Cut	Approximate Weight (in pounds)	Meat Thermometer Reading	Cooking Time * (in minutes per pound)
Loin			
Center	3 to 5	170° F.	30 to 35
Half	5 to 7	170° F.	35 to 40
End	3 to 4	170° F.	40 to 45
Roll	3 to 5	170° F.	35 to 40
Boneless Top	2 to 4	170° F.	30 to 35
Crown	4 to 6	170° F.	35 to 40
Picnic Shoulder			
Bone-in	5 to 8	170° F.	30 to 35
Rolled	3 to 5	170° F.	35 to 40
Boston Shoulder	4 to 6	170° F.	40 to 45
Leg (fresh ham)			
Whole (bone-in)	12 to 16	170° F.	30 to 35
Whole (boneless)	10 to 14	170° F.	30 to 35
Half (bone-in)	5 to 8	170° F.	35 to 40
Tenderloin	½ to 1	170° F.	45 to 60
Spareribs			1½ to 2½ hours

* Based on meat taken directly from refrigerator.

BRAISING

Cut	Approximate Weight or Thickness	Approximate Total Cooking Time
Chops, fresh	¾ to 1½ inches	45 to 60 minutes
Spareribs	2 to 3 pounds	1½ hours
Cubes	1 to 1¼ inches	45 to 60 minutes

Are a fresh ham and leg of pork the same thing? Yes. It's uncured pork and one of the most delicious cuts of meat you can imagine—cooked properly. Pork must be cooked thoroughly in order to kill any trichinae, the source of trichinosis. But that doesn't mean it has to be cooked to death. Recent research at Iowa State University showed that fresh hams cooked in a preheated 325° or 350° oven to an internal temperature of 170°—as against the old 185°—were more succulent and flavorful.

PORK IN A CASSEROLE

4 tablespoons butter
4 tablespoons vegetable oil
6-pound piece shoulder end of the loin of pork, cracked and tied
2 carrots, peeled and sliced thin
1 medium onion, peeled and minced
1 large (or 2 small) cloves garlic, peeled and crushed

2 tablespoons Calvados, brandy, or vodka
1 cup *vin rosé*
Salt
Freshly ground pepper
6 to 8 medium-sized new potatoes, peeled

Heat *half the butter and half the oil,* in a heavy enameled casserole. When hot, brown the meat on all sides, including both ends. Lift from the casserole and pour off all the fat. Add the remaining butter and oil, the carrots, onion, garlic, and meat. Heat the Calvados, ignite, and pour flaming over the pork. When the flames die out add the wine. Salt and pepper the meat. Bring the liquid up to a boil, then reduce heat to a simmer, cover, and cook in a preheated 350° oven for 30 minutes per pound (3 hours) or until a meat thermometer registers 165° to 170°. Thirty minutes before the meat is cooked, add the potatoes (if they are large, cut in two). Turn them in the juices to coat them well.

To serve, place the meat, surrounded by the potatoes, on a heated serving platter and keep warm. Skim off as much fat as possible from the sauce and taste for seasoning. Place over a high heat and bring to a brisk boil. Pour (do not strain) into a heated sauceboat.

Can pork chops be broiled? They can but it's not the best way to cook them since pork needs slow cooking. Broiling tends to dry them out and make them hard and tough. Braising or cooking in the oven gives better results.

What is brawn?   In France, called *fromage de tête,* it is usually made
with a pig's head but some English recipes call for the feet only, with
the addition of a piece of ham. The herbs, vegetables, and spices used
vary considerably from area to area. Essentially, brawn is a mold that
can be every bit as good as a pâté. It is customarily served cold with
a cold mustard sauce.

What is gammon?   The English term for the cured foreleg of a pig.
Gammon may or may not be smoked.

Is mold on bacon harmful?   Of course not and it does not necessarily
mean the bacon is spoiled. Usually it can be trimmed or scraped off.
Obviously, if the bacon smells rancid, it should be discarded.

What is maple-syrup-cured bacon?   Broadly speaking, all bacon available to us is cured with some sugar, but the introduction of maple
syrup (which started in Vermont) is relatively new. Not only bacon
but ham and sausage with a maple-sugar cure are now in our markets. Canada is currently sending us their famous Canadian bacon
with a maple-sugar cure. You'll find on eating any one of these products there is a mild, but distinctive, maple flavor.

Is it true that hot dogs are fully cooked when purchased?   Yes. Frank-
furters, wieners, franks, or hot dogs—whatever the name—are seasoned, smoked, and fully cooked. Recipes differ from packer to
packer but, generally, a frankfurter is made of 60% beef, 40% pork,
and varying spices. The kosher variety is all beef, with or without
garlic. Today, hot dogs are available in every size from the tiny cocktail frank to the gargantuan 12-incher spawned in Texas. Where else?

Are wieners (hot dogs) smoked?   Yes. Smoking is part of the processing, but it is not listed on the label.

Are pork sausages sold by the number of links or by weight?   By
weight. Since the sausage is packed in natural casings which vary in
size and diameter, there would be variance in the number of links.

What is Toad-in-the-Hole?   An English dish, as you might guess, beloved by children, essentially broiled sausages topped with a light
batter, then baked in the oven.

T O A D - I N - T H E - H O L E

1 pound pork sausage links	White pepper, freshly ground
2 cups flour	2 eggs, well beaten
½ teaspoon baking powder	1 cup milk, about
Salt	

Combine the flour, baking powder, salt and pepper. Then stir in the eggs. Add just enough milk to make a not-too-thin batter. It should just drop from the spoon. Now beat and allow it to stand until the sausages are ready.

Broil the sausages under a high heat until brown outside. Turn once. They do not need to be cooked through. Arrange in a medium-sized greased, ovenproof dish, pour the batter over all and bake in a preheated 375° oven for 40 minutes or until the batter has risen and is a lovely golden brown. Serves 4.

Are rabbits available in meat markets? The U.S. Department of Agriculture tells us they are. U.S.D.A.'s Consumer and Marketing Service inspects rabbits in all service plants that request it and also grades them for quality. The U.S. Grade A shield is your guarantee of a fully fleshed, top-quality animal. Most commercially produced rabbits are marketed when they are 8 to 10 weeks old (these are known as "fryers"), weigh from 1½ to 3½ pounds, and are ready to cook. The flavor of young rabbits is not unlike that of chicken. They can be roasted, broiled, barbecued, or fried. Mature rabbits, 8 months or older, weigh around 4 pounds, and have a firmer, more coarsely grained meat than fryers.

What is chine bone? The whole or a piece of the backbone of an animal with adjoining parts, cut for cooking. With ribs of beef, the rack or crown of lamb, and loin of pork—where the chops are all in one piece—you should always have the chine bone removed by the butcher. Some butchers tie it back onto a loin or crown to seal in the juices, and it is removed before serving. As a matter of record, the ribs must be cracked between for easy carving and serving.

What does civet mean in cookery? It's the French for a *ragoût* (meaning stew) of game. Primarily rabbit, hare, or venison.

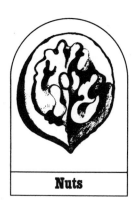

Nuts

What nuts originated in the Western Hemisphere?   Cashew and brazil nuts—Brazil; pinon nuts (also called Indian and pine nuts)—Mexico; Pecan—indigenous to both the United States and Mexico; peanut (not a true nut but a legume)—Peru and Uruguay.

How do you chop nuts?   Chopping can be done in the electric blender to the degree of coarseness needed or it can be done by hand with a good French knife. Hold the tip of the knife in your left hand and move the handle up, down, and around in a semicircle with the right hand, pulling the nuts together with the blade as you work.

How do you grate nuts?   It depends on how they are going to be used. For a very fine grind, you can use the electric blender but certain recipes (the torte family, for example, where nuts take the place of flour) call for a softer texture. For this the hand-operated nut grater is essential. An inexpensive little gadget that belongs in every "cooking" kitchen.

How many actual peanuts are there in peanut butter?   By law, peanut butter must be at least 90% peanuts with the addition of no more than 10% of other ingredients and it must not contain more than 55% oil. Seasonings and stabilizers may be added but non-sugar sweeteners, preservatives, artificial flavors, and color additives are illegal.

How are peanuts available today?   In the shell, salted or unsalted; salted, out of the shell, vacuum packed in jars, in cans or transparent bags; salted Spanish peanuts, the little ones with red skins, are packed the same way. Both types are available "dry-roasted" which means they have been roasted in the oven as against deep-fat fried (fewer calories).

How is processed coconut available today?   Flaked, in 3½-ounce and 7-ounce cans, and 7-ounce and 14-ounce bags; shredded, in 4-, 8-, and 16-ounce bags, and 4-ounce cans; cookie coconut, in 7-ounce bags; and toasted sweetened coconut, in 4½-ounce cans.

Where do macadamia nuts come from?   Those in our markets come from Hawaii but the nut was first discovered in Australia. Golden brown and tasting something like an almond but resembling an overgrown filbert, they are generally available roasted and salted, packed in glass jars. They make an interesting cocktail bite.

What are pignolias?   Pine nuts or pine kernels, also known as *pignons, Indian nuts, pinons* and *pinoli,* they come from the cones of the pine tree. About ¼-inch to ¾-inch long, cream colored and slightly oil flavored, they are used extensively in Italian cooking in meat and game dishes, salads, also sugared in small cakes, biscuits, and macaroons. Available in the United States roasted, salted, or plain. Generally marketed in jars.

What is walnut oil?   An oil made from walnuts, imported from France, used primarily in making salad dressings. The flavor is most distinctive and a taste for it often has to be cultivated.

Is an English walnut the same as a California walnut?   First, let's straighten out one thing. The English don't grow walnuts commercially. You will find walnut trees in England, however, and the English eat the walnuts. The Persian walnut brought to England by the Romans came to be known as Circassian walnut and was used extensively by English furniture makers. It was later erroneously called "English walnut," and that's the circuitous route by which "English" got tacked onto the nuts. The walnuts you buy in your market are grown, processed, and packed in California. Available in 1- and 2-

pound cellophane bags; shelled, in 3-ounce to 2-pound clear bags and in 4- and 8-ounce vacuum cans.

What are pickled walnuts? Walnuts that are picked green before the nutshell hardens, about the middle of July, my English friends tell me, pierced thoroughly with a needle or similar tool, then placed in a brine which is changed every three days for nine days. They are then washed and put in the sun on trays until they are quite black. At that point, they are placed in jars and covered with cold spiced vinegar. An English relish, pickled walnuts are served with cold meat or meat pies, sometimes in the pie.

What are dragees? Traditionally, almonds coated with an enamel-like, liqueur-flavored sugar in pastel colors. It is customary in France to give little boxes of dragees at christenings and weddings. For christenings, the coating is white; for other occasions usually pale tints.

Rice, Pasta, and Potato Substitutes

Should white rice be washed before cooking? The four types of white rice available are: regular milled (long grain, medium grain, and short grain—sometimes called pearl), converted, quick, and pre-cooked. Most good cookbooks call for washing the regular milled rice, prior to cooking, in cold water until the water is no longer cloudy—actually, to get rid of the starch. With converted rice, quick and pre-cooked, this is not necessary.

JULIA AUGIER'S RICE AND BEANS

This is one of those recipes that doesn't spell out, by name, what it really is since it's a combination of pork, kidney beans, seasonings, and tomato sauce served with freshly cooked rice. A hearty, good-to-eat, inexpensive stew right out of Puerto Rico.

3 pounds (6 slices) of pork, cut off the end of the loin
2 tablespoons butter
2 tablespoons vegetable oil
1 very large onion, peeled and coarsely chopped
1 bay leaf
½ teaspoon thyme

Salt
Freshly ground pepper
3 cans (8-ounce size) tomato sauce
1 tablespoon tomato paste
Grated rind of 1 lemon
3 cans (1 pound, 4-ounce size) kidney beans

When you buy the meat, have the butcher cut out the bone or do it yourself. Then cut each slice into 3 pieces about of a size, cutting off any surplus fat.

Heat the butter and oil in a large, heavy skillet. When hot, sauté the meat, a few pieces at a time (don't crowd the pan) until lightly browned on both sides. As you cook the meat, lift it to a heavy 4- to 5-quart oven-proof casserole that can go to the table. Add the onion, bay leaf, salt and pepper to taste, tomato sauce, tomato paste, and *1 cup of water*. Bring to a boil. Add the lemon rind and all the beans with their liquid. Fold the beans into the mixture with two spoons, taking care not to break the beans. Bring up to a boil again. Cover and place in a preheated 325° oven for 1 hour or until the meat is tender when pierced with a fork. Taste for seasoning.

While the beans are cooking, cook the rice and keep warm. Serve in large, heated soup bowls or on plates with a serving of rice. Serves about 8.

N O T E : In the event any beans are left (doubtful), purée them in the blender to make a nice bit of soup.

How long do you cook white rice when it is added to a soup? It depends on what rice you are using but, in any event, for a shorter time than if the rice were to be used as a separate vegetable, when it should be fluffy and dry. Long-grain rice dropped into the boiling liquid should cook about 15 minutes; converted rice, which takes somewhat longer than long grain, about 20 minutes; precooked rice or quick rice should be added to the hot liquid just long enough to heat through.

Is wild rice available in cans? Yes. Cooked, ready to serve. Although it does not match freshly cooked wild rice, it is surprisingly good. And the price for a 14-ounce can, which will serve 3 to 4, depending on how it's prepared, is modest indeed when compared with uncooked rice at around $8 a pound. Wild rice mixed with long-grain rice and seasonings is now available in 6-ounce packages. Good, too.

What is rijsttafel? It's the Indonesian name for "rice table." In Indonesia, where rice is the principal food, each person is served a plate of hot rice to which he adds any combination of many dishes, such as fish, shrimp, chicken, pork, beef—all very spicy—finely chopped, hard-cooked eggs, chutney, ground fresh coconut, fried and chopped bacon, raw or cooked raisins, chopped peanuts, thinly sliced cucumbers, fried onions, sliced bananas. In short, almost anything that is available.

How do you eat pasta correctly? Many Americans, to the horror of Italians, use a fork and a spoon, twirling the spaghetti in the bowl of the spoon to wrap it around the fork. Correctly, you use a fork only and this is how you do it: Push a small portion of the pasta on your plate away from the rest, then twirl it until most of it is entwined on the fork.

How do you serve pasta? Jack Denton Scott, who has written the most exhaustive study on the subject, perhaps in any language, *The Complete Book of Pasta,* recommends that rather than drain the pasta through a sieve, you lift it from the boiling pot with a long fork, letting the water drain off into the cooking pot, then place it in a large warm bowl in which you have melted some butter. He allows ½ cup (1 stick) of butter to a pound of pasta. When all the pasta is in the bowl, add a couple of turns of the peppermill, then toss the pasta gently with a wooden fork and spoon. Finally, add freshly grated Parmesan cheese, then toss again. At this point, the pasta is placed in individual heated bowls (big soup plates are ideal, actually) and is ready to receive a heaping tablespoon of sauce.

Is pesto available canned? Yes, but if you can get your hands on some fresh basil, you'd do well to make it yourself. Incidentally, basil is very easy to grow and not easy to buy—fresh, that is. The following recipe should inspire you to make some pesto yourself.

PESTO ALLA GENOVESE
(Genoese Basil Sauce)

This marvelous sauce, described by Elizabeth David as "the best pasta sauce in the whole of Italy," is served with spaghetti, lasagne, tagliatelle—in fact, any pasta you fancy. It is also used as a flavoring in minestrone (a tablespoon or so stirred in at the last minute gives a most delicious flavor). Further, it is very good mixed into baked potatoes in place of butter. The only hitch to this great sauce is that you must have fresh basil. However, once the sauce is made it can be frozen, so any foresighted pesto fan can make up a big batch in the summer and savor it in the dead of winter. We suggest freezing it in individual ice-cube containers.

2 to 3 cups fresh basil leaves, tightly packed
2 cloves garlic, peeled and minced
A little salt
1 tablespoon pine nuts or chopped walnuts

1 to 1½ cups olive oil
2 ounces Parmesan cheese (about 8 tablespoons, grated)
2 ounces Sardo cheese (about 4 tablespoons, grated)

In Italy pesto is made by pounding the mixture to a paste in a mortar, but we've found it much easier and just as good when done in the electric blender.

Combine the basil leaves (no stems) with garlic, salt, nuts, and 1 cup of oil in the container of the blender. Blend at high speed until smooth. Pour into a bowl and stir in both cheeses. If it seems too thick (the sauce should have the consistency of creamed butter) beat in more oil. This makes about 1½ to 2 cups. Since you allow about 2 tablespoons of pesto for each serving, this amount goes quite a long way.

To serve, place a serving of the pasta in a heated soup plate; add 2 tablespoons or so of the cold pesto and a big lump of sweet butter. The butter and sauce are mixed into the pasta, individually, at the table, Grated Parmesan cheese is served separately.

What are herb noodles? Invented by Rosa Tusa, food editor of *The Palm Beach Post,* they are egg noodles with a blend of aromatic herbs. An idea actually conceived years ago but only brought to fruition relatively recently. Now available nationally in 8-ounce packages.

HERB NOODLES, ROSA TUSA STYLE

1 8-ounce package herb noodles, cooked and drained
3 tablespoons butter

1 cup heavy cream
½ cup grated Parmesan cheese (about ⅛ pound)

Cook the noodles according to package directions. Place the cream and butter in a shallow ovenproof dish or casserole and keep warm in the oven (140°). Add the drained hot noodles and toss lightly. Add the cheese and toss again. Serve immediately in heated soup plates or bowls.

What are cellophane noodles? Fine, extremely delicate "noodles" made from meng beans, the same beans from which the Chinese get bean sprouts. They are air-dried and translucent. As China-born Dorothy Lee of General Foods tells us, "These noodles are not used like pasta, despite the name, but rather as an ingredient or garnish."

Are grits, corn meal, and corn flour related? Yes. They all come from corn. Grits are a medium grind; corn meal, a finer grind; and corn flour, the finest grind of all.

How are grits used? Originally, they were used interchangeably with hominy and were used as a vegetable or a breakfast dish (see below) but today they are used in more sophisticated ways. Such as: Creole shrimp in a grits ring; made into a ring with ham and cheese; used to make spoon bread, grits au gratin; etc. Grits, extremely popular in the Deep South, are used primarily in place of potatoes.

What's the difference between hominy grits and hominy? Grits are a medium grind of dry corn with hull and germ removed, and must be cooked before eating; modern hominy (the name comes from the Indian, "rockahominy") is the whole (hulled) grain of corn, soaked in lime water (in the old days, it was lye) until it swells. It is then canned with water and salt, ready to heat and eat.

Is there any difference between white and yellow corn meal? No, just color, and they can be used interchangeably, although there is a slight difference in the nutritional value and flavor.

JAMES BEARD'S POLENTA

1½ cups white or yellow corn meal   Butter
4½ cups water   Parmesan cheese, freshly grated
1 tablespoon salt

Bring 3½ cups of the water to a boil. Pour the corn meal into the top of a big double boiler, then stir in the remaining cup of *cold* water. When well mixed, add the boiling water, mix well, place over a very low heat and cook, stirring constantly, until the mixture comes to a boil. Stir in the salt, cover, and place over simmering water for 1½ hours. Take off the heat and stir in 2 to 3 tablespoons of butter and lots of freshly grated cheese.

Butter a pan about 10 x 12 inches in diameter and add the polenta. It should be no more than ½-inch thick. Smooth the surface with a wet spatula, then chill.

To serve, cut the polenta into small circles with a cookie cutter, then arrange, overlapping in a serving dish that can go to the table. Allow to stand at room temperature. Before serving, coat generously with melted butter and top that with a good coating of the cheese. Place in the oven until hot through, then slide under the broiler just long enough to brown lightly. Serves 6 at least.

CORN MEAL SOUFFLÉ

2 cups milk	1 teaspoon salt
⅓ cup white or yellow corn meal	Few grains cayenne
1 tablespoon butter	3 eggs, separated
3 tablespoons grated Cheddar or Swiss cheese	2 extra egg whites

Heat the milk to the boiling point. Stir in the corn meal and butter. Reduce heat to moderate and stir in the cheese. Cook, giving the mixture an occasional stir, until you have a thick mush. Season with salt and cayenne. Take off the heat. Beat the egg yolks until thick and creamy. Combine with the corn meal mixture and cook, stirring constantly, for 1 minute. Cool.

Beat the egg whites until they hold stiff shiny peaks when the beater is held straight up. Beat about a third of the whites into the batter with a wire whisk. Fold in the remainder with a rubber spatula. Pour into an ungreased 1-quart baking dish or soufflé mold and bake in a preheated 350° oven for 45 minutes or until the top is crusty. Serve to 3 with cold sliced ham and a green salad.

What is bulgar? Also spelled bulgur, burghol, and bourghol, it is a cracked wheat, a staple food for centuries in the Middle East. It has a rich, nut-like flavor, and is rather chewy. It is also known by other names such as kasha and groats or grits. It can be used in place of rice or substituted for rice in many recipes. "Kibby," the national dish of Syria and Lebanon, is made with bulgar. Bulgar is available in this country, precooked and packaged in three forms: fine, medium, and coarse.

What is couscous?   It's the name of a dish (an amazing mixture of chicken or mutton, beef, vegetables, chick peas, seasonings, etc.) extremely popular in Morocco and other Middle Eastern countries; and/or the name of the semolina or cracked wheat (bulgar; see above) that is served with it.

What is a couscous steamer like?   A large deep kettle with a steamer on top and a cover. While the meat, broth, vegetables, seasonings, etc., cook in the kettle part, the couscous (cracked wheat) steams on top, thus picking up some of the delicious odors that waft upward. *Couscousière* in French.

Sauces

What is meant by the "mother" sauces?   The four basic sauces used in French *haute cuisine* which are: sauce béchamel, sauce allemande, sauce velouté, and sauce espagnole, from which almost all other sauces are made.

What is sauce allemande?   Veal stock thickened with a roux (butter and flour) plus cream, egg yolks, nutmeg, and lemon juice. One of the "Mother" Sauces. Allemande or German style also means dishes garnished with sauerkraut, smoked sausage, pickled pork, or noodles tossed in butter.

Can white sauce be cooked over a high heat?   Yes, if the sauce (*béchamel*, in French) is stirred constantly. Chefs and experienced home cooks almost invariably use high heat, but we don't recommend it for novices.

Can you freeze hollandaise?   Yes. Pour into a suitable container and place in the freezer. To thaw, bring to room temperature then place the jar in a pan of tepid, *not hot*, water.

CLASSIC HOLLANDAISE SAUCE

4 egg yolks	White pepper, freshly ground
2 tablespoons water	Dash cayenne
1½ cups (3 sticks) butter	Lemon juice
Salt	

Place the yolks and water in the top of a double boiler and beat for 1 minute with a wire whisk. Then place over simmering water and whip vigorously for 8 to 10 minutes or until the mixture is thick and creamy. Take care not to curdle the eggs. The temperature should never be so hot you cannot dip your finger into it. When perfectly combined, you can see the bottom of the pan between strokes and the sauce will be slow to cover the lines made by the whip. While you are doing this, melt the butter in a separate saucepan.

Take the mixture off the heat, place on a damp cloth to keep the pan from turning while you beat and add the hot butter very slowly, actually in dribbles, whipping constantly. Season with salt, pepper, and cayenne. Stir in the lemon juice to taste last of all. Keep warm in a pan of tepid water, *not hot,* or your sauce will separate. Makes 2 cups.

What is a sauce béarnaise? Classically it is a marvelous sauce made with a reduction of wine or tarragon vinegar to which egg yolks, then butter are added, seasoned with fresh tarragon, parsley, salt and pepper, and, if available, fresh chervil. Like hollandaise, it is served lukewarm with filet mignon, fried or boiled fish. Said to have been invented by Maître Collinet, the chef of an inn at St. Germain-en-Laye, called Henri IV, which is now Pavillon Henri IV in a suburb west of Paris. Henri IV was born in Béarn, hence the name of the sauce. Collinet, apparently, is the same man who invented *pommes soufflées,* sliced potatoes, cooked twice in deep fat which makes them puff into golden shells of hot air. Difficult for the amateur to make successfully.

SAUCE BÉARNAISE FOR STEAK

½ cup wine or tarragon vinegar	Salt
4 to 5 shallots, peeled and chopped	4 to 5 sprigs parsley, minced
White pepper, freshly ground	Good pinch dried tarragon *
4 egg yolks, slightly beaten	2 or 3 sprigs fresh chervil, minced
1½ cups (1½ sticks) sweet butter	(if available)

* If fresh tarragon is at hand, mince about 6 leaves.

Combine the vinegar, shallots, and pepper in the top of the double boiler. Cook over a high heat until there is about ¼ cup left. Cool slightly. Gradually add the beaten yolks, whipping hard and constantly with a wire whip. Place over simmering water and cook to a creamy consistency, beating constantly. Take off the heat.

Melt the butter, taking care not to let it brown. Add to the yolk mixture, drop by drop, whipping steadily. Stir in the salt to taste. Strain and add the minced parsley, tarragon, and chervil (if you have it). Like hollandaise, sauce béarnaise is served lukewarm. Keep warm over tepid, *not hot*, water. Makes about 2 cups. Delicious with filet mignon, fried or boiled fish.

SAUCE BERCY FOR STEAK

¼ cup dry white wine	¾ cup canned beef gravy
2 shallots, peeled and minced, or	2½ tablespoons butter, softened
green onion bulbs, minced	Salt
Black pepper, freshly ground	Minced parsley

Combine the wine, shallots, and pepper from a few turns of the mill in a saucepan. Place over moderate heat and cook until about 2 tablespoons of liquid remain. Mix in the beef gravy. Simmer 5 minutes. Beat together the butter, salt to taste, and minced parsley. Stir in the wine sauce. Serve with steaks.

What does marchand de vin mean? Culinarily, it means a red-wine sauce; in the world of commerce, a wine salesman.

RED WINE SAUCE FOR STEAK

2 cups red Burgundy	1 bay leaf
6 shallots, peeled and minced, or	1 cup beef broth
green onion bulbs, minced	Juice 1 lemon °
Freshly grated pepper	3 tablespoons butter
Good pinch dried thyme	Salt and pepper to taste

° Boil lemon about 2 minutes to yield more juice.

Combine the wine, shallots, pepper, thyme, and bay leaf. Bring to a boil. Reduce heat then simmer until there is about ½ cup left. Stir in the beef broth and the lemon juice. Bring to a boil again. Finally, stir in the butter. Taste for salt and pepper. Pour over the steaks which have been seasoned with salt and pepper.

Why does my gravy sometimes curdle? Probably because you have too much fat in the roasting pan. To make good, smooth gravy, pour off all but about a tablespoon of the pan drippings. Off the heat, stir in a tablespoon of flour, stirring until perfectly smooth. Put back over moderate heat and cook, stirring constantly, for 2 to 3 minutes to cook and brown the flour. Then add whatever liquids (about 2 cups) and seasonings you are using. Place over high heat and stir until gravy has thickened sufficiently. Strain through a fine sieve. For a thicker gravy, use more flour and fat at the beginning. Taste for seasoning.

What is corn flour? It's the English name for what we, in this country, call cornstarch, a white granular substance that occurs naturally in corn. It is used as a thickener in place of flour in gravies, sauces, stews, puddings, and pie and cake fillings. If used in sauce or gravies you use less cornstarch: 1 tablespoon as against 2 tablespoons of flour. Unlike flour, it gives a translucent finish to sauces and gravies and does not brown when heated. This last feature makes it very desirable in Oriental or fruit sauces. The English, you may be interested to know, make a cake with cornstarch.

Does à la russe mean Russian dressing? No. A la russe means in the Russian style. It usually indicates dishes made with horseradish, sour cream, beetroot juice, or shredded beetroot. Russian dressing is simply a mayonnaise to which other ingredients have been added. The variations are endless.

What are the different types of prepared horseradish? There are three: (1) prepared horseradish, made with grated horseradish, vinegar, and salt; (2) cream-style, which looks much like the prepared but has had cream added to it (these two can be used interchangeably); (3) horseradish sauce (this varies considerably, depending on the manufacturer), which is really a sauce, with a consistency similar to mayonnaise, made with vegetable oil, vinegar, eggs, seasonings. It is served with boiled or corned beef, tongue, or ham and is not a substitute for either prepared or cream style.

What is the best way to prepare horseradish? Scrape or peel the roots, as you would carrots, to get rid of any defects; then cut the roots into cubes, about ¼ by ¾ inches. Place in white or distilled vinegar (do not use cider vinegar because it turns the horseradish dark) of 4½ to 5% strength in these proportions: one part vinegar to four parts horseradish. Some cooks add a little salt or sugar. Blend in the electric blender to make a smooth paste. Bottled, securely capped, and refrigerated, it will keep for weeks. There is nothing to compare with fresh horseradish; if it is not available, you can always reconstitute the dried horseradish powder, available bottled in supermarkets, but it will not give you as flavorful a condiment. As a matter of record and interest, the red prepared horseradish you see in stores is colored with beet juice.

How do you make French dressing properly? The standard proportions are three parts oil (olive, vegetable, or half olive and half vegetable) to one part vinegar (wine, herb, or cider) with salt and freshly ground pepper to taste. It does not need further seasoning. However, a soupçon of prepared mustard can be added, or garlic to the extent you like it, or fresh herbs, minced. Elizabeth David, the great English food authority, says: "To my mind, these proportions are too vinegary. I seldom use less than six times as much oil as vinegar." For the interested cook, it is worth doing a bit of experimenting.

   N O T E : This dressing is called *sauce vinaigrette,* and although some American recipes call for a dash of sugar, sugar is not used by the French nor is it an improvement.

Are salad dressing and mayonnaise alike? No. Commercial salad dressing is a cooked dressing made with vegetable oil, egg yolks, vinegar, sugar, seasonings, etc., while mayonnaise is an emulsion made by whipping oil into egg yolks with vinegar and seasonings. There are something like 3,000 different brands of commercial salad dressings on the market, which include the spoon types (salad and mayonnaise) and the pourable types. Mayonnaise is the most popular of all.

CLASSIC MAYONNAISE

2 egg yolks	Salt
1 teaspoon French Dijon mustard	Freshly ground white pepper
1 tablespoon tarragon or wine vinegar	1½ cups imported peanut oil, vegetable oil or olive oil *

* In some instances you may want the flavor of olive oil. In this case, make the mayonnaise with half olive and half vegetable oil.

Place the yolks, mustard, half the vinegar, and salt and pepper to taste in a bowl. Beat for 1 minute with a wire whisk. Add the oil slowly, drop by drop, whipping vigorously and constantly until all the oil is incorporated. If the finished mayonnaise seems too thick, beat in a little extra vinegar. Makes 2 cups.

Can you freeze mayonnaise? No.

Where did the word ketchup come from? Also spelled catsup and, at one time, catchup. The *Oxford English Dictionary* dates it about 1711 and suggests the word derives from the Chinese *kôechiap* or *kê-tsiap*—pickled-fish brine. In any event, British sailors picked it up somewhere in the Far East and tried to imitate "kechap" as they called it, using mushrooms, walnuts, cucumbers, and much later, tomatoes. Maine sea captains also developed a taste for exotic Oriental sauces and with the discovery of tomatoes in Mexico, they brought the seeds home; not long after, Maine wives were serving tomato "kechap" on codfish cakes, baked beans, and meat. It's possible that today it's the most popular sauce in the world.

Is it necessary to refrigerate ketchup? Catsup or ketchup, whichever you call it, needs refrigeration only if it is not used up within a comparatively short time, the H. J. Heinz Company tells us. By that they mean within a few weeks. Oxidation is unattractive but harmless, although there is probably a slight loss of flavor. So if you use a lot of ketchup, don't refrigerate; if you don't, do refrigerate.

What is orgeat? An almond syrup perfumed with orange flower water. Not easy to find in the United States, except in New Orleans, where it is used extensively.

What is caramel?   A sugar syrup cooked until it turns a light, nut brown. Used as a flavoring or coloring, for coating a mold, or for coating such things as cream puffs.

How do you make caramel syrup?   Combine ⅔ cup of granulated sugar with ⅓ cup of water in a small, heavy saucepan. Boil over a moderate heat, shaking the pan occasionally until the syrup turns a light, nut brown. This will take 3 to 4 minutes. Take off the heat as soon as the syrup has reached the right color. Do not allow it to darken too much or it will turn bitter.

    N O T E : It must be used immediately.

What is chocolate syrup?   A combination of chocolate or cocoa flavoring, sweetening, water, salt, and flavorings. Used to make chocolate milk or over puddings.

What is commercial chocolate sauce?   Just what you'd think. A sauce that is essentially the same as chocolate syrup but heavier in density because of the addition of milk, cream, and/or butter. Use as you would any chocolate sauce.

What exactly is maple syrup?   Pure maple syrup (the government seems to prefer to spell it "sirup" despite all the civilized people and packers who continue to spell it the original way) is made by boiling down the sap from maple trees. The Agricultural Research Service of the U.S. Department of Agriculture tells us that the government standards for table maple syrup are: U.S. Grade AA (Fancy), U.S. Grade A, and U.S. Grade B. "The principal grade-determining factor is color—U.S. Fancy being the lightest. Other considerations are density (thinness or thickness), flavor, and lack of cloudiness."
    Pure maple syrup, much more readily available than many people realize, can even be bought direct from the farm. It is worth noting that it is one of the few products still processed "down on the farm." Although most Americans are inclined to associate maple syrup exclusively with Vermont, it is also produced in New York (New York and Vermont lead in production), Maine, Maryland, Massachusetts, Michigan, New Hampshire, Ohio, Pennsylvania, West Virginia, and Wisconsin.

Blended syrups are made of sugar syrup with maple syrup added for flavor—the most usual proportions being 85% sugar syrup to 15% high-flavored maple syrup. Imitation maple syrup is sugar syrup with imitation flavor, and it tastes exactly like that. Other maple products include: maple cream (sometimes called butter); soft maple-sugar candies; and crystalline honey-maple spread, a combination of honey and maple syrup. Maple syrup is exclusively North American (Canada also produces it) and we have the Indians to thank for teaching us newcomers how to use it.

What is Apple Syrup?   Made from apple juice and cane sugar by a special formula, it is bright red in color and has the consistency of real maple syrup. The delicate flavor, reminiscent of apple jelly, is delicious over pancakes, waffles, etc., and very pretty and good over ice cream. It can also be used to baste a ham or, if you will, to make a Tom Collins. The makers suggest, too, that it can be used to bake apples, together with small cinnamon candies and a little water, resulting in an unusually delicious dessert. You'll find it is somewhat less sweet than maple syrup.

What makes the difference between light and dark corn syrup?   They are both pure corn syrup but the dark has had a small percentage of refiner's syrup which gives it its color and also adds some flavor. Light corn syrup, with the addition of sugar, salt, and vanilla, is blander than the dark. They can be used interchangeably, although you would not use the dark in light candies. Both are used to make candy, certain frostings, and sometimes a small amount is used to prevent sugar from crystalizing when making syrup.

Why does molasses sometimes taste bitter?   Because it has sulphur in it. There are three major types of molasses on the market: one unsulphured and two edible sulphured. Unsulphured molasses from the West Indies is made from sun-ripened sugar cane. It is not, as is true of sulphured molasses, a by-product of sugar cane that has been treated with sulphur fumes during the sugar-extracting process. The unsulphured is, obviously, the most desirable since it is an absolutely pure, natural sweetener that belongs in such old-fashioned American dishes as baked beans (see page 233) and molasses pie. For the record, blackstrap molasses, once popularized by food faddists, is primarily sold to producers of animal feeds and industrial alcohol. It is as black as the inside of your hat with a harsh, bitter taste.

HARD SAUCE

Work or cream ⅓ cup of sweet butter until soft. Then gradually work in 1 cup sifted confectioners' sugar. Flavor with 1 teaspoon of vanilla or 2 tablespoons of cognac. Good on apple pie as well as steamed pudding.

**Seasonings, Spices,
Herbs, and Sweeteners**

What is the shelf life of spices and herbs?　You can't be specific about
this. It depends on how quickly you use them up. Once there is no
longer a full, fresh pungency (take a sniff) they should be discarded
and replaced. Since they are relatively inexpensive it's false economy
to "use up" herbs and spices that no longer can contribute any flavor
to food. To store, both spices and herbs should be kept in a cool,
dry place away from light and care should be taken to replace the
covers securely after use.

How can you test the strength of spices and herbs?　By your nose.
Take the whole spices (cinnamon sticks, ginger roots, peppercorns,
etc.) and compare the difference in aroma when you break them up
a bit. Whole, their aromas and flavors are pretty well sealed, but
when you cut them up or break or grind them, you release the good
perfumes. With whole leaf herbs (oregano, thyme, basil, etc.) rub
them between the palms of your hands, then cup your hands and
savor their good smells. Or, chew a little bit of each spice or herb
(take a sip of water between so you won't mix flavors). By doing
this you can not only determine their strength but fix the flavors in
your mind. It seems superfluous to point out that fresh, high-quality
spices and herbs are a prerequisite if your cooking is to be high
quality, too.

What is the difference between sweet herbs, salad herbs, and pot

185

herbs? Sweet herbs are those whose leaves (fresh or dried), and sometimes seeds and roots, are used for seasoning cooked foods (thyme, tarragon, dill, parsley, basil, fennel, bay leaves, etc.); salad herbs are what you might assume, fresh herbs that can be chopped and used in salads (tarragon, dill, mint, parsley, basil, etc.). Broadly speaking salad herbs are interchangeable with sweet herbs. Since the pot was one of the earliest cooking utensils and remains one of the simplest ways of preparing a meal, everything went into the pot which was suspended over the fire. Thus the leaves of cabbage, spinach, etc., came to be known as "pot herbs."

What does quatre-épices mean? It means "four spices" and is actually a blend made in these proportions: 3 tablespoons ground white pepper, 5 tablespoons ground cloves, 3 teaspoons ground nutmeg, and 3 teaspoons ground ginger. Combine them all in a small jar, screw on a tight lid, and shake until they are well mixed. The French add *quatre-épices* to stews, sweet yellow vegetables such as carrots, to bean and bacon soup, and sprinkle it over sautéed mushrooms. If used over broiled meats, salt should be mixed into the blend so it will be distributed evenly.

When are herbs added to a cooked dish? You can't be specific about this. Take stew, for example. Suppose it calls for thyme; it would be added at the beginning of the cooking period. But if herbs are used to flavor vegetables, they are added during the last few minutes of cooking. With salads, fresh herbs are combined with the other greens and tossed in whatever-the-sauce just before serving. Dried herbs, on the other hand, should be added to the sauce sometime prior to serving to allow the flavor to develop.

What's the easiest way to mince fresh herbs? If you are French, you will use a big French chef's knife thus: Holding the knife blade by both ends, chop with rapid up-and-down movements, pulling the herbs together, as you work, into a pile with the knife. If you have an electric blender, you'll mince any quantity in that, although you will not get as fine a mince. In either case, make sure the leaves are on the dry side; otherwise they stick together, making them difficult to chop.

Are stalks used when you mince parsley?   No. Only the leaves. However, thrifty cooks and most chefs tie the stalks into little bundles and use them to season soups, stews, etc. because they're loaded with flavor. Parsley is extremely high in vitamin C (2 cups of sprigs will provide the daily allowance for an adult), iron, and vitamin A. They used to say that lovely actress, Lynn Fontanne, kept her youth and beauty by eating loads of parsley every day. A lesson to all of us: Always eat the parsley garnish.

What exactly is a sprig of parsley?   According to United Fresh Fruit and Vegetable Association and the U.S. Department of Agriculture, a sprig is one stem with the leaves attached to it. Not, as one might think, the individual clusters of leaves. When a recipe calls for several sprigs (in a stew, for example), toss in three or four. But when a recipe calls for minced parsley, you use only the leaves, discarding the stems. Recipes all too frequently specify a measured quantity of minced parsley. We think this is ridiculous. We suggest in such cases that you use your head and mince as many leaves as seems logical. A little minced parsley, more or less, will not make an iota of difference in the finished dish. Besides, it's good for you.

What is Chinese parsley?   Quoting from an excellent authority, *The Complete Book of Mexican Cooking* by Elizabeth Ortiz, it is also known as coriander (in Mexico as *cilantro;* in Puerto Rico, *culantro*). "It looks rather like a paler green Italian parsley, although its flavor is much more pronounced." Apparently, it is easy to grow from seed but does not dry well. Mrs. Ortiz writes, "It is sold with its roots still on; they should not be removed. Either wrap in paper towels or place in a plastic bag or glass jar and refrigerate. Do not rinse before storing, as it will rot very quickly. Because it is stored with the roots on, it comes up very fresh and green when soaked five minutes before using. It can be frozen."

What spices and herbs are used in marinades?   A marinade is, of course, a mixture of oil, vinegar, or wine with spices and/or herbs in which to marinate vegetables, meat, poultry, fish, and shellfish. It adds flavor and will help to tenderize less tender cuts of meat. The spice chart that follows, prepared by the American Spice Trade Association, is a useful guide.

Spice	Description	Good in Marinades for:
Basil	Dried, crushed leaves and stems from a plant of the mint family. Light green color—mild pleasantly sweet flavor. Grown commercially in United States and imported from Bulgaria, Hungary, France.	Vegetables, beef, and and chicken
Bay Leaves	Usually sold as dried, whole, light green leaves ranging in size up to 3 inches. Flavor is basically mild, but increases in strength with cooking. Turkey, Greece, Yugoslavia, and Portugal are suppliers.	All meats and vegetables
Celery Seed	Small, brownish-green seed of a parsley type plant. Not the same as the vegetable celery. Bitter celery flavor. Imported mostly from India and France.	Fish and vegetables
Caraway Seed	Dark brown, crescent-shaped seed with light stripes. Fresh, slightly sharp, flavor, associated with rye bread because it gives rye bread its flavor. Comes mostly from Netherlands, and Poland.	Sauerbraten and beef à la mode
Cloves	Dark brown, unopened buds of a tree flower. Nail-like shape, spicy sweet penetrating flavor. Mostly from Malagasy Republic and Tanzania.	Beef, mutton, and shrimp
Fennel Seed	Sand-colored seeds with brown stripes, ranging up to 5/16 inch long. Licorice-like flavor. Imported from India and Bulgaria.	Vegetables and fish
Garlic	Garlic powder, granulated garlic, and garlic salt are considered in the realm of spices. All these processed forms are made in the United States. You can always use fresh, minced garlic.	May be used in any marinades
Marjoram	Crushed, gray-green leaves. Delicate, distinctive flavor. France, Mexico, Canada, main sources.	Vegetables, pork, and lamb
Mixed Pickling Spice	A blend of from 10 to 16 whole spices.	Beef and lamb

Onion	Minced onion or onion powder, onion flakes, and onion salt are part of the spice realm and are all processed in the United States. A new form—instant minced onion, which reconstitutes to the size of minced onions, is especially suited to marinades.	May be used in all marinades
Oregano	Crushed, olive-green leaves. Distinctive, pungent flavor. Imported from Greece and Mexico.	Pork and beef
Parsley	Fresh parsley or dried, crushed, bright green leaves of parsley plant. Grown in the United States.	All marinades
Pepper	Dried berries of a vine. Black pepper is the whole berry (or peppercorn). For white pepper, the dark outer husk of the berry is removed and only the light colored kernel is used. Comes from India, Brazil, Indonesia, Malaysia.	All marinades
Rosemary	Dried leaves resemble pine needles. Distinctive, delicate flavor. France, Spain, and Portugal are suppliers.	Venison and mutton
Thyme	Crushed, gray-green leaves with pleasantly penetrating flavor. Imported from France and Spain. Fresh can be used, if available.	Lamb, beef, pork, venison, and vegetables
Tarragon	Crushed green leaves with fresh, pleasant flavor. Grown commercially in United States and imported from Yugoslavia. Fresh can be used, if available.	Vegetables

Do you season differently in raw and cooked marinades? Somewhat. The soul of any good marinade is its seasoning. All marinades have a base of oil and some will include wine, others vinegar and water. But what produces a good marinade for each individual food depends on the proportion in which the spices and herbs are used. You'll note from the chart that follows how the seasonings change for cooked and uncooked marinades. You'll note, too, that spices (cloves and peppercorns, for example) are used whole, the reason being that you want a gradual release of flavor throughout the marinating period. If ground spices were used, the flavor would be dissipated more quickly, perhaps too quickly. Whole spices, obviously, are easily removed when the marinade is adequately flavored or if the marinade is to be used as a sauce. Usually recipes tell you to tie up the *bouquet garni* (parsley, bay leaves, peppercorns, etc.) in a little cheesecloth bag for easy removal. It is not necessary if the liquid is to be strained. It is important to remember that cooked marinades are usually not as heavily spiced as uncooked because the heating develops a stronger flavor and not a large quantity is needed. As is true of most things, there are exceptions to this: If the uncooked marinade is to be used later to make a sauce (beef à la mode or sauerbraten, for example), the seasonings should be much stronger than in a cooked marinade because in making the sauce, cooking is involved.

Ingredients	Raw	Cooked
Instant Minced Onion *	⅓ cup	⅓ cup
Carrot	1 carrot, coarsely chopped	1 carrot, sliced
Celery Salt	1 teaspoon	½ teaspoon
Garlic Powder *	1 teaspoon	½ teaspoon
Dried Parsley Flakes *	1 teaspoon	2 teaspoons
Peppercorns	1 to 12	10
Bay leaf	2	1
Cloves	4	2
Thyme	1 teaspoon	½ teaspoon
Water		2 quarts
Basil	1 teaspoon	
Salt	2 tablespoons	1 tablespoon
Oil	1 cup	
Vinegar	2 cups	3 cups

* You can use fresh onion, garlic, and parsley.

Should marinating foods be refrigerated?   If they are to marinate for longer than a couple of hours, yes.

What's the easiest way to marinate meat, fish, fowl, etc.?   The easiest way we know is to place whatever food is to be marinated in a plastic bag with the marinade, making certain the bag is intact and tied securely so it won't leak. Take special care with any food that has sharp corners, such as bones. Then, as frequently as possible,

turn the bag so that all the food (or foods, as the case may be) bene-
fits by the marinade. This is much easier than before we had these
wonderful bags, when you had no choice but to place the food in
a container that rarely accommodated the food's shape. It is advisa-
ble to set the bag in a pan so that, should there be any leakage,
the marinade will drip into it.

Do macerate and marinate mean the same thing? In this sense only,
they both mean to place foods in a special liquid for a given length
of time so they can absorb the flavors. Macerate is the term used
for fruits and the maceration is usually spirits, sometimes with the
addition of sugar (cherries, for example, macerated in kirsch); while
marinade is used for meats. The marinade can be wine and/or broth
usually with seasonings (for example, beef marinated in red wine).

What are the differences between the many vinegar types? Pale-gold
apple cider vinegar is used in salad dressings and some cooking.
White or distilled vinegar, made from cereal grains, is best for
pickling, although it has other uses. Then we have the wine vinegars,
red and white, usually used only in making salad dressing. The
flavored vinegars include tarragon, chili, shallot, and garlic—all used
in making salad dressing—and England sends us a honey vinegar
that is quite interesting; it, too, is used for salads.

Where does the word mustard come from? It is derived from the old
French *moustarde* which, in turn, came from the latin *mustum,* meaning "must." In this sense, "must" refers to the fresh or pulp of grapes
or other fruit with which ground seeds of mustard were once mixed
and used as a condiment.

What is Chinese mustard? We can do no better than quote Grace
Zia Chu, whose book, *The Pleasures of Chinese Cooking,* remains
the best available. Madame Chu says, "It is simply dry mustard
mixed with enough cold water to make a fairly thin, smooth paste.
Sometimes a little vinegar or a little sherry is added." As is true
of English mustard (made the same way, except thicker), it should
be mellowed for 10 minutes before using, and any not used up
should be discarded.

How do you crush whole peppercorns? A chef usually crushes them

in a mortar with a pestle. Lacking this equipment, peppercorns can
be crushed in a bowl (preferably wooden) with the bottom of a
bottle. This writer does it by placing the corns in a heavy polyethy-
lene bag and crushing them with a meat pounder. Ingenuity is a
good thing to have in your kitchen when confronted with such
problems.

   N O T E : Cracked black pepper in 2½-ounce jars is available commercially in stores specializing in fine foods.

Do chefs always use freshly ground black pepper?   No. Professional
chefs are purists about this and always use finely ground white
pepper, known as the table grind, or white peppercorns ground in
a mill, in any dish where the pepper might show. Very particularly
white dishes (chicken or fish in a white sauce, for example) and
sauces such as hollandaise, velouté, etc., where tiny specks of black
pepper would stand out like sore thumbs. It's a matter of aesthetics,
really, not taste.

What are green peppercorns?   *Poivre vert* in French, they are unripened and undried peppercorns. Pungent, with a marvelous aroma,
and so soft you can mash them into a paste. As Elizabeth David
writes in her book, *Spices, Salt and Aromatics in the English Kitchen*
(Penguin), "it is virtually a new spice, discovered or launched by
French." Adding, "It has great potentialities for spicing sauces, and
butter, and for spreading on meat, chicken or duck that is to be
grilled." Obviously, it can be used to make Steak au Poivre in place
of the dried peppercorns. Jacques Pépin, who has cooked with it,
tells us it is much stronger than dried peppercorns and must be used
with a judicious hand. Those being imported into the United States
are packed in glass jars (3½ ounces net weight) in wine vinegar,
come from Madagascar (the French ones come in cans packed in
water) and are not as soft or as green as the French pack. The
price is high, the flavor great, and you can track them down in
stores specializing in fine foods.

Is there any substitute for fresh ginger root?   Yes. From our experience
Jamaica ginger, which is the dried root, is every bit as satisfactory
as the fresh. The pieces must be soaked in a cold liquid, water or
milk, for several hours. Then, use them as you would the fresh;

chopped, grated, or shredded—in marinades; added to sauces; in pickling or preserving; whole, rubbed over the skin of a chicken or turkey or a leg of lamb before roasting; etc. A half teaspoon, grated, mixed with salt and pepper, then rubbed on a steak before broiling, is delicious. Available in 2½-ounce jars.

What types of salt are available? Iodized, for one, which provides iodine for those who live in areas where there is little of the trace mineral iodine in food naturally; *free-flowing table salt,* which has been treated to retard moisture absorption and, thus, caking. There are special forms of salt for pickling, labeled *"pickling salt"; kosher,* the purest of all salts, can be used for pickling most satisfactorily but it should be used in a somewhat larger quantity than pickling salt; table salt tends to cloud the brine in pickling. Both *granulated* and *flake salt,* available only in certain parts of the country, have the same strength but do not measure the same. If flake is used, the measure should be increased by about one third. *Kosher,* because of its large, sparkling crystals, absorbs moisture very slowly, if at all, so is ideal in high-humidity weather. Chefs and good cooks find it an excellent substitute for *gros sel,* used extensively in France.

Can one salt be saltier than another? Oddly, yes. It depends on whether the salt is granulated (crystalline) or flaked. Actually, both salts have the same strength but you would use more of the flaked than you would of the granulated to achieve the same amount of "saltiness." New York seems to use more of the flaked than other parts of the country where the granulated seems to be more widely available. It seems you must just learn, by taste, to cook with the salt you buy.

Is ground rosemary available? Yes, although not nationally. Certain herb houses pack ground rosemary but the chances of your finding it in your supermarket are remote. Stores specializing in fine foods may have it on hand. However, you can pulverize it yourself in the electric blender (it will not be a powder) or you can crush it with a mortar and pestle. Whatever, it should be crushed and it should be used with caution since it is very powerful stuff.

What is monosodium glutamate? It is a salt of glutamic acid, derived from a variety of natural foods (such as sugar beets, wheat, soy beans) and is, in itself, a natural ingredient of every protein food (meat, fish, poultry, cheese, tomatoes, mushrooms, even mother's milk). In his book *Eating for Good Health,* Frederick J. Stare, M.D., Professor of Nutrition and Chairman, Department of Nutrition, Harvard School of Public Health, says, "Protein, the body's building block, is essential for growth and life." Monosodium glutamate, colorless and tasteless, has been known and used for centuries in the Orient to enhance food flavors, but it is important to point out here that while it will emphasize flavor it will not cover up bad flavor.

Is it safe to use monosodium glutamate?   In his syndicated column, "Food and Your Health," Dr. Frederick Stare has said: "In my judgment the potshots at MSG are unwarranted at best and premature at least. I still regard it as completely safe as it is used in foods even in baby foods, and as far as I know, so does the Food and Drug Administration."

How do you use monosodium glutamate?   In *The Pleasures of Chinese Cooking,* an authoritative book on Chinese cooking, Grace Zia Chu says: "In using monosodium glutamate, remember that a little goes a long way. A pinch of the powder will enhance any dish, be it vegetable, soup, seafood, meat, or poultry." As a rule of thumb, ½ teaspoon is sufficient in a dish that will serve 4 to 6. It is not, of course, used with sweets and should not be used in egg cookery. We are told that prior to roasting, a sprinkling in the cavity of turkeys, which are inclined to be dry, tends to make the turkey meat juicier.

What are cassia buds?   The dried flowers of *cinnamon cassia,* the bark of which provides us with cinnamon. They are not readily available these days, but if a recipe calls for cassia buds you can substitute cinnamon in these proportions: ¼ ounce *ground* cinnamon for 1 tablespoon cassia buds. In pickling, we recommend using 1¼-ounce *stick* of cinnamon for 1 tablespoon of the buds.

Why do recipes sometimes call for both vanilla and almond?   We've wondered about this ourselves. So we wrote to McCormick & Co., Inc., the spice and flavoring people, and this is what they say: "The theory that vanilla used in combination with almond makes the almond more apparent simply isn't true. Almond is far more potent than vanilla. Adding vanilla tends to mellow and soften the overall flavor." If you want a vanilla flavor, use vanilla; if almond, use that. Ignore any recipe that calls for both. It's probably out of date, anyway.

How is garlic available?   It is sold by the head but it is also available in small bags and windowed pasteboard containers holding several cloves or two whole heads. You can also buy garlic powder, garlic flakes, garlic chips, and garlic salt.

How do you keep garlic?   In an open jar in the refrigerator. The garlic doesn't dry out and stays fresh much longer than if it is kept at room temperature.

When do you add garlic to a dish?   It depends on what dish you are talking about. You can tuck it into the cavity of a bird, skin on, to give the roasted chicken a soupçon of flavor but if you burn peeled garlic, it turns very bitter. So, it is added to a stew when the liquid is added. If you cook it with tomatoes, for example, again you add it after the tomatoes begin to "throw" some juice. However, in the recipe that follows, which is loaded with garlic, the finished dish has only a very subtle garlic flavor because the garlic cloves are cooked a very long time with some moisture.

J A M E S   B E A R D ' S
C H I C K E N   W I T H   4 0   C L O V E S   O F   G A R L I C

10 whole (thighs and drumsticks) chicken legs, split	6 sprigs parsley
	1 teaspoon tarragon
40 cloves garlic (about 4 heads), peeled	1 tablespoon salt
	Freshly ground pepper
⅔ cup olive oil	Good dash freshly ground nutmeg
4 ribs celery, sliced thin	

Choose nice, plump legs from broiler-fryers and cut them apart or have the butcher do it.

Break the heads of garlic apart and drop into boiling water for a couple of seconds. Cool under cold water, then drain. This makes them easy to peel. Set aside when peeled.

Pour the oil into a large, heavy casserole that has a cover. Turn the chicken legs over in the oil. Add the garlic cloves, celery, and parsley. Crumble the tarragon over all and sprinkle with the salt, lots of pepper, and the nutmeg. Now, using your hands, mix everything together. To cook, place double-duty foil over the top and down the sides of the casserole. Add the lid, then cover that with foil, too. Finally, seal with masking tape. The original recipe called for sealing with a heavy flour paste but this method is easier.

N O T E : It is absolutely essential to have a very tight seal. *Can be prepared to this point early in the day* and set aside, at room temperature.

Cook in a preheated 375° oven for 1½ hours. Do not take off lid or foil until serving time. Serve straight from the casserole with soft toast or thin slices of pumpernickel that you "butter" with the soft garlic.

A red wine such as Beaujolais is flawless with this interesting dish and we think you need nothing more than a big green salad, with vinaigrette dressing, followed by a simple dessert—ice cream, perhaps.

How do you use freeze-dried shallots?   They are little chips. Mix 1 tablespoon with 1 tablespoon of water and allow to stand 5 minutes 'to reconstitute. Presto, shallots ready to use. Drain before using in a recipe. Available nationally.

What is fenugreek?   An herb whose seeds are ground and used in curries. It has a celery-like flavor and derives its curious name from *Foenum Graecum* (Greek hay). In Oriental countries it is eaten by women who want to get fat.

Is there any difference between beet and cane sugar?   None whatsoever. In *Today's Food Market,* of the Kansas State University, it is noted: "Beet and cane sugar are identical in chemical composition."

Are Demerara sugar and coffee sugar the same thing?   No. Demerara sugar is a coarse brown shiny sugar that comes from the West Indies and is usually offered on the table of English restaurants. Coffee sugar, also known as pure cane sugar candy crystals, is an expensive form of brown sugar that is served with coffee after lunch or dinner in chic English homes. A product known as brown sugar candy, the equivalent of the crystals, is available in this country at shops specializing in fine foods; also expensive.

Can you use superfine sugar in place of regular granulated? Yes, weight for weight or measure for measure. Actually, this beautiful sugar makes superb cakes and of course, it is ideal when you want to sprinkle sugar over fruit, for example. Obviously, it's just dandy in mixing drinks because it dissolves so readily.

What is milk chocolate? The best known kind of eating chocolate in the United States made by combining chocolate liquid, extra cocoa butter, milk or cream, sweetening, and flavorings. Usually available molded into bars. It can, in certain instances, be used in cooking.

What is sweet chocolate? It is also identified as semisweet chocolate. Like bitter, it is packaged in 1-ounce squares, 8 to the box. Chocolate pieces, also semisweet, come in 6-ounce bags. Both can be eaten or used as an ingredient.

What is bitter chocolate? It is unsweetened chocolate, sometimes called baking or cooking chocolate. Packaged in 1-ounce squares, 8 to the box.

What is Dutch process cocoa? A cocoa powder that has been treated with alkali to neutralize the natural acids. Dutch process cocoa (it has nothing to do with the Netherlands) is darker in color and the flavor is slightly different from that of natural cocoa.

Can chocolate be overcooked? Yes. When this happens the cocoa butter separates. To restore the chocolate, cool to the solid stage, and reheat, over simmering water, taking care not to go beyond 90°. If the melted chocolate is combined with butter and/or cream it should be done gradually, mixing each ingredient in thoroughly or the mixture, too, will separate.

How should chocolate, once opened, be stored? Ideally, any kind of chocolate should be stored in a cool, dry place at a temperature below 78°; otherwise the cocoa butter will soften, rise to the surface, and form a gray film known by professionals as "bloom." It detracts from the attractiveness of the chocolate, but in no way affects the eating or cooking quality. Once melted, the bloom disappears. Chocolate from opened packages should be stored in airtight glass jars, securely covered. Since it is not always possible to maintain the desired temperature, the jars can be refrigerated, but bring the chocolate to room temperature before using.

What is ready-to-use cocoa?   A mixture of cocoa powder, sweetening, and flavorings.

What is vanilla sugar?   It is nothing more than sugar given a vanilla flavor by burying a vanilla bean in a jar of granulated sugar. Tuck one or two beans into a jar with two cups of sugar, and cover tightly. After a week or so, the sugar will have taken on a mild vanilla flavor. Add more sugar when needed to keep the bean covered. Keep right at hand to flavor whipped cream and soft custards or to sprinkle over freshly made cakes and cookies.

What can you do with hardened brown sugar?   Here's what: Combine 2 cups (1 pound) of the sugar in a saucepan with about ⅔ cup of water and a good knob of butter. Place over low heat until the sugar has completely melted. Stir occasionally. Serve over pancakes or waffles. A good substitute when your larder is shy on maple syrup and a happy solution for the brown sugar that's too hard to use.

Vegetables

What vegetables originated in the Western Hemisphere? Tomatoes —Mexico; sweet potatoes—West Indies; Irish potatoes—Peru, Bolivia, Chile, Ecuador; corn—Peru; lima beans—Guatemala, Peru, or Brazil; snap beans, green beans, navy beans, kidney beans, etc.—Central America; Hubbard squash—Argentina; pumpkin—Mexico and Central America; chili peppers—tropical America.

How long can you store fresh vegetables? If, as so many of us do these days, you buy a week's supply at one time, here is a general guide from Western Growers Association. The vegetables listed under 1 to 2 days lose their flavor very quickly, it is well to note. Before putting vegetables in the hydrator of your refrigerator, pull off any yellow leaves, and place vegetables, separately, in a plastic bag, all air squeezed out, and tied.

1 to 2 days	*3 to 4 days*	*Week*	*Week or more*
Asparagus	Cauliflower	Anise	Artichoke
Fresh Beans	Collards	Beets	Cabbage
Fava	Kale	Broccoli	Carrots
Lima	Swiss Chard	Cucumbers	Celery
Wax or Snap	Iceberg Lettuce	Eggplant	Celery Root
Brussels Sprouts	Okra	Endive	Garlic
Corn	Pink Tomatoes	Escarole	Parsnip

199

1 to 2 days	3 to 4 days	Week	Week or more
Mustard Greens	Watercress *	Kohlrabi	Rutabagas
Fresh Peas		Leeks	Winter Squash
Bunch, leafy		Green Onions	Turnips
Lettuce Varieties		Parsley †	
Spinach		Green Peppers	
Ripe tomatoes		Radishes	
		Romaine	
		Summer Squash	

* *Watercress* will keep a week or more if its "feet" are placed in a glass of cold water (an old-fashioned glass is just the ticket), the cress completely encompassed in a plastic bag and secured with a rubber band so no air can reach it. Then refrigerated.

† *Parsley*, once you've got it home, should be run under cold water, shaken to get rid of as much water as possible, then placed in a jar (such as a Mason) with a tight cover—preferably screwtop. Stored in the refrigerator it will keep as long as a couple of weeks. However, when you use it, pull off and discard any wilted, yellow or decaying leaves.

Can you "hold" defrosted vegetables? No. Once defrosted, they should be cooked at once. Further, don't buy packages of frozen vegetables that are stained by the contents which indicates they have been defrosted and refrozen, and don't buy packages that are limp, wet, or sweating—all signs of defrosting.

When should lemon juice be added to vegetables? Add to green vegetables just before serving. Otherwise, the vegetables may turn olive green. If the lemon juice is added at the beginning, the vegetables will take longer to cook. (Always cook green vegetables uncovered so they will retain their bright color.) Add to *white* vegetables while they are cooking, to help them stay white.

How are canned vegetables available?
Asparagus, spears or tips, from 8¾ ounces to 1 pound, 3 ounces; cut spears, with or without tips, from 8 ounces to 1 pound, 3 ounces.
Beans (green, Italian, wax, cut, French-style or whole), from 8 ounces to 1 pound, 12 ounces.
Kidney beans, from 8 ounces to 1 pound, 14 ounces.
Lima beans, from 8½ ounces to 1 pound.
Beets, in glass and tin, 8½ ounces and 1 pound.
Carrots (diced, shoestring, sliced or whole) from 8¼ ounces to 1 pound (this size in both tin and glass).

Corn (cream style or whole grain, golden or white), from 8½ ounces to 1 pound; corn, vacuum packed, from 7 ounces to 12 ounces.

Hominy, from 1 pound to 1 pound, 13 ounces.

Mushrooms (all drained weight), from 2 ounces to 14½ (vacuum packed) to 1 pound.

Okra, 15½ ounces.

Okra and tomatoes, 15 ounces.

Onions, from 8 ounces to 15¾ ounces.

Peas, from 8½ ounces to 1 pound.

Peas and carrots (same weight as peas).

Peppers (diced, red or green), 1 pound.

Pimientos, from 4 ounces to 1 pound, 12 ounces.

Sweet potatoes, in heavy syrup, from 8 ounces to 1 pound, 13 ounces; in light syrup, from 8 ounces to 1 pound, 7 ounces; vacuum packed, 1 pound, 1 ounce.

White potatoes, from 8½ ounces to 1 pound, 13 ounces.

Pumpkin or squash, from 1 pound to 1 pound, 13 ounces.

Rutabagas, diced, 1 pound.

Sauerkraut, from 8 ounces to 1 pound, 11 ounces.

Spinach, kale, turnip, or other greens, from 7¾ ounces to 1 pound, 11 ounces.

Cut squash, 1 pound.

Succotash, whole kernel corn, 1 pound.

How long should you cook canned vegetables?   They should not be cooked. Canned vegetables or those packed in glass containers are already cooked and *should only be heated through* over a low heat, then drained thoroughly, seasoned, and dressed with butter or a sauce.

What are crudités?   Crudité, from the French, means raw. Culinarily, *crudités* means raw food, especially fresh vegetables—radishes, baby carrots, turnips, scallions, green pepper rings, thinly sliced zucchini, cucumber strips, tomatoes, etc.—that taste good served raw as hors d'oeuvres, with salt or mayonnaise.

How do you keep washed salad greens fresh?   Wash the greens thoroughly, then dry as well as you can. Line the hydrator of your refrigerator with several layers of paper towels or use a fresh dish towel. Lay the greens, leaf by leaf, in the hydrator right on top of each other. That's it. By actual test, washed greens including even delicate ones, have kept fresh and beautiful much longer this way than if wrapped. It's the best method we've discovered so far.

How do you make a watercress salad? Break off the sprigs, which should be 2 inches long, and discard the stalks. Make a good vinaigrette dressing (allow 1 tablespoon per person, see page 179) and pour into a salad bowl. Just before serving, add the watercress sprigs. Toss the salad at the table. *Another way:* Arrange the fresh sprigs in a salad bowl, without dressing. Give each person at the table small, individual bowls with a tablespoon or so of dressing in each bowl. The cress is then eaten by each person dipping the sprigs into his own little bowl of sauce. For the record, watercress, like parsley, makes a beautiful garnish with meats, fowl, etc.

What is samphire? A hardy plant which grows naturally on cliffs by the sea. Also known as "Peter's cress" and "sea fennel," it can be raised in gardens in dry, rocky soil. Although it can be cooked, it is usually served as a salad.

What are mustard greens? A member of the *Brassica* family which includes broccoli, Brussels sprouts, cabbage, cauliflower, Chinese cabbage, collards, kale, kohlrabi, rutabaga, red cabbage, Savoy cabbage, turnips, and mustard. Mustard greens (they can be easily raised in the home garden) are used to make salads, alone or combined with other greens. In the South, where they are very popular, they are cooked with salt pork or ham. The principal varieties are the plain-leaved type, sometimes called Elephant Ear, and the two curly varieties, Forkhook Fancy and Southern Curled. In buying, the smaller leaves—6 to 12 inches long—are preferred.

What is mustard cress? Correctly, it is "mustard and cress." Mustard and cress comprises two plants. Cress, being slow to germinate, must be sown three days before the mustard and takes about a week to mature. They are miniature plants with tiny leaves and you eat the whole lot. Mustard and cress is available at greengrocers in England but some firms sell mustard and cress "farms." The seeds being sown on "carpets" need only the addition of water. The English use it to make sandwiches, mixed with a little mayonnaise, served at teatime. It is also used as a garnish. The flavor is pleasantly hot.

What is the best way to store celery?   To keep it firm and fresh, place it in a plastic bag, all air squeezed out, tie and refrigerate. By the way, one rib of celery adds up to a mere 40 calories. Good news for nibblers.

Where did we get Bibb lettuce?   This beautiful lettuce with its flower-like heads, ruffled leaves, and elegant flavor, "born" behind an old mansion in Frankfort, was first produced by Jack Bibb, a soldier in the war of 1812 and a one-time member of the Kentucky legislature.

He never gave his lettuce a name but his neighbors always called it "Mr. Bibb's lettuce." Eventually, and logically, it came to be known as Bibb lettuce. It can be raised in one's own garden and such well-known seedsmen as Burpee's carry the seeds.

Is there any easy way to clean Bibb lettuce?   Yes. Paul Kovi, director of New York's splendid The Four Seasons Restaurant, tells us that if you slosh the heads up and down in warm, not too hot, water the leaves wilt and release any dirt that has crept into their little indentations. Then drop the heads into a basin of very cold water to tighten up the heads again. To dry, shake off as much water as possible, then wrap the heads, root side turned up, in fresh dish towels and chill in the hydrator of your refrigerator. We tried it, and it works.

How can you separate whole lettuce leaves from a head to make lettuce cups?   Easy. Core the head of lettuce first. Then holding the cored end up, place it under a strong stream of cold water. The weight of the water will start to separate the leaves from the head. Beginning at the stem end, where the leaves are the strongest, peel off each leaf with care. Blot dry with a fresh dish towel, wrap, and refrigerate. This method works well with either iceberg or Boston lettuce.

How do you peel, seed, and slice cucumbers?   Chop off both ends. Then, with a potato peeler, peel off the skin in long, thin strips. Slice in half lengthwise. Scoop out all the seeds with a teaspoon. If you are going to cook them, slice each half into three even strips.

Line up strips and cut across in half or in thirds. If you are using them uncooked, peel, seed, then slice seeded halves very thin.

BAKED CUCUMBERS

6 cucumbers
2 tablespoons wine vinegar
1½ teaspoon salt
Big pinch sugar
¼ cup (½ stick) butter, melted
½ teaspoon dried basil or 4 to 5 leaves fresh, minced

4 green onions, minced, tops and all
Big pinch white pepper, freshly grated
Handful parsley sprigs, minced

Peel the cucumbers, then cut in half lengthwise. Scoop out seeds from each half, slice lengthwise into 3 even strips, then cut across into 2-inch pieces. Combine the cucumber pieces with the vinegar, salt, and sugar in a plastic bag. Place in a pan in case of leakage. Marinate at least 30 minutes or, better, several hours, turning whenever you think of it. Drain and pat dry with paper towels.

Pour the butter into a shallow (about 1½ inches) baking dish about 12 inches wide. Add the cucumbers, basil, onions, and pepper. Toss the cucumbers until well coated with the mixture.

Place in a preheated 375° oven for about 35 to 45 minutes or until the cucumbers are tender but still crisp. *Can be prepared to this point and reheated. If so, do not cover.* Sprinkle with minced parsley just before serving. Serve with poached or sautéed fish to 4, perhaps 6.

CUCUMBER SALAD

2 firm, large cucumbers
⅔ cup white or cider vinegar
6 tablespoons sugar
2 teaspoons salt

Dash freshly ground pepper
Small handful parsley sprigs, minced

Prepare the cucumbers by slicing in two, lengthwise. Then scoop out the seeds. Slice very thin. Place in a bowl.

Combine all ingredients, *except the parsley,* and stir until sugar has dissolved. Allow to stand for 10 minutes, then pour over the cucumbers. Refrigerate for 3 hours. Sprinkle with parsley just before serving.

Do you pare, peel, or scrape carrots? In the 1896 edition of *The Boston Cooking-School Cook Book* (now known as the *Fannie Farmer Cookbook*), it reads, "wash and scrape." The latest edition (1959) of this famous book says, "Wash or scrub *young* carrots with a stiff brush. Scrape *old* carrots with a wire brush, metal sponge, or with a vegetable peeler." Actually, since scrape means to "remove the outer surface," scrape and peel are the same thing. It is worth noting that pare and peel are also synonymous. Carrots used to season—in a broth, for example—need only a good washing.

How do you slice, julienne, and dice carrots? Using a vegetable peeler, peel, then cut a thin strip off one side so the carrot will lie flat. Trim off tip and the tap root. To slice: Cut across the length of the carrot to thickness called for in recipe, pushing the pieces away as you work. To julienne: Cut lengthwise in ⅛-inch-thick slices, then place 2 or 3 slices one on top of the other and slice into thin strips. To dice: Cut crosswise into size needed.

CARROT AND ORANGE MARMALADE

2 pounds carrots, about	Grated rind 1 large navel orange
Grated rind 2 lemons	Juice 1 large navel orange, strained
Juice 2 lemons, strained	6 cups sugar

Chop the ends off the carrots, peel, then cut into cubes. Drop into a big pot of boiling salted water and cook at a fast boil, uncovered, until they can be pierced easily with the point of a paring knife. Drain thoroughly; cool in cold water to stop the cooking. Drain, then chop fine. Measure 3 cups (if you have any carrots left over, use them in soup).

Combine the chopped carrots with all remaining ingredients in a large, heavy enameled saucepan. Place over moderate heat, stirring until the sugar is dissolved. Cook over low heat (a Flame Tamer * works fine here) for about 40 minutes or until the marmalade jells or the syrup reaches 220° to 222° on a candy thermometer. Ladle into hot sterilized pint jars, leaving ½-inch headroom, and seal. When cold, label and store. Makes about three pints.

* A Flame Tamer is a double metal device made for both gas and electric stoves that can be used in place of a double boiler because it distributes heat so evenly.

CARROTS IN CREAM

1 pound young tender carrots   1 egg yolk
  (about 12)   ¼ cup heavy cream
1 small onion, peeled and minced   Salt
4 tablespoons butter

Peel the carrots and slice into thin rounds.

Melt the butter in a heavy saucepan and add the onion with ½ cup water. Cook over medium heat until all the water has boiled away and the onions are very soft. If necessary, add more water. Add the carrots to the onions with a good pinch of salt. Cover and simmer gently over a low heat until the carrots are tender.

Beat the egg yolk together with the cream. When the carrots are cooked, pour the sauce over them and place back over a very low heat until hot through. Do not cook further. Serve at once.

What are carrots Vichy?   Carrots cooked in Vichy water. Cook as you would glazed carrots. That is, with butter, salt, and a little sugar, substituting imported bottled Vichy water or plain bottled water with a pinch of soda in place of broth. The theory is that pure non-calcareous bottled water produces a more delicately flavored carrot. More likely, it is a result of all those French who have gone to Vichy to drink the water for the sake of their livers, with which the French are often so preoccupied.

Why do my carrots sprout tops and roots?   They're old to start with and are stored at too high a temperature. United Fresh Fruit and Vegetable Association tells us that if carrots are picked young, washed, topped, cooled, and moved to market quickly, they can be held from 4 to 6 weeks at about 32°, but they also tell us that the average home refrigerator is too warm—45° or warmer. Hence your problem and that of most cooks. Further, in a busy household with lots of youngsters opening and shutting the refrigerator door, it is virtually impossible to maintain a sufficiently low temperature to keep vegetables happy. The cold facts are, the Association tells us, home storage is not recommended for more than a couple of days. But you might try this trick, with which we've had some success: Wash the carrots, cut off tops and tips, place in a container such as a large bottle, cover with cold water, and cap securely. Then refrigerate; but no longer than a week because the carrots change flavor and become bitter.

How do you make onion juice?   Cut the onion in half and squeeze on reamer just as you would an orange.

Can raw onions be frozen?   Yes, slices or rings. They will keep several days refrigerated tightly covered. They also can be frozen on a cookie sheet, then packaged for the freezer. A handy trick for the cook who looks ahead.

Is it true that onions lose some flavor when frozen?   Yes. But that's easy to solve. Simply adjust your recipes accordingly. Use more onions.

What are dry onions?   Onions that have been cured by having hot dry air blown over them in the field or by fresh air and sunshine. They are not dry in the sense that they have been dried out. Inside, they are juicy and delicious.

Other than fresh, how are onions available?   In can or jar, boiled whole; pickled. Onion juice and, of course, onion soup; frozen (chopped); mixed with peas; creamed. Then we have the dried or freeze-dried onion products: instant onion, onion flakes, scallions, onion soup mixes, onion bouillon cubes and, even, some onion gravy mixes. In addition, onion powder, onion salt, and a combination of the two are all available. Onions, anybody?

How can you get rid of the smell of onion on hands?   Rub your hands with lemon juice, vinegar, or salt, then wash in soap and water. A little cream worked into your hands following this is a good idea.

Is there a difference between a scallion, a green onion and a shallot?
Dr. Gilbert D. McCollum, Jr., research geneticist with the U.S. Department of Agriculture, wrote us as follows: "It appears that originally scallion and shallot referred to the same plant, the 'onion of Ascalon' (Ascalon is a seaport in old Palestine), which today we call shallot, but somehow scallion became a descriptive word for green shoots of any onion or related plants, including the leek, be-

fore bulbs have formed." Scallions are known in the trade as "bunching" onions and are described in *Onions and Their Allies,* by Dr. Henry Jones and Dr. Louis K. Mann, as "non-bulbing onions that continue to grow and divide at the base to form new shoots throughout the growing season." M. A. de Farcy, of Northrup, King & Co., the well-known seedsmen, writes: "The term scallion is applied to young leeks or shallots and is almost a generic term for any *young* member of the onion family . . . the onion that, in a sense, never had a chance."

N O T E : Many recipes suggest scallions when shallots are not available.

How do you peel, slice, and dice scallions?   Chop off root ends, then using your hands pull off the outside layer and any film that clings to the stem. Chop off any damaged or wilted green tops. Slice the entire length of each scallion, down the center. To dice, gather the slices into small bundles and cut across, using a firm stroke, to the size dice called for in recipe.

Is there any way to keep fresh chives?   They're extremely fragile but I've had some luck sticking their little "feet" in a small glass of water (an old-fashioned, for example), covering them completely with a plastic bag, secured with a rubber band, then refrigerating. They'll keep a few days.

Is the long, cyclindrical eggplant a new species?   No. According to the Fresh Fruit and Vegetable Association it is quite common (both Ferry-Morse and Burpee, the seedsmen, list it in their catalogues) but it is grown primarily in home gardens, whereas almost all commercial eggplants are the familiar egg shape. Actually, there are many variations of the eggplant and the colors include purple, purple-black, yellowish-white, white, red or striped. It depends on the variety. They got their name from English-speaking people for the rather obvious reason—their colorful egg shape. It is interesting to note that until about 50 years ago eggplants were grown in this country primarily for ornamental purposes. An amusing side note: Eggplants have been known in China since the 5th century and at one time, Oriental ladies made a black dye with eggplant which was used to stain their teeth, which were then polished to gleam like metal. Styles change.

What is moussaka? A meat and eggplant dish found in many Middle Eastern countries. The Greek spelling is *mousaka*; the Arabic, *musakka's;* and the Turkish, *musakka.* Commonly spelled "moussaka."

MOUSSAKA FOR 10

This is an excellent dish to serve at a buffet for it can be made the day before and reheated in a low oven. Serve with a big green salad.

4 medium-sized eggplants	Few twists of the peppermill
Salt	¼ teaspoon cinnamon
Flour	2 whole eggs, beaten until frothy
½ cup vegetable oil	¾ cup freshly grated Parmesan
10 tablespoons (1 stick plus 2	cheese
tablespoons) butter	½ cup fine bread crumbs (about 2
3 large onions, peeled and minced	slices firm white bread)
2 pounds ground lean lamb	3 cups milk, heated
3 tablespoons tomato paste	Freshly ground nutmeg
Big handful parsley sprigs, minced	4 egg yolks, slighten beaten
½ cup dry red wine	

Peel the eggplants, using a vegetable peeler, then slice lengthwise into pieces about ½ inch thick. Sprinkle with salt on both sides, place in a bowl and allow to stand for 30 minutes. Cover with cold water and allow to stand 10 minutes longer. Squeeze out the water and blot the pieces dry with paper towels. Coat lightly with flour. Heat the vegetable oil in a large skillet. When hot, fry the eggplant until golden on both sides. Don't crowd the pan. Drain on paper towels. Set aside.

Add 4 tablespoons of the butter to the skillet. Add the onions and meat. Sauté until the meat has browned, giving it an occasional stir. Stir in the tomato paste, parsley, wine, salt and pepper to taste, and ½ cup of water. Simmer, stirring frequently, until all the liquid has been absorbed. Take off the heat and cool. Then stir in the cinnamon, the two beaten whole eggs, ½ cup of the cheese and ¼ cup of the bread crumbs. Set this aside, too.

To make the sauce: Melt the remaining butter in a saucepan over a low heat. With a wooden spatula, stir in 6 tablespoons of flour until smooth. Cook, stirring constantly, for about 3 minutes. Do not brown. Then add the hot milk, beating constantly with a wire whisk. Place back over moderate heat and cook, whipping constantly, until the sauce is thick and smooth. Stir in salt, pepper, and nutmeg to taste. Beat a little of the hot sauce into the egg yolks, then combine the two, whipping steadily. Cook over very low heat for 2 minutes, still whipping. Do not cook further or the sauce will curdle.

Butter well a 10 x 16-inch ovenproof baking dish (you may have to use a big baking pan). Sprinkle the remaining bread crumbs over the bottom. Cover with a layer of the eggplant slices, then a layer of the meat mixture. Continue, layer after layer, until all ingredients are used, finishing with a layer of eggplant. Cover with the sauce, sprinkle with the remaining cheese and bake in a preheated 350° oven for 1 hour or until the top is golden. Cool for about 25 minutes before serving. Serves 10.

How long do you cook asparagus? First of all, you chop off—in one fell swoop—the tough root ends. Don't bother with that silly business of bending each spear so that it breaks at the most flexible point. As for cooking, and again we say *peeled* asparagus is the most delectable, we cook it about 3 minutes or until a paring knife will pierce the end easily. Further, cook it in lots of briskly boiling, salted water, *uncovered.* Uncovered because it stays a brilliant, beautiful green. If cooked in advance, and often that is the most convenient (also you may want to serve it cold), cool quickly in cold water to stop the cooking. Then heat up in hot, melted butter or in boiling water just long enough to heat through.

How long will asparagus keep? It should be used within one or two days of purchase because it ages rapidly after cutting. Like corn, ideally it should be rushed from the garden to the boiling pot. To store, place in plastic bags or in the dehydrator of the refrigerator until ready to use.

What do you consider high-quality asparagus? Specialists at the U.S. Department of Agriculture say to look for closed compact tips, round spears, and a fresh, bright appearance. A rich color should cover most of the spear and the stalks should be tender—almost down as far as the green extends. Tender asparagus, you might well note, is brittle and easily punctured. Avoid, and we emphasize this, asparagus with tips that are open and spread out, moldy, decayed, or broken; also "ribbed" spears—that is, spears with up and down ridges—signs of aging, toughness, and poor flavor. Also avoid excessively sandy asparagus but if you peel asparagus, as we strongly recommend (a swivel-bladed vegetable knife is ideal), this is not a problem.

How do you judge beets?   The important thing to remember is that elongated beets with round, scaly areas around the top surface are tough, fibrous, and strong flavored.

SWEET AND SOUR BEETS

1½ pounds fresh beets or 1	½ teaspoon cornstarch
1-pound can baby beets	¼ cup cider vinegar
¼ cup sugar	1½ tablespoons orange marmalade
½ teaspoon salt	2 tablespoons butter

Drain canned beets thoroughly (see below for cooking beets) and set aside. Combine sugar, salt, and cornstarch in the top of a double boiler. Add the vinegar and cook over direct heat, stirring constantly, until smooth and bubbly. Add beets, marmalade, and butter. Place over simmering water for about 30 minutes. Serves 4.

To cook fresh beets: Cut off the tops, leaving about 1-inch stem. Wash well. Place in a heavy kettle, cover with boiling salted water, add the lid, and cook for ½ to 1 hour, or until tender when pierced with a sharp knife (longer if they are old beets). Cool slightly, then peel. Slice or dice.

What exactly are "new" potatoes?   Freshly harvested potatoes that are not fully mature. Often they have skinned areas because the skin is tender and not "set" as is true of mature potatoes that have been stored before marketing.

Is it true the color of the skin of potatoes makes a difference in their cooking performance?   No. What does make the difference in potatoes is not the color but rather the specific gravity of the potato. Specific gravity means the ratio of solids to water. The higher the specific gravity, or the ratio of solids to water, the more mealy or flaky the potato will be when cooked.

Should raw potatoes be refrigerated?   "No," says Cornell University's Consumer Education Program (New York City), because "Long storage below 40° turns potato starch to sugars and causes a sweet taste to develop." Potatoes should be stored away from light (light causes the surface to turn green and the potatoes to develop a slightly bitter flavor) in a cool but not cold temperature; 50° to 70° is okay for short storage periods.

Do you start potatoes in cold or boiling water? Such great cookbooks as those of Fannie Farmer, Mrs. Beeton, and James A. Beard, and *The Joy of Cooking* and *Mastering the Art of French Cooking* all say "cover with boiling, salted water." But such great chefs as Jacques Pépin, former *chef de cuisine* to de Gaulle, and Roland Chenus, chef and co-owner of New York's four-star Veau d'Or Restaurant, start their potatoes covered in *cold* salted water. So you can string along with either the cookbooks or the chefs.

How do you test potatoes for doneness? Chefs use the point of a small knife for the plain and simple reason it doesn't make a hole as a fork does. It's a matter of aesthetics from the chefs' point of view and we hold with them.

Can you reheat boiled potatoes? Not successfully, they get soggy. That's why you rarely see plain boiled potatoes in restaurants. It takes too long to cook potatoes to order.

Other than raw, how can you buy potatoes? Name it and you can undoubtedly find it. Canned (whole, julienned, sticks); package chips, fried shoestring; frozen (see below); plus, of course, instant potatoes.

How can you buy frozen potatoes today?
Straight-cut frozen French fried (sticks or strips) in 9-ounce and 16-ounce cartons, bags up to 80 ounces (5 pounds).
Crinkle cut frozen French fried (sticks or strips, with crinkly shape) in 9-ounce and 16-ounce cartons and bags up to 80 ounces (5 pounds).
Frozen shoestring (straight cut) very thin sticks or strips in 8- and 12-ounce cartons up to 72-ounce bags (4½ pounds).
Frozen shoestring (crinkle cut), thin sticks or strips with crinkle shape, in 8- and 12-ounce cartons up to 72-ounce bags (4½ pounds).
Frozen potato rounds (finely shredded frozen potato), in bite-sized morsels in 9-ounce and 16-ounce cartons and bags up to 32 ounces (2 pounds).
Frozen hash browns (shredded frozen potato), in patties, in 12- and 16-ounce cartons up to 32-ounce (2-pound) bags.
Frozen Southern-style hash browns (diced frozen potatoes, in 12-

ounce cartons, 16-ounce oven wrap and bags up to 80 ounces (5 pounds).

Other frozen potatoes include whole peeled potatoes, cottage fries, steak cut (thick) French fries, stuffed baked, and potato puffs (mashed potato balls).

Are mashed potatoes necessarily fattening?   The poor potato has taken a terribly beating in this weight-watching era—and unjustly. One half cup of mashed potatoes made with milk, but without butter, add up to a mere 86 calories, about the same as a glass of skim milk. So, what's wrong with that?

Are there different types of instant mashed potatoes?   Yes. There are three forms, all available nationally; flakes, granules, and puffs. The end result of all forms is the same thing—good, and very good, mashed potatoes. Certainly, one of the best of the instant products on the market. They can be used in any recipe that calls for mashed potatoes—meat loaves or balls, stuffings, bread dough, and in such old classic American recipes as cakes and doughnuts. Broadly speaking, instant mashed potatoes are packaged loose in cartons, cans or plastic bags.

Should sweet potatoes be cooked in their jackets?   Yes, for two reasons. You get more flavor and more nutrition. It takes 35 to 55 minutes, depending on size, in boiling water and about 35 to 60 minutes in a preheated 425° oven.

How can you buy canned mushrooms?   Whole or sliced, caps or stems, packed in their own juice, in 2-, 4-, and 8-ounce cans or 2½-ounce glass jars; also whole, sliced, and chopped, broiled in butter, packed in butter-mushroom broth, in 3- and 6-ounce cans. In addition, mushroom gravy, canned mushroom soups (creamed and golden) and sliced button mushrooms in a dietetic pack are available. Furthermore, there are two wild varieties of mushrooms, imported canned from Europe: the large, strong flavored *cèpes*, and the bright-yellow, delicate *chanterelles*.

NOTE WELL: Canned mushrooms are already cooked and only need heating although there are instances, in certain recipes, where they would be cooked briefly.

QUICK MUSHROOM SAUCE

1 4-ounce can sliced mushrooms	1 tablespoon lemon juice
2 tablespoons butter	White pepper, freshly ground
1½ tablespoons flour	Salt
1 cup heavy cream	2 tablespoons dry sherry

Open the can of mushrooms and drain off the liquor into a bowl. Set aside.

Heat the butter in a small heavy saucepan. Stir in the flour until smooth, then cook over a low heat, stirring constantly, for about 3 minutes. Do not allow the *roux* to brown. Add the liquor from the mushrooms, the cream, lemon juice, and pepper and salt to taste. Bring up to a boil, whipping until the sauce has thickened slightly. Add the mushrooms and bring up to a boil again. Do not cook further. Stir in the sherry.

Serve with cold braised beef, cold roasted turkey, or fresh cold tongue. Use as a filling for omelets or serve over hot toast.

How can you reconstitute dried mushrooms? Soak in fresh, warm, unsalted water for 20 to 30 minutes. Then squeeze out all liquid. Once reconstituted they will keep, refrigerated, for several days.

What are russet mushrooms? The right name is golden cream and it's a new variety, a sister actually of the more familiar snow-white mushroom. More readily available in California than in the East.

How many sliced mushrooms equal a pound? If they are raw, 1 pound makes 5 cups sliced; if sautéed, it cooks down to about 2 cups.

How many whole mushrooms are there in one pound? This is a good question and especially useful since you often must know how many you will need for a given number of people or a particular recipe. One pound is about 12 to 15 large mushrooms, best used to stuff; 25 to 30 medium (1½ to 2 inches), which might be called all-purpose, are excellent for garnishing dishes; 36 to 46 small or button, best used for chopping. Size, it is well to point out, has nothing to do with quality.

NOTE: In buying mushrooms, remember they should be firm, clean, white to creamy, with closed caps—that is, the gills (the fluted formation between the cap and the stem). If gills are showing, they are old, tired mushrooms. However, if they get "tired" in your refrigerator, they can always be used in soups, etc. Note, too, that if the recipe doesn't call for the stems, they can be turned into a very good soup.

How do you mince or chop fresh mushrooms? Place the mushrooms in a heap on a chopping board (do not attempt to mince more than ½ pound at a time). With a big, sharp, straight-edged French knife, holding the tip in your left hand, the end of the blade in your right, chop in rapid up-and-down motions. Keep pulling the mushrooms back into a heap as you work. Minced means very fine. Diced means in approximately ⅛-inch pieces.

Are dried mushrooms interchangeable with fresh? It depends. If the mushrooms are to be used to flavor sauces, soups, gravies, stews, casseroles, omelets, stuffings, etc., the dried are excellent. On the other hand, if the mushrooms play an important role, such as a *duxelles* in a Beef Wellington, or are sautéed or stuffed and used for a meat garnish, or are served with a sauce as an hors d'oeuvre, fresh mushrooms are essential.

Are dried mushrooms readily available? Yes. But note: There are both dried and freeze-dried mushrooms, and there is a marked difference. Freeze-dried, imported from France, come in ½-ounce cans and rehydrate to 5½ to 6 ounces. Available in stores specializing in fine foods. Dried mushrooms, imported from Poland, Czechoslovakia, Rumania, as well as from France, are available in food stores nationally and are also usually packed in ½-ounce containers. However, in foreign-food stores, dried mushrooms are available loose, sliced, caps with stems attached, and caps only. When rehydrated, dried mushrooms about double in weight. Excellent as these products are for flavor, they do not have the crispness of fresh mushrooms.

Can you buy frozen mushrooms? Yes. Whole mushrooms in 10-ounce plastic bags and whole mushrooms frozen in butter sauce in 6-ounce packages are generally available. Use exactly as you would fresh mushrooms.

How do you keep shallots? The United Fresh Fruit and Vegetable Association tells us to run them under cold water or spray them, shaking off any excess, then place them in a plastic bag, tied securely, and refrigerate. Since the flesh is not as well protected as that of onions or garlic, they need this additional moisture. Obviously, this makes sense only when you buy shallots in quantity, such as by the pint box.

What are water chestnuts?   In one of the best books on Chinese cooking ever written, *The Pleasures of Chinese Cooking,* Grace Zia Chu, the author, says: "Water chestnuts, as the name implies, are grown in a flooded field. It is a type of vegetable and not to be confused with the chestnuts sold roasted on the street, or those used so extensively in French cooking. When the bulb-like roots of the water chestnuts are fully matured, the field is drained and the chestnuts continue to grow for a few more days before they are harvested. Freshly gathered, they are especially tasty and juicy and can be eaten as fruits or sliced and added to dishes for flavor or texture. When dried and ground into powder, they are used as a binder or thickener."

Why do artichokes sometimes have brown-tipped leaves?   You have a sharp eye. It's because the artichokes have matured slowly in a late California sun and received a light frostbite. To put it euphemistically, they've been "winter kissed." As is true of some root vegetables, a light frost improves the flavor, and epicures consider winter-kissed artichokes the finest. For the record, artichokes are in season from September through June but are at their peak from November through January.

What is Chinese cabbage?   Also known as celery cabbage, it resembles cos lettuce or romaine, compact, with slightly wrinkled, fresh green leaves. It makes a delicious salad, but can be cooked as you would cook other green cabbage. It is in good season most of the year but reaches its peak in the fall.

Can you inhibit the smell of cooking cabbage?   This gives us a chance to remark that one of the crimes often perpetrated in the American kitchen is overcooking cabbage. Hence the unpleasant smell. Shredded cabbage should be cooked in a small amount of boiling, salted water about 4 minutes and quartered cabbage should be boiled in salted water 6 to 8 minutes. If you have a problem, *The Blue Goose Buying Guide* for fresh fruit and vegetables says: "The typical cabbage odor can be appreciably decreased by dropping a whole walnut into the water in which the vegetable is cooked."

What are the signs of a good turnip?   When buying turnips or rutabagas (sometimes called yellow turnips or Swedes), avoid those that are soft or shriveled, cut or punctured. Best to choose ones that are small or medium size, smooth, fairly round and firm. For good flavor in your soups, add some turnips or rutabagas. They work taste wonders.

What are mango peppers?   Curiously, in the Midwest, large sweet garden peppers are often called mangos. Hence, the confusion when a recipe calls for mangos and means sweet peppers.

What are soup greens?   It means the same thing as pot herbs (see page 186).

What precisely is a cherry tomato?   Apparently, it was originally a wild tomato and the U.S. Department of Agriculture in its experimental farms actually grows wild tomatoes (of the familiar "baby" size) to use in its work. They're sweeter, as you know, than the standard tomato and you may be interested to know they're affectionately called "sugar lumps," "small fries," and "tiny Tims." Whatever, they are certainly having a great vogue among tomato lovers. In season the year round and aren't we lucky? Although we are inclined to serve them with drinks or in salads, James Beard, with his usual imagination, turned them into a dessert and here it is.

JAMES BEARD'S
CHERRY TOMATO COMPOTE

3 boxes cherry tomatoes	1 lemon, sliced thin
4 cups sugar	Commercial sour cream

On first tasting this unusual compote, a taster said, "This is the best dessert I ever ate."

Choose firm tomatoes. If they are overripe, they are impossible to peel. First remove all stems, leaving—and make sure you do this—the stem end in. Cover with boiling water and allow to stand briefly. Drain. Then peel, with the greatest care, so the tomatoes remain intact.

Combine the sugar with about ½ cup of water. Place over medium heat until the sugar has dissolved, giving mixture an occasional stir. Bring to a boil, reduce heat, and simmer for 5 minutes. Add the tomatoes and the lemon slices. Bring to a boil again. Reduce heat to very low and simmer for about 20 minutes. Chill. Serves 6. Serve cold with sour cream.

The syrup: Since the tomatoes yield a good deal of juice, there will, inevitably, be some left over when you've eaten all the tomatoes. Strain this. Then reduce to about half. Use to glaze a ham, fruit tart, or an apple pie.

When is the greenhouse tomato in season?   There are two seasons; the one that starts in October and runs through December; and the one that starts in February and runs to about July. Grown under rigidly controlled conditions in glass "farms," this is a really remarkable fruit (the government calls the tomato a vegetable)—firm, fine-textured, tender, with a distinct fresh-from-the-vine flavor. One of the secrets of their perfection is that the tomatoes are hand pollinated (no bees around), which means that all sections of the fruit develop into perfect shapes with good, solid, flavorful fruit. You can distinguish greenhouse tomatoes by the green calyx (stem) which is left on, and by the perfect shape and flawless skin. These tomatoes are "babied" from the day they are planted until they reach you. Naturally, you pay a premium for such perfection. One of their many virtues is their staying power. They will stay fresh and firm for days at room temperature. In fact, the growers suggest you do not refrigerate them, thus savoring them at their best.

TOMATOES PROVENÇALE

1 tomato per person	Butter
Olive oil	Minced parsley
Salt	Minced garlic
Freshly ground pepper	

Slice the tomatoes in half, across. Heat a good film of oil in a heavy skillet large enough to accommodate all the tomatoes. Season the tomatoes well, cut side, with salt and pepper. Place in the hot oil, cut side down, and sear. Turn, season again. Then place in pan in a preheated 450° oven for 10 minutes.

Add a good lump of butter to the remaining oil in the pan. When melted, stir in parsley and garlic. Pour over the tomatoes just before serving.

Is it true tomatoes should be ripened in the dark?   No. This editor and all her confrères in the food field have been saying for years, "Put your unripened tomatoes in a brown paper bag [nothing but brown would do] to ripen." Well, the Agricultural Research Service of the U.S. Department of Agriculture did some extensive research on the subject and this is what they reported:

1. The best way to ripen fruits at home is to place them in a bag —any bag—or box along with a ripe apple (it must be really ripe).

2. For tomatoes, peaches, pears, and apples, a *transparent* container would be best.

3. The container, whatever it is, should not be airtight, but have a few holes punched in it. Here's why: The ripe apple, or any other ripe fruit for that matter, gives off ethylene, a gas which stimulates unripe fruit to ripen. Ripe apples are recommended companions for the unripe fruit because they give off a lot of ethylene. The fruit container should not be airtight because fruit breathes—taking in oxygen and giving off carbon dioxide. High concentrations of carbon dioxide can prevent ripening. The punched holes allow the excess carbon dioxide to escape, and although some ethylene from the apple will escape, too, enough will remain to speed up the ripening process. In addition, the air holes also prevent a high-humidity condition that might encourage growth of decay organisms.

A temperature range of 65° to 75° is best for ripening. At 80° to 85° fruit ripens very quickly but loses quality. Below 65°, ripening is retarded.

Hence, the refrigerator, when slow ripening is your objective. Once ripe, if not eaten immediately, tomatoes and other fruits should be refrigerated.

Are tomatoes native to Mexico? No. The tomatoes we know apparently originated in wild forms in the Peru-Ecuador-Bolivia area of the Andes. Presumably cultivated species of the tomato were carried north from there to Central America and Mexico, perhaps in the last two thousand years, much the way maize (corn) was carried by a migration of Indians long before the arrival of white men. For more than 200 years after 1554, when the first-known record of the tomato was written, this vegetable was gradually carried over the globe. Italians were the first to grow it for food (circa 1550). A few years later, the English, Spanish, and mid-Europeans were growing tomatoes in their gardens for ornamental purposes only. By the middle of the 18th Century, tomatoes were grown for food extensively in Italy and, to some extent, in other European countries. The French called the tomato *pomme d'amour;* from which came the English and early American term "love apple."

It was not until after 1776 that we find any record of tomatoes being raised in the United States. In 1781, Jefferson, a great gardener, was growing them in Virginia. It is said that a French refugee from Santo Domingo introduced the tomato to Philadelphia in 1789, and an Italian house painter, in 1802, to Salem, Massachusetts (Newport, Rhode Island, makes the same claim). However, the Newport Historical Society has in its possession a handwritten cookbook by a Mrs. Samuel Whitehorne, *Sugar House Book*, dated 1801, with a recipe for Tomato Ketchup. It seems safe to assume that Mrs. Whitehorne, and other good New England housewives, had been putting up tomato ketchup for some time and that the Italian-painter story should be taken with the customary amount of salt.

BAKED STUFFED TOMATOES

My friends Jean and Luca Salvadore were horrified when I said I served these tomatoes hot. In Milan, where they live, they are served cold as a first course. In my opinion, they are good hot or cold. Allow 1 ripe tomato per person, and choose firm, ripe tomatoes. Cut out the stem end, then cut the tomatoes in half, crosswise. Score by making shallow slashes in both directions across the cut surfaces of the tomatoes. Sprinkle with salt, turn upside down, and allow to drain for about an hour. Squeeze the halves gently to extract the seeds.

For 4 tomatoes, grate 2 slices of firm, day-old bread, broken up, in the electric blender, along with a big handful of parsley sprigs. Blend until very fine. Mince 1 clove of garlic very fine and combine with the crumbs and just enough olive oil to dampen them. Add salt and pepper to taste. Sprinkle a little olive oil over each tomato half, then pack with the crumb-parsley mixture. Add another light sprinkling of oil.

Place on a cookie sheet in a preheated 450° oven and bake for about 10 minutes or until the tomatoes are tender when pierced with a fork.

What are beefsteak tomatoes? An old, large-fruited variety whose origin, says Burpee, the seed growers, has been lost in antiquity. Their presumption is that it earned the name "beefsteak" because the fruit is very large (from 12 ounces to 20 ounces by weight), red, and juicy.

Ponderosa, Belgian Giant, and Turkish Red, the U.S. Department of Agriculture writes, are frequently called beefsteak, and it adds, "There are relatively few beefsteak tomatoes grown any more. The fruit is very rough, crack susceptible, and also susceptible to fruit rots. Newer varieties are resistant to several diseases, have equal flavor, and more attractive fruit."

NOTE: Burpee lists only one beefsteak tomato in its catalogue.

How are canned tomatoes available currently? More ways than you will believe. Sliced, in 8-ounce, 14½-ounce, and 16-ounce cans, suggested for sandwiches, salads, or as an addition to main dishes; whole peeled, in 14½-ounce, 1-pound, and 1-pound, 12-ounce cans, ready to heat and eat as a vegetable or to use as an ingredient in cooked dishes (the number of tomatoes per can will run from 4 to 5 up to 9 or 11, depending on size of tomatoes and can size); pear-shaped tomatoes, in 14½-ounce and 1 pound, 12-ounce cans, yielding somewhat more tomatoes, per can, because of the shape. Tomato sauce with chopped onions, in 8-ounce and 15-ounce cans; and tomato sauce packed with tomato tidbits, in 15-ounce cans; and tomato sauce with mushrooms, in 8-ounce cans.

The old familiar tomato products still around are: the standard 8-ounce can of tomato sauce; tomato purée; tomato paste; seasoned, stewed tomatoes; tomato juice; pizza sauce; cocktail sauce; chili; and tomato ketchup (catsup).

What is sorrel? In his *Herb and Spice Cook Book,* Craig Claiborne says, "It has been characterized as a sour-leaf version of spinach." Sorrel, which derives from the Greek for sour, is a leafy vegetable which applies to several species of the genus *Rumex.* In an impressive book, *The World of Vegetable Cookery,* by Alex D. Hawkes (Simon & Schuster), the author writes: "In this country we have both native and naturalized sorrel," adding that "Sour Grass is another well-known North American vernacular, and the name Dock is also applied regionally to some of these plants, such as the Belleville Dock, Spinach Dock, the Curled and Narrow-leafed Dock, the Bitter or Broad-leafed Dock, and so on." The French are great admirers of sorrel and have created a most delicate soup, *potage crème d'oseille,* also called *potage germiny.* Sorrel can be braised; cooked, then puréed and served with heated heavy cream; a small amount, chopped, added to salads gives a special flavor. Sorrel grows readily in the garden (only a limited number of seedsmen carry the seeds but they're worth tracking down) and occasionally bunches of fresh sorrel will turn up in good markets in our large cities.

What is poi? The bulbous root of the taro plant, cleaned, chopped, steamed, and crushed into a paste. It is a staple food in the Hawaiian diet and essential to an authentic luau (feast).

What is Kukkakaalikeitto? It translates into cauliflower soup. Here's how (our translator is Heikki Ratalahti, a country boy [sic] from Finland): *Kukka* means flower, *kaali,* cabbage, and *keitto,* soup. Now put them all together and pronounce it, if you can. If you can't, consider the soup a rival to Vichyssoise.

HEIKKI RATALAHTI'S MARVELOUS CAULIFLOWER CREAM SOUP

1 large head firm, white cauliflower (about 2½ pounds)
1 medium onion, peeled, sliced thin
Salt
4 cups cold water

3 egg yolks
2 cups heavy cream
½ teaspoon nutmeg, freshly grated
Freshly ground pepper

Break the flowerets off the cauliflower. Discard the main stem and all leaves. Place the flowerets in a large heavy saucepan with the onion, salt, and water. Bring to a boil. Reduce heat to simmer, cover, and cook until the cauliflower is very tender—about 10 minutes. Blend, a small amount at a time, in the electric blender, until you have a very smooth purée. Pour back into the saucepan.

Combine the egg yolks and cream in a bowl and beat until well mixed, then stir into the cauliflower purée. Place over a very low heat and cook, whipping constantly with a wire whisk, until the mixture has thickened, and shows the first bubbles of coming to a boil. *Do not allow it to boil.* Take off the heat. Season to taste with salt, nutmeg, and pepper. If you plan to serve the soup cold, it is wise to step up the seasonings as chilling reduces them somewhat.

To serve hot: Garnish with lemon slices and, if you like, a dollop of sour cream.

To serve cold: Garnish with chopped chives or fresh dill. Here, too, you may like a spoonful of sour cream.

Can you keep cauliflower from yellowing while cooking? Yes, just add a little bit of lemon juice.

Is there a purple cauliflower? Yes, and sometimes confused with broccoli in that the flavor, when cooked, is like a mild broccoli. The large heads are a deep purple on top (very pretty) but turn green when cooked.

What is gnocchi? It means dumpling and James A. Beard suggests it derives from *nokki,* a Balkan word. In any event, *gnocchi* is Italian and the singular is *gnoccho.* There are innumerable variations: *gnocchi de ricotta* made with ricotta or cream cheese, flour, eggs, and seasonings; *gnocchi verdi* (also known as green ravioli or gnocchi), made with spinach and cream cheese or ricotta; these are formed into little croquettes and simmered—fabulous!;*gnocchi de patate* (potato gnocchi), a purée of potatoes, flour, eggs, butter, poached in salted water; *gnocchi de semolino,* milk, semolina, eggs, seasonings; *gnocchi au gratin* made with *pâte à choux,* milk, seasonings, eggs, etc.; *gnocchi à la romaine* made with semolina, milk, seasonings, eggs; *gnocchi de pommes de terre,* made with puréed potatoes, eggs, flour, seasonings, etc., turned into balls and poached in boiling water. All recipes call for Parmesan cheese.

What is guacamole? A Mexican recipe calling for very ripe avocado, which is mashed and traditionally mixed with fresh tomato, onion, serrano chilies (very hot peppers), fresh coriander, salt, pepper, and a pinch of sugar. Actually, there are many variations on the theme. Although Mexicans customarily place an avocado pit in the center of the serving dish to keep the avocado from turning dark, we have found lemon juice mixed in with the avocado is more effective. Frozen guacamole is now available, and we have found it excellent. Guacamole is usually served as a dip with fried tortillas in Mexico, but in this country on crackers or toast.

How do you extricate the seed from an avocado without damaging the meat? Cut the avocado lengthwise, twisting gently to separate the halves. Then whack a heavy, sharp knife directly into the seed and twist to lift out. A sprinkling of lemon juice is called for to keep the avocado from darkening if it is not to be used immediately.

AVOCADO SOUP

4 ripe avocados	Salt
2 10½-ounce cans condensed chicken broth or 3 cups home-made	Good dash cayenne
	2 cups half-and-half or light cream
	Garnish: Toasted sesame seeds*
Juice 2 lemons	

* To toast, place in a shallow baking dish and bake in a preheated 300° oven until lightly browned. Allow about one tablespoon ot see.'s per person.

Cut each avocado in half lengthwise, then twist to separate. Whack a heavy sharp knife directly into the seed and twist to lift out. With cut side down in palm of hand, strip or peel off skin. Chop coarsely.

Purée, a small amount at a time, with some of the broth in an electric blender. Pour into a large bowl, stir in the lemon juice and salt to taste. Add the cayenne and stir in the half-and-half. Seal securely with Saran Wrap flat on the surface so no air can reach it. Chill. This serves 6 to 8.

N O T E :   Because avocado discolors when exposed to air, this soup should not stand more than three or four hours. Serve in chilled bowls, sprinkled with sesame seeds.

How many calories are there in an avocado?   Far less, we wager, than you'd think. Half a medium avocado, which is an average serving, has only 150 calories, the equivalent of a couple of glasses of champagne or, to put it another way, one small slice has the same number of calories as a small carrot.

Is it true we now have black avocados?   Yes. Outside, not inside. The pebbly skin is almost coal-black with green overtones; available from April through October with summertime the peak months. So, with the green, smooth-skinned avocado available during the remainder of the year, we can now enjoy avocados the year round.

What are the various types of hot peppers?   Known generally as chili peppers, there is the Anaheim chili, mild compared with other varieties but still with a distinct nip. Available fresh, they are also canned whole or diced. The dried Anaheim is ground and used as an ingredient in chili powder; pasilla or ancho, used mostly by Mexicans, usually in gravy, available in the Los Angeles area dried; Armenian yellow wax pepper, much like the Hungarian yellow wax, both sweet and hot, usually added to salads and pickled; yellow chili, with a sweet flavor nip, used raw in salads, pickled or as a seasoning in cooked dishes; floral gem chili, a hot pepper, usually found canned or pickled rather than fresh; yellow Cascabel chili, a hot variety, rarely found in the fresh market but a great pickling favorite; Caribe chili, looks like the yellow chili, very hot, used primarily for pickling; jalapeno chili, not perhaps the hottest but very fiery, used in hot green sauce or pickled in vinegar; serrano chili, devilishly hot, mostly pickled, but people with asbestos throats eat them raw; pulla chili, about as hot as the serrano, usually sold dried; fresco chili, sold fresh, used widely in making hot sauces, as a flavoring for meat dishes, sometimes pickled. All chili varieties are green and turn shades of red as they mature.

How do you prepare dried red chilies? In *The Complete Book of Mexican Cooking*, an authoritative book, Elizabeth Ortiz, the author, says, "Wash the chilies in cold water, remove veins, stems, and seeds; tear them roughly into pieces. Place in a bowl and soak them in hot water, about 1 cup to 6 chilies, for about an hour. They are then ready to be puréed in the electric blender." She also suggests, "Add the water in which they soaked." One final bit of advice, always wash your hands with soap and warm water after working with the chilies because the hot chile rubbed into the eye can be devastatingly painful.

What is jicama? A root vegetable, also known as "yam bean," whose major use is as a fresh vegetable. It is raised throughout the Latin countries and particularly in Mexico. The fleshy root is peeled and cut into small segments which are eaten directly, garnished with chilies, lemon juice, or simply salted. Occasionally, the root is boiled or pickled. Jicama is imported from Mexico into the United States only in small quantities. Some also comes from Hawaii. Available in the late fall or winter.

What are chickpeas? Sometimes mistakenly spelled *chic*, they are the *garbanzos* beloved of the Spaniards and Mexicans; the *ceci* of Italy, the *pois chiches* of France; and the *Kichererbsen* of Germany. Corn-yellow in color, with a unique flavor, very hard when dried, some-what larger than regular peas, they need long soaking in water before cooking, and lengthy simmering. Also available canned. A native of western Asia, known since ancient times, they are used by most Mediterranean countries. They are also popular in India.

What exactly are dry peas? The Dry Pea Commission tells us "There are many varieties, types and strains of dry edible peas which are generally classed as 'dry greens' or 'dry yellows.'" Whatever the type, they are interchangeable in recipes.

Are dry peas and split peas the same?   A split pea is essentially a dry pea that has had its hull removed, the Research Service of the U.S. Department of Agriculture tells us. What is left are the two halves (technically, the cotyledons) of the pea seed itself, which split apart when the skin (hull) is removed.

SPLIT PEA SOUP

4 cups quick cooking split peas
Ham bone*
2 onions, peeled, each stuck with 2 cloves
2 cloves garlic, peeled
2 bay leaves
Freshly ground pepper

3 celery ribs, with tops, cut in two
3 large carrots, washed, coasely chopped
2 tablespoons tomato paste
Heavy cream
Minced parsley garnish

* If you haven't a nice bone on hand, buy the butt end of a ham, cut off a thick slice and bake or broil, then use the real butt to make your soup.

Place all the ingredients *except the tomato paste and the cream* in a large heavy kettle. Add enough cold water to cover (5 to 6 quarts), and bring up to a boil. Reduce the heat, then simmer, covered, until the peas are very soft—several hours. Lift the ham bone out of the kettle. Cut off any meat on the bone, and sliver it. Discard the bone.

Push the soup and all the vegetables through a fine sieve to make a thick purée. Then stir in the tomato paste. This should make about 4 generous quarts.

To serve, dilute the purée with heavy cream (a cup or so to a quart). Taste for seasoning. At this point, you'll probably need both salt and some freshly ground pepper. Bring up to a boil, but do not cook further.

Present the soup in a large heated tureen with a garnish of slivered ham and parsley. Serve with croutons fried in butter on the side.

N O T E : This pea soup freezes perfectly. Add heavy cream after thawing.

What exactly is a lentil?   The seed as well as the name of a leguminous plant (known since biblical times) which has been used as food in Mediterranean countries for thousands of years. They look very much like split peas and like all other legumes, they are very nutritious. Today, lentils are grown extensively in the United States.

LENTIL SOUP

2 cups dry lentils	1 bay leaf
Salt pork, about ¼ cup diced	2 whole cloves
1 carrot, washed and diced	Dash cayenne pepper
1 medium onion, peeled and diced	2 teaspoons salt
1 rib celery, diced	Several twists of the peppermill
1 clove garlic, peeled and minced	Minced parsley
1 ham bone*	

* If you haven't a nice bone on hand, buy the butt end of a ham, cut off a thick slice and bake or broil, then use the real butt to make your soup.

Pick over the lentils (see below) and place in a large kettle with 2½ quarts of water. Sauté the pork in a heavy skillet until nicely browned. Add the vegetables and the garlic and cook, over moderate heat, for 10 minutes. Add to the kettle with the lentils. Add the ham bone, the bay leaf and cloves tied in a cheesecloth bag, both peppers, and salt. Bring up to a boil. Reduce heat and simmer for about 2 hours or until the lentils are cooked.

Lift out the cheesecloth bag and ham bone. Strip any meat off the bone. Combine with the lentils and push through a food mill or fine sieve. Reheat the soup and taste for seasonings. Serve with a garnish of minced parsley. Serves 6 to 8.

Do lentils need picking over before cooking?   Although not all cookbooks say it is necessary, it may be, since odds and ends such as weed seed, dried soil (known as "dobie"), even tiny stones which cannot be removed mechanically, may be mixed in with the lentils. This is particularly true of lentils bought loose, not packaged. The simplest way to pick them over is to spread the measured amount on a cookie sheet and look for any foreign matter. Then pour the lentils into a colander, place it in the sink and run cold water over the beans. Swish the colander around in the water. Drain sink, then repeat the rinsing process.

How good are legumes nutritionally?   We quote Dr. Ancel Keyes, of the School of Public Health, University of Minnesota, Director of International Research on Nutrition and Health, author of *Eat Well and Stay Well* (Doubleday), who says, "Beans and the like are high-protein foods, matching meat in this respect but with the difference that meat is high in fat." Legumes are also rich in minerals, having worthwhile amounts of iron, calcium, and phosphorus, along with other vital minerals. Too, they are "wealthy" in B vitamins and supply valuable thiamine and riboflavin as well as a liberal amount of vitamin A. Because of their high protein content, the average person needs, in addition, only a small amount of meat, cheese, milk or other animal proteins in order to make legumes adequate for the job of body-building and tissue-repairing.

What are the types of dry beans available? The most popular are the *white beans* (marrow, Great Northern, navy, and pea), used interchangeably in baked beans (see page 232) whether Southern, New England, or Western style; and *pinto*, pale pink, speckled with brown, also called "red Mexican" and "red miners," popular in the Southwest in hearty stews. There are also red and white *kidney beans* (see cassoulet, page 229), also available in cans; light to bright red-purple, used in chili con carne, soups, and salads; *lima*, both large and small, flat and kidney-shaped; in the South, large limas, mottled with purple, are called "calico" or "speckled butter beans," often used in combination with meat, such as lamb. *Red beans,* darker red than pink beans, also known as Mexican "chili beans," essential in chili con carne and other Spanish dishes. *Black-eye* and *yellow-eye*, oval with either a black or yellow "eye," called peas in the South; black eyes are the very heart of Hoppin' John, an old Southern dish traditionally served on New Year's Eve. *Chickpeas, also* known as Spanish, garbanzo, or *ceci* peas; good in stews, soups, and puréed with seasonings to make a dip for hors d'oeuvre. *Black* or *turtle beans*, from South America: white inside, oval-shape used primarily in soups in U.S. South but in South America in many bean dishes. *Cranberry beans*, known in Ohio and Indiana as "shellouts," similar to pintos, except markings are pink rather than brown; popular in New England, where they are used interchangeably with young limas in succotash.

PURÉED KIDNEY BEANS

2 cups dry kidney beans	1 or 2 stalks parsley
Salt	Pinch thyme
1½ cups dry red wine	2 slices bacon
1 carrot, scrubbed and coarsely chopped	2 teaspoons flour
	3 tablespoons butter
½ onion, peeled and coarsely chopped	Salt
	Freshly ground pepper
1 bay leaf	

Wash beans well in cold water. Drain, cover with cold water, and soak overnight. Bring to a boil *in the soaking water* and cook until tender. To determine tenderness, squeeze them. They should feel soft and look plump. The length of time will depend on the age of the beans. Shortly before the beans have finished cooking add 2 teaspoons of salt. Drain and reserve liquid.

Push beans through a sieve; set aside. Combine the wine with the carrot, onion, bay leaf, parsley, and thyme. Bring to a boil. Reduce heat and simmer until you have about ¾ cup left. Cook the bacon until crisp and drain on paper towels. Pour off all but 1 tablespoon of the fat from the skillet. Stir in the flour until smooth and cook the *roux*, stirring constantly, for a couple of minutes. Take off the heat and strain the wine into the *roux*. Whip with a wire whisk until smooth. Place back over a moderate heat and cook until the sauce thickens. Stir into the puréed beans. Add the butter, salt, and pepper to taste. If the purée seems too thick add a little of the reserved cooking liquid.

This dish can be made in advance and heated over simmering water. To serve, spoon the purée into a heated serving dish and crumble the bacon over the top. Delicious with lamb. Serves 6.

JACQUES PÉPIN'S CASSOULET
Will Serve 10 or Even 12

The cassoulet is an excellent dish but as the *Dictionnaire de l'Académie des Gastronomes* points out, "It is first of all a peasant dish," sturdy, country fare. Although many recipes make the preparation of a cassoulet a formidable task, this one can be prepared, all told, exclusive of the time the beans soak, in exactly four hours.

2 pounds white peas, or navy beans
1 tablespoon salt
1 leek, well washed and split
1 onion, stuck with 2 cloves
1 carrot, scraped, cut in two
2 fresh tomatoes, peeled, seeded, and chopped
3 cloves garlic, crushed
1 tablespoon tomato paste
1 bay leaf
1 teaspoon dried thyme
4 or 5 stalks parsley
¾ pound pork skin, tied in 3 or 4 bundles

1 pound lean, cured bacon, all in one piece
4 cups chicken broth, your own or canned
1 1-pound garlic sausage, such as Keilbasa (Polish sausage) or Genoa salami
Freshly ground pepper
1 4- to 5-pound duck, thawed
1 to 2 pounds pork shoulder, boned, rolled, and tied
5 slices bread made into fine crumbs (1¼ cups)
½ cup fat from the pork and/or duck

Cover the beans with cold water and allow to soak for 2 to 3 hours. Lift the beans from the water to an 8- to 10-quart, heavy, enameled casserole. Add the salt, leek, onion, carrot, tomatoes, garlic, tomato paste, *bouquet garni* (bay leaf, thyme, parsley) tied in a piece of cheesecloth, pork skin, bacon, broth, and *6 cups of cold water.* Bring up to a boil slowly, reduce heat, cover, and simmer for about 1¾ hours. At this point pierce the sausage with a fork and add to the casserole. Cook another ½ hour. At the same time, salt and pepper both the duck and the pork. Place each in a separate roasting pan and roast in a preheated 375° oven for 1½ hours.

When the beans are cooked (they should be tender but not mushy) turn off the heat. Lift the sausage, pork rind, bacon, onion, carrot, leek, and *bouquet garni* from the casserole into a pan and cool slightly. Discard the *bouquet garni.*

When the duck and pork are cooked, pour ½ cup fat from the roasting pans into a measuring cup and set aside. Discard any extra fat. Deglaze the pork pan by adding a few tablespoons of the juice from the beans. Bring up to a boil, then simmer, stirring together all the coagulated cooking juices. Add to the beans. Chop the onion, carrot, and leek very fine and return to the beans.

Prepare the meats to combine with the beans like this: Slice the sausage about ¾-inch thick; the pork skin and fresh bacon in strips 1½-inches long, 3-inches wide. Slice the pork in half, lengthwise, then into 1-inch slices; cut the duck in half with a heavy sharp knife, and then cut each half into five pieces, bones and all.

Pour the beans into another container. Then rinse out the casserole. Layer the various ingredients in the casserole starting with about a third of the beans, followed by layers of each of the five meats, more beans, the remaining meats, ending with beans. Add the remaining liquid so the beans are completely covered. Spread the bread crumbs over the entire surface, then spoon over the ½ cup of reserved fat. Place in a preheated 350° oven for about 1½ hours. After 30 minutes, when a crust has formed on top, break the crust into the beans with a large spoon. Allow to brown again, leaving the crust intact for serving. At the end of the cooking time, the *cassoulet* can rest, out of the oven, for 20 to 30 minutes before serving.

Serve straight from the casserole, giving each one at the table a serving of the various ingredients. Serves 10 or more generously.

Serve with a good dry red wine or a chilled *rosé* and a green salad, followed by a light dessert.

How can you determine when beans are properly cooked?   As is true of many foods, the taste test is the best test. Squeeze them, if you

like, but also look at them. They should look soft and plump, yet still
shapely. If undercooked the skins will appear "hidebound."

How can you determine the quality of packaged beans?   It's best,
we're told, to buy beans, peas, and lentils in see-through packages
so you can actually see the color. Beans, peas, lentils should be
bright. If not, it indicates long storage and means longer cooking
but the quality is in no way affected. Also, they should be uniform
in size, otherwise you'll have a problem in cooking. Cracked seed
coats, foreign material, and pinholes caused by insect damage are
signs of low quality.

Is it necessary to skim the foam off dry beans while they are cooking?
No. Add 1 tablespoon of butter, drippings (bacon fat, for example)
or vegetable oil which helps to keep down the foam. In any event,
the foam eventually sinks to the bottom of the cooking pot and disappears.

Can you cook dry beans in advance?   Yes. Once cooked, drain well,
cool, and refrigerate, well covered. Or freeze in suitable freezing
containers. As thrifty cooks know, and all cooks should, the liquid
from the beans makes an excellent base for a good soup.

Do all beans and whole peas need soaking?   Yes. The important thing
to remember is that they are dry and all must be soaked to restore
the moisture lost during the drying process. The two methods used
are:
  Overnight soaking method: This is the old traditional method and
the one this writer has found to be the most successful. The beans
and whole peas are first washed in cold water, then covered with
cold water and allowed to soak overnight. The exceptions are split
peas (when used in soup) and lentils which do not call for soaking.
Always cook beans in their soaking water. Then follow recipe
instructions.
  Quick method: Bring measured amount of water to boiling point
(allow about 3 quarts of water to 1 pound of beans). Add the
washed beans. Bring to a boil again and boil exactly 2 minutes.
Take off the heat, cover, and allow to stand for 1 hour. Follow
recipe from this point on.

Are quick-cooking beans available? No. At one time they were on the market but the processor has since withdrawn them.

What are refried beans? Frijoles refritos, a Mexican peasant dish, customarily served with *coachella albondigos*, which simply means meat balls, Spanish-style.

What are brown beans? Until recently, they were all imported but they are now grown successfully in Idaho, although in somewhat limited production. The favorite of Scandinavians, they are traditionally served with meat balls (Swedish style) and usually turn up on a real Smörgåsbord in homes and restaurants. Highly recommended by bean connoisseurs, they can be used in recipes calling for pinto beans and in any baked-bean recipe. Soak and cook as you would any dry bean.

BOSTON BAKED BEANS

Although Boston is credited with having originated baked beans, actually it was the Indians who soaked their beans (just as we do), then combined them with deer fat and onion in a stout clay pot, baking them overnight. The method proved to be a godsend to Pilgrim housewives because their religion forbade all worldly activities, even cooking, on Sunday. So the beans were prepared Saturday, cooked all night and served hot on Sunday. Eventually, beans became a Saturday night tradition in New England. They also taste mighty good on Sunday morning for breakfast.

2 pounds (4 cups) dry peas or Great Northern beans	Good pinch powdered cloves
¾ pound salt pork	½ cup dark molasses
1 large onion, peeled	2 teaspoons salt
2 tablespoons tomato paste	1 generous teaspoon black pepper, freshly ground
2 tablespoons cider vinegar	1 cup dark brown sugar

Soak the beans overnight in enough cold water to cover them generously. Drain, place in a large kettle, cover with fresh water by 2 inches. Bring to a boil slowly, reduce heat to simmer, and cook gently until the beans are almost tender. If the water boils away, add more boiling water to keep them well covered. Drain, saving the cooking water.

Meanwhile, scald the pork in boiling water. Cut half of it into pieces about 1-inch squares, leaving the other half whole.

In the bottom of a large earthenware casserole or bean pot with a lid, place the onion. Add half the drained beans, top with the cubes of pork, add the remaining beans. Place the chunk of pork on top. Mix together all remaining ingredients and pour over the beans. Heat 2 cups of the remaining bean liquid and pour it over all. Cover and bake in a preheated 250° oven for 6 to 8 hours. Keep an eye on the beans to see if the liquid boils away. In which case, add any remaining bean liquid heated to the boiling point or boiling water. The beans must always be covered. During the last hour of cooking, uncover the pot and allow the beans to finish cooking. Do not add any more liquid. Serve with steamed Boston Brown Bread (this is available in cans).

Does it make any difference when you add salt and acid foods to dry beans?   Yes. Salt, about 1 teaspoon to each cup of uncooked beans, is added only *after* the soaking period since salt tends to toughen the beans and increases the cooking time. If you are combining the beans with a salty meat (ham or salt pork), hold off on the salt for the same reason until the beans are cooked, then taste to see how much seasoning they need. As for acid ingredients such as tomatoes, lemon juice, vinegar, wine, etc., they, too, should be added only when the beans are almost tender since they also tend to delay softening.

Do dry beans need picking over and washing before cooking?   The Idaho Bean Commission tells us they should be washed but if they are packaged, it is not necessary to pick them over. If on the other hand they are loose, picking over is recommended.

Does the age of dry beans make a difference in the cooking time?   Yes. If the beans have been stored at too high a temperature and/or for too long a time, they will take longer to cook. Although the cook can't do much about these problems, it's worth knowing when beans seem to take forever to finish cooking. Further, hard water and the altitude are factors in the cooking time.

The U.S. Department of Agriculture recommends adding ⅛ teaspoon of baking soda to hard water for every 1 cup dry beans *at the start of the soaking*. Do not be tempted to add more soda or it will affect the flavor and nutritive value of the beans.

What are flageolets? A type of bean used widely in France and Belgium that resembles a lima except that it is smaller and greener. They are not available fresh in the United States but they are imported, dry, in 1-pound packages, also water-packed in 15-ounce tins and 14-ounce jars. Stores specializing in fine foods usually stock them. In France they are used in soups, salads, etc. White pea or navy beans can be substituted in such French dishes as the cassoulet (see page 229). In Arpajon, the heart of the flageolet country, a *foire aux haricots* (Bean Fair) is traditionally held in June.

FLAGEOLETS EN CASSEROLE

1 cup dry flageolets
1 onion, stuck with 1 clove
1 bay leaf
2 or 3 sprigs parsley
Salt
Freshly ground black pepper
2 tablespoons (¼ stick) butter

1 onion, peeled, chopped
1 clove garlic, minced
3 tomatoes, peeled, seeded, coarsely chopped
10 to 12 sprigs parsley, chopped
3 tablespoons natural juices from roast leg of lamb

Place the beans in heavy saucepan with enough water to cover, and allow to soak overnight. Or bring to a boil, simmer 2 minutes, cover, and allow to stand 2 hours.

When the soaking period is over, add the whole onion, bay leaf, parsley, and salt and pepper to taste. Bring up to a boil and simmer until the beans are tender but not mushy. About 1½ to 2 hours. Drain.

Heat the butter in a large saucepan, add the chopped onion, garlic, and *½ cup water*. Bring to a boil, then boil over a moderate heat until all the water has evaporated and the onion is limp and transparent. If necessary, add more water. Add the tomatoes and simmer 5 minutes. Add the beans, parsley, and lamb juices. Bring up to a boil, then simmer for 10 minutes longer. Serves 6. Serve with roast leg of lamb.

ACKNOWLEDGMENTS The author is extremely grateful to the following individuals, organizations, and publications for their generous assistance and cooperation.

Abraham & Straus
Adams, David
Agricultural Research Service of the U.S.D.A.
Albertson, Sarah D.
All About Baking
Almadén Vineyards
Alsace Wine Information Bureau
American Dairy Association
American Institute of Baking
American Lamb Council
American Meat Institute
American Mushroom Institute
American Spice Trade Association
America's Table
The Art of British Cooking
Art of Fine Baking
A Taste of Ireland
Augier, Julia

Beard, James A.
Beverage Executive
The Blue Goose Buying Guide
The Blue Sea Cookbook
The Boston Cooking-School Cook Book
Boui-boui Restaurant
Brown, Philip S.
Brownstone, Cecily
Bureau of Commercial Fisheries
W. Atlee Burpee Co.

California Prune Advisory Board
Châlet Suisse
Chenus, Roland
Child, Julia
Chu, Grace Zia
Claiborne, Craig
The Complete Book of Mexican Cooking
The Complete Book of Pasta
Consumer Education of Cornell University (N.Y.C.)
Cooking for All Occasions
Cooking with Herbs and Spices
Cornell University Consumer Education Program (N.Y.C.)

David, Elizabeth
de Farcy, M. A.
Department of Nutrition, Harvard School of Public Health
Dictionnaire de L'Academie des Gastronomes
The Dictionary of Food and Cookery & Menu Translator
The Dry Pea Commission
Duck Joint
Dunham, Ellen-Ann

Eating for Good Health
Eat Well and Stay Well
The Economic Research Service of the U.S. Department of Agriculture
Edelman, Edward
Egg and Poultry Board
Egli, Konrad
Elysée Pastries
Encyclopedia of Wines and Spirits
Enea, Joseph
Essers, Florence M.

The Fannie Farmer Cookbook
Ferry-Morse Seed Company
Fessaguet, Roger
Fisher, Kathleen
The Fishery Council
Fitzgibbon, Theodora
Fitz Market
Fleischmann's
Food for Us All
The Four Seasons Restaurant

General Electric Company
General Foods Corporation
General Foods Kitchens
General Mills, Inc.
Giambelli, Frank
Giambelli Restaurant

Hawkes, Alex D.
Hempstead, Eleanor
H. J. Heinz Company

Idaho Bean Commission
Ideal Cheese Shop
International Milling Corporation
Iowa State University

James Beard's Fish Cookery
Jones, Henry, Ph.D.
The Joy of Cooking

Kan, Johnny
Keys, Ancel, M.D.
Kovi, Paul

La Caravelle
Larousse Gastronomique
Law's *Grocers Manual*
Lee, Dorothy
Le Poulailler
Le Veau d'Or
Lianides, Leon
Lichine, Alexis
Lutèce Restaurant

McCollum, Gilbert D., Jr.,
McCormick & Co., Inc.
Mann, Louis K.,

Mastering the Art of French Cooking
Metric Study Team, U.S. Department of Commerce, National Bureau of Standards
Moore-Betty, Maurice
Mount Holyoke College
Mrs. Beeton's Cook Book

National Academy of Sciences
National Livestock and Meat Board
News from the Vineyard
The New York Times Cookbook
New Zealand Department of Agriculture
Northrup, King & Co.

Ocean Spray Cranberries Inc.
Odeurs, Anita
Onions and Their Allies
Ortiz, Elizabeth Lambert
Oxford English Dictionary
Oxford French Dictionary

The Palm Beach Post
Peck, Paula
Pépin, Jacques
Pisacane Fish Shop
The Pleasures of Chinese Cooking
Poultry and Egg National Board
Private Guide to Restaurants

Ratalahti, Heikki
Robbins, Ann Roe
Robin Hood Flour
Ross, Bow

Salvadore, Jean
Salvadore, Luca
The Sandeman Newsletter
School of Public Health, University of Minnesota
Schoonmaker, Frank
Scott, Jack Denton
Shelton, Jack
Smith, Henry
Soltner, André
Spices, Salt and Aromatics in the English Kitchen
Stare, Fredrick J., M.D.
Steindler, Paul
Szurdak, Jean-Claude

A Taste of Ireland
Taylor Instrument Companies
Terrail, Claude
Today's Food Market, Extension Service of Kansas City University
Tour d'Argent

Tusa, Rosa

United Fresh Fruit and Vegetable Association

U.S. Bureau of Commercial Fisheries

U.S.D.A. Consumer and Marketing Service

U.S.D.A. *Food and Home Notes*

U.S. Department of Agriculture

U.S. Department of Agriculture and Marketing Service

Vehling, Joseph D.

Webster's International Dictionary

Western Growers Association

Wilson, José

The Wise Encyclopedia of Cookery

The World of Vegetable Cookery

Index